T0133270

Retelling Journalism

GRONINGEN STUDIES IN CULTURAL CHANGE

GENERAL EDITOR
G.Th. Jensma

EDITORIAL BOARD
J.N. Bremmer, J.J.H. Dekker, G.J. Dorleijn,
H.W. Hoen, B.H. Stolte

Volume XLIX

Retelling Journalism

Conveying Stories in a Digital Age

EDITED BY

Marcel Broersma and Chris Peters

PEETERS
LEUVEN - PARIS - WALPOLE, MA
2014

Illustration on cover: Word cloud of the content of this volume, created by the editors using the online programme Tagxedo.

A catalogue record for this book is available from the Library of Congress.

D/2014/0602/23

ISBN: 978-90-429-3016-2
© Peeters, Bondgenotenlaan 153, 3000 Leuven

CONTENTS

PREFACE AND ACKNOWLEDGEMENTS

In 1999, the local Groningen Research School for the Study of the Humanities, and the Groningen members of the national Netherlands Research School for Medieval Studies succeeded in obtaining a grant for an innovative, large-scale, collective research programme entitled *Cultural Change: Dynamics and Diagnosis*. Supported by the faculties of Arts, Philosophy and Theology and financed by the Board of the University of Groningen, the *Cultural Change* programme constitutes an excellent opportunity to promote multidisciplinary approaches to phenomena characteristic of transformation processes in the fields of politics, literature and history, philosophy and theology. In order to enhance programmatic cohesion, three crucial 'moments' in European history were selected: 1) Late Antiquity to the Early Middle Ages (*c.*200–*c.*600), 2) Late Medieval to the Early Modern period (*c.*1450–*c.*1650), and 3) the 'Long Nineteenth Century' (1789–*c.*1918). In 2000 and 2002 further grants were obtained for *Cultural Change: Impact and Integration* and *Cultural Change: Perception and Representation* respectively. Several international conferences and workshops have already been organised and more are planned.

This volume focuses on storytelling, which lies at the centre of journalism practice. Journalism is an industry of narrative, however, in the digital era the way in which journalists tell stories is undergoing a dramatic shift. New media offer new possibilities to convey information and simultaneously stimulate traditional media to search for original ways to convey attractive and authoritative stories. How journalism adapts is this volume's focus.

It is the second volume generated from an expert workshop, *Trust, Truth and Performance: Diverse Journalisms in the 21st Century*, held in December 2009 at the University of Groningen. This event brought together approximately 25 international scholars to discuss key transformations impacting the industry, resulting in this collection and *Rethinking Journalism: Trust and Participation in a Transformed News Landscape* (Routledge 2012). The editors would like to thank the University of Groningen and ICOG for the financial support given to support these endeavours.

The editors are also particularly grateful to Marijke Wubbolts for her stalwart assistance in organizing the workshop, and to Gorus van Oordt who gave tips on preparing this volume. Finally, they would like to thank their production editors, Liselotte Schuren and Judith Katz, for their herculean efforts to ensure a consistently-formatted and well-polished text.

G. Th. Jensma, General Editor

INTRODUCTION: RETELLING JOURNALISM
CONVEYING STORIES IN A DIGITAL AGE

Chris Peters and Marcel Broersma

Storytelling is at the core of journalism practice. It is the key for communicating with the audience and it exerts a heavy influence over how news is perceived in the public sphere. The idea of 'just the facts' journalism is a caricature – and an inaccurate one at that – as the type of news that circulates, that breeds discussion and reaction, that is both remarkable and memorable, is based around conveying a narrative that generates meaning. In this respect, one could call journalism an industry of narrative.

It has been argued that journalists actually come to see the world through narratives, a sort of ontological narrativity.[1] Frequently, they will refer to their articles and pieces as 'stories' and one of the first exercises most aspiring journalists encounter at university is being told to go out, 'find news', and return in a short period of time; the idea being that the first essential ability for a journalist to develop is to learn how to spot a story. This rationale is captured within professional discourse as well. Many of the common industry terms, from lead, to background, angle, developing and breaking news, refer to the idea of sorting events and characters into some sort of narrative arc with a beginning, middle, and end. As Tuchman notably called it, the 'what-a-story' is at the heart of journalistic lore even if it is not an everyday part of the journalistic endeavor.[2] Certain scoops or stories capture the journalistic imagination and, if we are to take our cues from popular portrayals of journalism, cause the editor to 'stop the presses!'

Simply put, whether we are dealing with this type of 'what-a-story' or the more banal and mundane daily 'NIB's (news-in-brief), storytelling is ubiquitous at all levels of journalism. At first glance, typical event-based stories, the types which populate newspapers and news reports on a daily basis, may not be heavily infused with meaning, thematic development and complex narrative structuring. However, such reports bring a certain order-

---

[1] Jacobs, R. 'Producing the News, Producing the Crisis: Narrativity, Television and News Work', *Media, Culture and Society* 18 (1996), no. 3, pp. 373-397.

[2] Tuchman, G., *Making News: A Study in the Construction of Reality* (New York, 1978).

ing and clarity to the seeming ambiguity and randomness of events. They meet the criteria of verisimilitude, credibility, and fidelity to some extent, and they help us to make sense of the world through narrative.[3] In other words, the simple facts and observations that populate news reports are not in-and-of-themselves all that remarkable. What makes an issue stand out is its encapsulation in a progressive account that unfolds to demonstrate some transgression of societal norms or cultural expectations. As one of the more cynical maxims of the profession notes: 'never let the facts get in the way of a good story.'[4]

In the contemporary digital age, the different ways in which journalists construct and tell stories is undergoing a number of dramatic shifts. New and social media offer novel possibilities to tell stories, while at the same time they stimulate traditional media to search for new venues and approaches to convey their stories in an attractive and authoritative way. Interaction with audiences is increasingly possible, which impacts the relation and notion of sourcing as well as the dominant mode of address. Notions of truth and trustworthiness are reinterpreted in the era of digital media and we are only beginning to understand how these transitions stimulate new journalistic practices and shift the institutional function and ethics of journalism. The broader commercial and global context in which journalism now operates impacts the types of stories that are desired, sought out and produced, and may even change how we conceive of the societal role of journalism in an increasingly connected and ubiquitous media ecology. This volume addresses how journalism tries to find and craft new forms and genres of storytelling within this environment, considering what it means to tell 'newsworthy' stories in a digital age. Its Parts look at different lines of research that reflect on the broader themes of truthful, personal, and sensational stories, as well as the journalistic practices that underlie them.

Of course, claiming the novelty of such developments should always be subject to caution and histories of journalism are littered with such examples. Charges of tabloidization have been heard with increasing regularity in the midst of the media proliferation and fragmentation of the past few decades, yet aspects of tabloid content and form stretch back centuries, even

---

[3] Cf. Aucoin, J., 'Epistemic Responsibility and Narrative Theory: The Literary Journalism of Ryszard Kapuscinski', *Journalism* 2 (2001), no. 1, pp. 5-21.

[4] Fulford, R., *The Triumph of Narrative: Storytelling in the Age of Mass Culture* (Toronto, 1999).

pre-dating the actual tabloid format itself.[5] Emerging technologies are frequently accused of heralding the dawn of an impoverished form of journalism, though history teaches us that the news industry quickly overcomes
such fears and embraces innovation to enliven and enrich its breadth of storytelling possibilities.[6] Yet awareness of this historicizing caveat to academic inquiry must also be cautious not to teeter too far in the opposite direction. Just because there are traces and parallels of previous aspects of news
within contemporary equivalents, one needs to be careful to balance the
tendency of claiming that 'there's nothing new under the sun' with the
sense that what we are witnessing is 'something we have never seen before.'[7] Journalism has changed and is changing. While its rhetorical claim
about its social role may appear stable, there are structural changes occurring which are certainly challenging its societal relevance.[8] Playing with the
conventions of storytelling and platforms upon which they are told is central
to journalism's strategies of adaptation in this changing context and impacts
the way that information is communicated and flows. Here a parallel with
another form of 'professional' storytelling might prove instructive. As
Schudson notes, while we could plausibly imagine eminent authors of the
1850s, early 1900s and modern age sitting around to discuss 'the novel' and
understanding themselves as being engaged in a similar project, envisioning
journalists from these same time periods participating in a comparable conversation about journalism seems far less likely, if not impossible.[9] He notes
that a key development historically was the change from journalism simply
chronicling or recording instances to an increasing awareness by journalists
that they were involved in a field that claimed to offer some form of
knowledge. It thus becomes essential to consider the particulars about the
social-cultural space, technological affordances, and economic context that
provide a fertile network for emergent forms of journalism to appear and

---

[5] Conboy, M., *Tabloid Britain: Constructing a Community through Language* (New
York, 2006); Sparks, C. and Tulloch, J., *Tabloid Tales: Global Debates over Media
Standards* (Oxford, 2000).
[6] Zelizer, B., 'Foreword', in: Sparks, C. and Tulloch, J., eds, *Tabloid Tales: Global
Debates over Media Standards* (Oxford, 2000), pp. ix – xi.
[7] Bourdieu, P., *On Television* (New York, 1998), pp. 43.
[8] Broersma, M. and Peters, C., 'Introduction: Rethinking Journalism: The Structural
Transformation of a Public Good', in: Peters, C. and Broersma, M., eds, *Rethinking
Journalism: Trust and Participation in a Transformed News Landscape* (London,
2012), pp. 1-12.
[9] Schudson, M., 'Would Journalism Please Hold Still!', in: C. Peters and M.
Broersma (eds.) *Rethinking Journalism* (London, 2012), pp. 191-199.

potentially thrive.[10] In this volume, the notion of storytelling is utilized as a guiding analytic to bridge these different levels of inquiry.

Narratives have the effect of making the unique or unusual appear familiar, to give order, flow, and meaning to otherwise disparate events.[11] For instance, the use of photos of children in wartime is a powerful rhetorical component of common conflict narratives, such as liberation or suffering.[12] Including accounts from 'ordinary' individuals is not only used for such dramatic fare but is also commonly used to situate and contextualize stories that are otherwise quite remote or abstract, such as those about the economy or foreign events. These techniques are so commonplace in the telling of news that we likely often overlook their significance. However, description, narration and exposition are ascending narrative techniques used to infuse feeling and experience into news discourse.[13] Fulford notes that 'a story is always charged with meaning, otherwise it is not a story, merely a sequence of events.'[14] Coherence in news reports is built up through narrative, which is then bundled with an enticing veneer of presentation to capture our interest. This interweaving helps to distinguish and brand journalistic products. If we accept this premise, what becomes interesting is to interrogate how the frames, forms, and genres of communicative action are currently being reconfigured to tackle and capture the news on a daily basis. By relying on new approaches, technologies and contexts to retell old stories, this is what allows new forms of journalistic storytelling to take hold; to appear, Janus-faced, both new and familiar; simultaneously forward-looking while staying true to tradition.[15]

An understanding of narratives, consequently, facilitates an exploration of how the news is 'held together'.[16] As such, it is important to recognize

---

[10] This parallels the methodological approach and mode of inquiry seen in approaches such as critical discourse analysis and actor-network theory. For the former, see Fairclough, N., *Media Discourse* (London, 1995); for the latter see Latour, B., 'A Dialogue on Actor-Network Theory with a (Somewhat) Socratic Professor', in: Avgerou, C. et al., eds, *The Social Study of Information and Communication Study* (Oxford, 2004), pp. 62-76.

[11] Tolson, A. *Mediations: Text and Discourse in Media Studies* (London, 1996).

[12] Wells, K., 'Narratives of Liberation and Narratives of Innocent Suffering: The Rhetorical Uses of Images of Iraqi Children in the British Press', *Visual Communication* 6 (2007), no. 1, pp. 55-71.

[13] Chouliaraki, L., 'Aestheticization of Suffering on Television', *Visual Communication* 5 (2006), no. 3, pp. 261-285.

[14] Fulford, *The Triumph of Narrative*.

[15] Peters, C., 'No-Spin Zones: The Rise of the American Cable News Magazine and Bill O'Reilly', *Journalism Studies* 11 (2010), no. 6, pp. 832-51.

[16] Cf. Desrosières, A., 'How to Make Things Which Hold Together: Social Science, Statistics and the State', in, Wittrock, B., Wagner, P. and Whitley, R., eds, *Dis-*

what is both new and familiar within emerging styles of journalism and focus on how they alter the craft. Successfully delimiting these elements becomes quite relevant when we evaluate how the seemingly endless possibilities of information, events, and personalities come together into a coherent assemblage every day that we can identify as 'news'. However, in the contemporary digital age, technology has made it such that what is call news is no longer entirely self-evident. Not only are the possible sources and sites of news more accessible and instantaneous, the question of who can create the news and the different forms that stories take also seems to be rapidly fluctuating.

This relates to a whole host of questions with which journalists and journalism studies scholars are grappling with as they seek to make sense out of what is happening to communication, media, and information and the news industry's role in our contemporary digital age. As the ease with which not just journalists but also the public can create, distribute, and interact over stories increases, questions are raised about what resonates as important and truthful. Communication has been democratized, and while it would certainly overstate matters to say that everyone is now a journalist, there is no question that what counts, as an authoritative and authentic voice is no longer just the purview of communication professionals. Our encounters with personal stories are no longer confined to the realm of close contacts and immediate social network but are part of the everyday media landscape, be this in the form of Twitter updates or reality television programming. In this respect the formality of communication is also in flux. Whether it be journalism or politics, storytelling forms which more explicitly align with audiences and empathize with their wants and fears are finding a place in mainstream (mediated) public discourse.[17] Of course, different genres of storytelling are still quite varied. However, the shifting boundaries between public and private spheres of life have had significant consequences for the types of stories that journalism feels warranted and perhaps even obliged to tell. Broadly speaking, this impacts journalism practice and the everyday way that news organizations go about 'making news'.

These issues roughly map onto the different themes and sections in this volume. More specifically, Part I looks at how the idea of journalistic truth

---

courses on Society: The Shaping of the Social Science Disciplines (Dordrecht, 1991), pp. 195-218; Somers, M., 'The Narrative Construction of Identity: A Relational and Network Approach', *Theory and Society* 23 (1994), pp, 605-649.

[17] Peters, C., 'Emotion Aside or Emotional Side?: Crafting an 'Experience of Involvement in the   News', *Journalism: Theory, Practice and Criticism* 12 (2011), no. 3, pp. 297-316.

is shifting in the contemporary age, and how personal and involved narratives are changing the way that stories are told. While mainstream professional journalism, at least within an Anglo-American context, still generally strives for a sense of truth that is firmly grounded in the objectivity regime, alternative approaches to convey the appearance of truth are gaining impetus. In his analysis of 'featurized journalism', Frank Harbers looks at an alternative to the tabloidization hypothesis, specifically considering how news organizations are incorporating literary elements into their coverage of everyday events in an effort to re-engage public interest in social issues. Rather than simply being a crass commercial imperative, Harbers considers how placing the individual central in the story and introducing storytelling elements potentially results in less distanced and more 'authentic' forms of journalism. Using the case of the Dutch quality newspaper *NRC Handelsblad*, Harbers' research considers how papers have looked to develop and integrate new discursive forms of journalism under the pressures of competition and commercialization. He investigates one of the more prominent examples of this, namely the reportage in *NRC* by Arnon Grunberg, a literary author who has produced various stories on 'hard' political topics. This analysis highlights the challenges between engaging the public and providing information, and looks to how storytelling forms which migrate away from the objectivity paradigm illustrate a growing (but at times reluctant) recognition on the part of news organizations to experiment with new definitions and understandings of 'quality' coverage.

The second chapter, by Gitte Meyer and Anker Brink Lund, delves further into the question of what makes a narrative appear truthful and authentic, in their analysis of the '*Publicizt*' tradition of journalism, an approach to storytelling built upon the pluralist political systems of Northern Europe, which necessitate compromise. Grounded in notions of truthfulness rather than a single overarching truth, this approach as outlined by Meyer and Lund is raised to challenge the predominance of Anglo-American understandings of the current shifts in the journalism field. They claim that many of the goals that new forms of digital storytelling are said to foster, from democratizing communication to incorporate diverse viewpoints; to recognition of multiple points of view; and public discussion and pragmatic compromise over the slavish pursuit of Universal Truths, are actually well-established within this lesser known framework of journalism. Their chapter can be read as a call for journalism scholarship to engage more actively with traditions outside its dominant intellectual paradigm, as it searches to make sense of the growing diversity of storytelling forms in a digital age.

If their chapter is a call to look outside of traditional paradigms to understand contemporary storytelling, the following chapter by Susan Aasman urges us to look beyond traditional orientations and platforms to make sense of how stories circulate and gain meaning in our current times. Journalists, documentary film-makers, and citizens (or news 'prosumers', as they are sometimes referred), increasingly take their own experiences as a point of departure for stories that give the public a feeling of authenticity. Aasman examines three examples of documentary first-person filmmaking over the past fifty years and notes that the successive phases illustrate two key transitions: that of the genre shifting from 'objective' to more inward-looking approaches and the shift from professional to amateur storytelling. Her chapter traces the changes in recorded self-expression and argues that it would be a fallacy to assume this is only a net-based development that began with YouTube. Rather, she looks at these changes as part of a series of slow developments beginning back in the 1960s, which became stronger over time and entered the mainstream in the 1990s.

Part II moves on from personal truths to considers personal revelation as a bastion of contemporary news. These chapters investigate instances when storytelling is seemingly employed in the name of entertainment, rather than the public interest. Though journalism is essentially a market-driven enterprise, the influence of commercial interests on actual practice has long been withstood through a process whereby journalists attempt to gain autonomy through professionalization. In the digital age journalism faces increasing competition on the information market and entertainment, as a selling point, becomes more prominent. Anniek Dubied and Magali Dubey take a broad look at this trend in the profession through interviews with showbiz reporters who produce celebrity news in Switzerland and France. Within the past decade, there has been a quantitative increase in showbiz and celebrity-focused content in French-speaking Europe and their study looks at what impact this has in terms of the identity and reputation of the news industry. They look to the ethical conundrums faced by reporters assigned to cover the showbiz beat and what storytelling techniques and approaches they use to craft their stories while also maintaining a sense of professional status and detachment. They look to how these journalists attempt to craft meaning and utilize professional storytelling skills to 'write about nothing'. Indeed, for such journalists one of the key ways that they manage to maintain their personal and professional integrity when assigned to this beat is to utilize narrative techniques and writing skills to write thick, engaging stories that appeal to audiences. In essence, while they eschew the informational importance of journalism, these reporters fall back on storytelling as an alternatively crucial part of the news enterprise.

Staying within the realm of celebrity, Tim Hoebeke, Annelore Deprez and Karin Raeymaeckers use the coverage of Belgian cyclist Tom Boonen and American golfer Tiger Woods as case studies that on the surface illustrates the increasing importance of 'heroes' to sell newspapers. However, their point goes beyond the commercial. Viewing modern journalists as following in the tradition of bardic storytellers, they look to how traditional myths are used in the process of newsmaking to create stories that journalists know how to tell and with which audiences are familiar. These stories of heroism, tragedy, villainy and compassion help convey moral values and when it comes to the portrayal of heroes, their status helps to reinforce and confirm social mores and norms. In this sense, these tales told in the press are not simply for entertainment's sake. According to Hoebeke, Deprez and Raeymaeckers, mass media are the primary contemporary storytellers in society. The mythological narratives they craft are significant in terms of their ability to help the public make sense of reality by relying on established narratives rather than a bland rational recitation of facts.

However, this is not to say that what appears as sensational coverage may not also have economic benefits. In the final chapter of this section, Nicolas Hubé ponders the makeover of front page design in French newspapers and how this is used to make papers attractive to a broader audience. Looking to the way that design and marketing strategies have become interwoven with professionalism, Hubé points out the crucial aspect of the front page and how it brands newspapers, considering the way that informational focus has translated to a concentration on appeal and connection with potential readers. His argument points to the necessity of considering storytelling and design changes in the context of broader economic and political imperatives, a perspective that illustrates the interrelated nature of three essential poles of the journalistic field, namely: production, content and audiences. Hubé encourages academic caution in terms of overemphasizing blanket evaluations of journalistic change, such as tabloidization, without considering its many manifestations and divergences in different contexts.

The final Part III of this collection gets away from different trends in storytelling proper to look more specifically at changing practices in terms of how journalistic stories are told. Chris Peters looks to the top of the American broadcast hierarchy, the network newscast, to examine to what extent evening newscasts are changing their storytelling practices as they adapt to a tumultuous journalism landscape. He compares one of the bastions of broadcast journalism, the *CBS Evening News*, under what appears to be two vastly different stewardships – that of Walter Cronkite and that of Katie Couric – to critically interrogate the claim that journalism mainstays have begun to incorporate elements associated with 'soft' news storytelling into their production. His textual investigation reveals that, in many respects, the *CBS Evening News* remains faithful to many of the 'professional' traditions established, and often valorized, under Cronkite. However, his study also illustrates that Couric's version of the *Evening News* incorporates elements that would more aptly be described as personal and conversational in its storytelling, something traditionally eschewed in the performance of the objectivity paradigm. By considering the complexity of how the newscast is being reconfigured, Peters argues that equating this creeping of informal storytelling techniques to a broader trivialization of journalism seems a knee-jerk and empirically-suspect charge.

Dan Jackson picks up on another broader critique often levied against journalism to interrogate the proposition that the news media increasingly report about the 'process' of politics over the 'issues'. Looking at UK-based meta-coverage of politics, Jackson looks more closely at process news and investigates the political and democratic implications for using these sorts of narratives in campaign coverage. He considers whether reporting politics using different storytelling techniques helps to demystify the political process, and whether such narratives can be harnessed to enhance citizenship. He relates such coverage to questions of cynicism and obfuscation, asking whether these stories clarify and build confidence in the journalistic coverage of politics and in the electoral system itself. Jackson argues that the purpose of all political storytelling is to promote broader understandings of issues and he proposes a number of injunctions that might help journalistic coverage to facilitate the conditions under which active citizenship can flourish.

Moving over to the continent, Yael de Haan and Jo Bardoel study actual measures that Dutch media organizations have implemented to try to establish a trustful relationship between their organizations and readers. The authors assert that trust in journalism and media constitutes a crucial prerequisite for the democratic function of professional journalism and journalism's ability to make sense of issues to the public can only be assured when this relationship is firm. In this sense, de Haan and Bardoel look to the necessary precondition for contemporary storytelling, which they identify as a press that satisfies demands for accountability and responsiveness. When the press is perceived by the public to transgress, its ability to create meaning through storytelling is curtailed. Looking at specific measures and instruments introduced at *de Volkskrant*, a quality paper in the Netherlands, the authors investigate how the journalistic performance is impacted by accountability instruments and discuss how trust, responsibility, responsiveness and accountability shape the terrain upon which the news can be told.

In this volume's final chapter, Bernadette Kester examines the way that stories are constructed when the context within which they are produced deviates from the environment where the journalist typically operates. Specifically, she investigates the storytelling strategies that Dutch foreign correspondents have developed as they try to tell stories from China. She argues that the main way that we understand the 'other', that which is foreign, is through the stories told to us by foreign correspondents of our national media. The way we perceive countries and other cultures is shaped by the meanings portrayed in these narratives and such stories do not only influence our personal perception, but the lay the grounds for foreign policy supported by the populace. Authenticity in these reports demands proximity, however typical storytelling routines often need to be adapted and reconfigured in these foreign contexts. Kester's contribution provokes a fascinating question with which to close this collection, namely: how is storytelling impacted in regimes where they are used to determining and controlling what stories are told?

This collection is the second book generated from an expert workshop that was held in December 2009 at the University of Groningen. The event, *Trust, Truth and Performance: Diverse Journalisms in the 21ˢᵗ Century*, brought together approximately 25 international scholars from around Europe to discuss some of the key transformations currently impacting the industry. The first collection on this theme, *Rethinking Journalism: Trust and Participation in a Transformed News Landscape*, looked at issues of public trust, participatory forms of journalism, and emerging news forms, which were challenging the established rhetoric and discourse surrounding the profession.[18] This volume follows a related but slightly more content-based theme, to consider the key practice of professional enactment, namely the construction of different news stories. It looks at how the personal and sensational are impacting the content of news and considers these changes in conjunction with changing practices, systems and contexts of news production.

---

[18] Peters and Broersma, *Rethinking Journalism*.

CONTRIBUTORS

Susan Aasman is Assistant Professor of Contemporary History at the University of Groningen.

Jo Bardoel is Professor of Journalism and Media at the Radboud University Nijmegen.

Marcel Broersma is Professor of Journalism Studies and Media at the Centre for Media and Journalism Studies, University of Groningen.

Annelore Deprez is Assistant Professor of Journalism Studies at Ghent University.

Magali Dubey is a Researcher in the Department of Sociology at the University of Geneva.

Annik Dubied is Associate Professor of Sociology at the University of Geneva.

Yael de Haan is a Senior Researcher at Utrecht University of Applied Sciences.

Frank Harbers is a Researcher and Teacher at the Centre for Media and Journalism Studies, University of Groningen.

Tim Hoebeke is a former Research and Teaching Assistant in Journalism Studies at Ghent University.

Nicolas Hubé is Associate Professor of Political Science at the University Paris 1 Panthéon-Sorbonne.

Daniel Jackson is Senior Lecturer of Media and Communication at The Media School, Bournemouth University.

Bernadette Kester is Senior Lecturer of Media and Communication at Erasmus University.

Anker Brink Lund is Professor at the Department of Business and Politics, Copenhagen Business School.

Gitte Meyer is Senior Lecturer at the CBS Center for Civil Society Studies, Copenhagen Business School.

Chris Peters is Assistant Professor at the Centre for Media and Journalism Studies, University of Groningen.

Karin Raeymaeckers is Professor of Journalism Studies at Ghent University.

Part I

———

PERSONAL AND TRUTHFUL STORIES

DIFFERENT FORMS OF FEATURIZED JOURNALISM

THE COLLABORATION OF *NRC HANDELSBLAD* AND ARNON GRUNBERG

Frank Harbers

Introduction

This essay concerns itself with the development of the Dutch quality daily *NRC Handelsblad* over the last few decades. In this period the ownership has changed several times and many of these owners were focused mainly on profitability.[1] This has incited a debate about the paper's alleged increasingly strong focus on profitability over journalistic quality, which connects to a more broadly shared concern about the commercialization of journalism. In an interview a former editor-in-chief of *NRC Handelsblad*, Birgit Donker, commented on this widely perceived threat to quality journalism, acknowledging the belief that journalism in the 21st century has to deal with increasing economic pressures is well-founded, and that these demands do pose a serious threat for the daily press. Nevertheless, she claimed that her paper had maintained and even strengthened its profile as high-quality newspaper by publishing daring and innovative articles. As an example she pointed to a series in which literary authors became reporters for a week and followed a specific politician: 'We have put those pieces prominently on the front page, which means we show more courage in flaunting our qualities.'[2] She argued that journalism is in a state of major flux and quality newspapers, like *NRC*, need to innovate to keep afloat. Her mention of the reportage series by literary writers indicates that one of the ways dailies do this is by looking for innovative discursive ways to appeal to readers.[3] Looking at

---

[1] Wijfjes, H., 'Kranten voor de Zondvloed? Het Krantenlandschap in de Lage Landen anno 2010', in: *Ons Erfdeel* 53 (2010), no 1, pp. 46- 55.

[2] Van Dam, L. and De Jong, B., 'Winstgevendheid is een Waarborg voor Onafhankelijkheid', in: Van Dijck, J., *The Culture of Connectivity: A Critical History of Social Media* (New York, 2013), p. 54.

[3] While in English the term reportage is often considered synonymous with 'coverage', on the European continent the word 'reportage' typically refers to a specific

these innovative elements can shed light on the way journalistic discourse in the 21st century is developing.

This essay therefore focuses on forms of featurized journalism and the underlying conception of journalism within *NRC Handelsblad*. In the broader framework of featurized journalism specific attention is devoted to a recent phenomenon, in which literary authors are hired as reporters. As argued below, I believe this form of collaboration resulting in literary jour-nalistic contributions should be regarded as part of the different discursive elements of featurized journalism. By conducting a quantitative content analysis of the editorial content of *NRC Handelsblad* in 1985 and 2005, and analyzing the collaboration of the paper with esteemed Dutch novelist Ar-non Grunberg, I hope to shed some light on the particular way in which *NRC* has tried to innovate without hurting its profile as a quality daily.[4] Journalistic standards play an important role in this context and for that rea-son, it is interesting to relate the forms of featurized journalism within *NRC Handelsblad* to the concept of the tabloidization that is intricately related to the debate about the alleged dumbing down of the daily press.

Tabloidization refers to the idea that as the result of an increasing commercialization of the media system, the journalistic developments since roughly the 1990s have brought journalism on a path towards abandoning its role as democracy's watchdog. Claims and efforts to present thoroughly researched and 'objectively' presented news that serves the public interest have been discarded for a more superficial journalism practice focusing on entertaining the reader, in which the traditional norms of the objectivity paradigm are left behind.[5] However, more recently the negative tone of this debate has given rise to voices that assess these supposed journalistic devel-opments less negatively. They acknowledge the pluriformity of the journal-istic developments that fall under the umbrella of tabloidization, and see some of these new discursive practices as an opportunity to re-engage the readership in democracy.[6] This is the reason why I have introduced the term

---

class of journalistic texts in which the experience of the event or situation – not just the facts of it – is what the author tries to convey

[4] This part is based on the results of a quantitative content analysis, which has been conducted within the framework of a larger research project into European journal-ism 'Reporting at the boundaries of the public sphere', for more information: http://www.rug.nl/staff/f.harbers/research

[5] Cf. Sparks, C., 'The Panic over Tabloid News', in: Tulloch, J. and Sparks, C., eds, *Tabloid Tales: Global Debates over Media Standards* (Oxford, 2000), pp. 1-40.

[6] Cf. Steensen, S., 'The Featurization of Journalism', in: *Nordicom Review* 32 (2010), no. 2, pp. 49-61; Cf. Van Zoonen, L., 'I-Pistemology: Changing Truth Claims in Popular and Political Culture', in: *European Journal of Communication* 27 (2012), no.1, pp. 56-67.

featurized journalism, for it enables a more nuanced and comprehensive perspective on the different discursive innovations to keep appealing to the public.

The *NRC*'s collaboration with Arnon Grunberg is an interesting attempt to reconcile quality journalism with a stronger public appeal. In 1995 Grunberg made his debut with the novel *Blauwe maandagen*. Since then he has become one of the most prolific, highly esteemed, and best-known literary writers of the Netherlands, who has won almost every Dutch literary prize there is. Grunberg is thus firmly rooted in the literary field. However, from the start of his literary career he also operated in the journalistic field as a columnist. From 2006 onwards, he has presented himself more pointedly as a journalist by contributing a reportage series to *NRC Handelsblad* on a regular basis. In these literary-journalistic pieces he left the traditional journalistic norms pertaining to objectivity aside and wrote highly personal accounts, in which emotions and the human angle are emphasized.

Literary journalism is generally regarded as a type of journalism, in which valuable topics that transcend the 'news of the day' are treated in-depth.[7] For that reason it is generally presented as being unrelated to journalism's move to superficiality. However, the more neutral and nuanced umbrella of featurized journalism opens up a perspective in which literary journalism, with its emphasis on the human angle, can be meaningfully related to other discursive developments towards a stronger focus on human interest and lifestyle. The publication of these articles in *NRC Handelsblad* led to both positive and negative responses, garnering the attention of readers, journalists, and social commentators.[8] The analysis of the way *NRC* presented this collaboration and the way Grunberg positioned himself as a literary journalist conveys the complexity of the discussion around the current development of journalism and offers a nuanced perspective on the different positions within the normative discussion about the recent developments in journalism.

In this essay I will first discuss the fuzzy notion of tabloidization in more detail and show that it refers both to a shift in the topical nature of the editorial content and to a shift in the choice of genre and narrative characteristics. To get away from the normative connotation of tabloidization, and to get away from the idea that it entails a uniform development towards more 'soft news' or 'infotainment', I will use the more neutral term of fea-

---

[7] Cf. Hartsock, J. C., *A History of American Literary Journalism: The Emergence of a Modern Narrative Form* (Amherst, 2000).

[8] Cf. Harbers, F., 'Defying Journalistic Performativity. The Tension between Journalism and Literature in Arnon Grunberg's Reportage', in: Boucharenc, M., Martens, D. and Van Nuys, L., eds, *Interférences littéraires* (2011), no. 7, pp. 141-163.

turized journalism, emphasizing the pluriformity of the discursive practices that this notion encapsulates. Furthermore, I will argue that literary journalism, like that of Grunberg, is a particular manifestation of featurized journalism, and thus both should be regarded as two sides of the same coin. In either case what is referred to is a form of reporting in which typical elements of storytelling, like subjectivity, personal experience and emotions play a central role. Finally, I argue that whereas storytelling conflicts with the rhetorical claims of the objectivity paradigm, our current postmodern society, in which objective truth claims have become suspicious, seems to offer a more fertile ground for a broader valorization of such forms of journalism.

Featurized Journalism and Literary Journalism

In the above-mentioned interview, in which Birgit Donker spoke about her time as editor-in-chief of the *NRC*, she touched on a key issue in the current debate about journalism: the profession is in a state of major flux and has to adapt to rapidly changing circumstances. News has become ubiquitous, and seems to be losing its appeal as a commodity. Via blogs, RSS feeds, Podcasts, Twitter, Facebook and all kinds of mobile phone and tablet 'apps' it is possible to get the latest updates anytime and anywhere, free of charge. This is part of the reason why especially the newspaper business, with its traditional pay models and high distribution costs, is said to be on its last legs. The dropping circulation rates and subsequent diminishing advertisement revenue indicate that dailies are losing the battle for readership, which puts the continued existence of the newspaper as a mass medium in danger.[9] Quality dailies have the hardest time dealing with these new commercial realities, for the increasing time pressure, one of the effects of the competition with online news media, combined with decreasing financial means, makes it more difficult to invest in time-consuming routines like fact checking or doing additional research. They thus have an increasingly hard time to live up to their quality profile.

But that is only part of the story by which the decline of the quality press is explained. It is part of a broader discussion about the decline of people's civic engagement. In our current postmodern society people move away from institutional politics, which seem increasingly distant from them.

---

[9] Cf. Compton, J.R., 'Newspapers, Labor and the Flux of Economic Uncertainty', in: Allan, S., ed, *The Routledge Companion to News and Journalism* (New York, 2010), pp. 591-601; Wijfjes., 'Kranten voor de zondvloed?', pp. 46- 55; Fuller, J., 'The Collapse of the Old Order', in: *What is Happening to News: The Information Explosion and the Crisis in Journalism* (Chicago, 2010), pp. 1-11.

Under the influence of an increasing individualism and fragmentation of society the traditional collective ideologies, which generated some connection with institutional politics, fail to engage the public. This development is seen as one of the reasons why many are no longer interested in the news – or at least in the type of news that is provided by quality newspapers. Such dailies relate strongly to the idea of being democracy's watchdog, and therefore have the strongest focus on 'serious' subjects, like politics, international affairs, and (social-) economic issues.[10]

This is also the reason for the heated debates around the decline of quality journalism. What is ultimately at stake in this debate is the watchdog function of journalism, in which it critically monitors democratic society from an independent position within society. This image of journalism as the fourth estate is a very successful discursive strategy, one upon which journalism has built its autonomous and authoritative position, and it is therefore not surprising that developments that seemingly undermine this foundation and have even been prophesied as ushering the end of quality journalism infuse such strong reactions.[11]

To what extent quality journalism is actually drawing to its end is hard to say, but it is clear that above all quality newspapers have to adapt or reinvent themselves in order to stay in business. Next to implementing technological innovations to keep up with the developments in new and social media, quality newspapers are therefore also looking for new discursive ways to attract and appeal to readers. Such developments are feared to result in what is dubbed the 'tabloidization' of journalism: an increasingly superficial and less reliable journalism practice that focuses on so called 'soft news' or 'infotainment', consisting of sensational content, insignificant knowledge about the private lives of celebrities and politicians, and lifestyle topics like food, housing, fashion, and holidays aimed to entertain the readership rather than inform them. For these reasons these developments have been considered by several journalists and journalism scholars as the 'dumbing down' of newspaper journalism.[12]

---

[10] Cf. Bardoel, J., 'Het Einde van de Journalistiek? Nieuwe Verhoudingen Tussen Professie en Publiek', in: Bardoel, J. et al., *Journalistieke Cultuur in Nederland* (Amsterdam, 2005), pp. 360-366; Cf. Drok, N., 'Civiele Journalistiek: Het Belang van de Professie voor het Publieke Domein', in: Bardoel, J., et.al, *Journalistieke Cultuur in Nederland* (Amsterdam, 2005), pp. 378-380.

[11] Sparks, C., The Panic over Tabloid News', p. 4-5; Broersma, M., 'The Unbearable Limitations of Journalism: On Press Critique and Journalism's Claim to Truth', *The International Communication Gazette* 72 (2010), no.1, pp. 21-33.

[12] Cf. Franklin, B., ed, *The Future of Newspapers* (New York, 2009), pp. 1-12; Broersma, M., 'De Waarheid in Tijden van Crisis: Kwaliteitsjournalistiek in een Veranderend Medialandschap', in: Ummelen, B., ed, *Journalistiek in Diskrediet*

Unfortunately, the indignation and anxiety underlying the claim of tabloidization has muddled the debate, and it has certainly confused the analysis of the journalistic development. It has already been pointed out that the concept of tabloidization lacks refinement and is highly normative, which has obscured the much more complex developments that underlie the notion. Tabloidization is often presented as a uniform process, in which the increasing influence of a commercial media logic results in newspaper that are filled with relatively more soft news, like portraits of celebrities, human interest stories, and lifestyle columns, apart from the traditional 'serious' news coverage. Along the same lines of Nick Couldry's critique on the oversimplifying notion of 'mediatization', I would like to suggest that the developments underlying tabloidization should not be conceived as a uniform result of a commercial media logic, but as a more complex process that can entail different discursive practices with different characteristics depending on the specific context of the development. It can certainly manifest in a journalism practice in which celebrity news and human interest and lifestyle stories dominate, but it is not the only inevitable line of development.

To get away from the normative perspective and the suggested uniform development of tabloidization, I have adopted the term 'featurized journalism'.[13] Apart from the already mentioned shift to human interest and lifestyle over politics and economics, featurized journalism also refers to coverage with a stronger human angle, in which a story is told by recounting the events around one or more individuals. It also refers to a form of journalism that entails incorporating storytelling elements, like personal experience, human emotions, tension building and dialogue.[14] Distinguishing between the three different types offers a more nuanced perspective on, and therefore a more refined analysis of, the recent developments in journalism.

(Diemen, 2009), pp. 23-40; Broersma, M., *De Associatiemaatschappij: Journalistieke Stijl en de Onthechte Nieuwsconsument*, Unpublished Inaugural Lecture, available from:
http://www.rug.nl/staff/m.j.broersma/Oratie_MarcelBroersma_170309.pdf (2009);
Cf. Steensen, S., 'The Featurization of Journalism', pp. 49-61; Sparks, C., 'The Panic over Tabloid News', pp. 1-40.

[13] Cf. Steensen, 'The Featurization of Journalism', pp. 49-50. My term featurized journalism is inspired by Steensen's ideas on featurization, in which he refers to the same developments in journalism that tabloidization denotes without automatically dismissing them as superficial.

[14] Cf. Sparks, 'The Panic over Tabloid News', 9-13; Steensen, 'The Featurization of Journalism', pp. 49-61; Wahl-Jorgenson, 'The Strategic Ritual of Emotionality', p. 1-17

These characteristics, especially the latter two, link up to the debate on literary journalism. In this form of journalism, which operates on the fuzzy boundary between journalism and literature, storytelling characteristics also play a pivotal role. The people publishing this work are mostly esteemed reporters, but highly regarded novelists also operate in this gray area between journalism and literature. These authors cover issues or events they are writing about in a way that is considered to exceed – and sometimes defy – the regular requirements of objective reporting. Their stories try to convey an authentic experience and often adopt a more personal approach and a clearly subjective perspective, in which their own experiences and emotions play an important role.[15] Such accounts are said to be literary, because they are believed to surpass the news of the day and deal with the *condition humaine*, awarding them a longer lasting relevance and appeal.[16] The use of narrative means and the storytelling characteristics of focusing on personal experiences and emotions show the similarities between featurized journalism and literary journalism.[17]

Although these storytelling elements are overrepresented in prize-winning journalism, showing their implicit importance in quality journalism, they conflict with the rhetoric of objective journalism, a rhetoric which has legitimized journalistic practice and cultural authority for an important part of the 20th century.[18] The authority of objective journalism's authority resided in its claim to a reporting practice in which information was decontextualized by cutting it off from the subjective perception and emotional experience it is rooted in.[19] The way journalism and literature are demarcated from each other rhetorically can elucidate this paradox further.

Journalism vs. Literature in the Age of I-Pistemology

Journalism and literature are seen as inherently distinct domains. However, both discourses share certain discursive aspects – which is not to deny that there are also are fundamental differences. One way or the other both offer a representation of the world for which they use certain narrative means and

---

[15] Cf. Hartsock, *A History of American Literary Journalism*, p. 53-68; Lehman, *Matters of Fact*, p. 14; Cf. Kostenzer, C., *Die Literarische Reportage: Über eine Hybride Form Zwischen Journalismus und Literatur* (Innsbruck, 2009), p. 90-91.

[16] Cf. Harbers, 'Defying Journalistic Performativity', pp. 145-149; Cf. Rigney, A., 'Teksten en Cultuurhistorische Context', in: Brillenburg Wurt, K. and Rigney, A., eds, *Het leven van Teksten: Een Inleiding tot de Literatuurwetenschap* (Amsterdam, 2006), pp. 295-331.

[17] Cf. Steensen, 'The Featurization of Journalism', 52-57.

[18] Cf. Wahl Jorgenson, K., 'The Strategic Ritual of Emotionality', pp. 1-17.

[19] Cf. Hartsock, *A History of American Literary Journalism*, pp. 55-60.

forms. These means and forms show some overlap, which has created a gray area of texts that have an ambivalent status in both fields. Rhetorically however, the journalistic and literary domains are strongly positioned as opposites. The former is presented as dealing with factual reality, whereas the latter is believed to be concerned with imaginary worlds.[20] This opposition goes back to the second half of the 19th century, when both domains grew apart and developed into separate fields with a (semi-) autonomous position.[21]

Cultural sociologist Pierre Bourdieu's field theory offers an elucidating perspective on the social dynamics underlying the organization of and relation between cultural fields. He argues that society is built up of different fields, which compete with each other for autonomy and power. They are organized according to a set of field-specific rules through which they attempt to establish their autonomy and authority. The journalistic and literary field are thus in competition with each other for cultural autonomy and authority.[22] Since their establishment the fields have positioned themselves as two domains with different objectives and journalists and literary authors continuously reinforce such differences rhetorically.[23]

Looking at the organizing norms behind both domains, it becomes clear that they are almost opposite to one another. Journalism derives its autonomy and authority from its widely perceived ability to capture 'the truth', and provide a trustworthy image of the world to the public. If, for example, a news report does not manage to make a successful truth claim it is robbed of its most vital function, and loses all journalistic authority. The field has successfully conceptualized itself rhetorically as a passive mirror of reality.[24] The autonomous position of the literary field and the prestige of a literary author revolve around the persisting conviction that literature is the result of an individual and original creative act of a writer, who reflects in their work on issues that exceed everyday reality.[25] For that reason literature

---

[20] Cf. Harbers, 'Defying Journalistic Performativity', p. 141; Lehman, D., *Matters of Fact*; Frus, P., *The Politics and Poetics of Journalistic Narrative: The Timely and the Timeless* (Cambridge, 1994).

[21] Cf. Roggenkamp, K., *Narrating the News: New Journalism and Literary Genre in Late Nineteenth-Century American Newspapers and Fiction* (Kent, 2005).

[22] Bourdieu, P., 'The Political Field, the Social Science Field, and the Journalistic Field', in: Benson, R. and Neveu, E., eds, *Bourdieu and the Journalistic Field* (Cambridge, 2005), pp. 33-41; Bourdieu, P., *Opstellen over Smaak, Habitus en het Veldbegrip* (Amsterdam, 1992), pp. 171-178.

[23] Bourdieu, Broersma, Dorleijn & Van Rees.

[24] Broersma, M., 'The Unbearable Limitations of Journalism', pp. 24-27.

[25] These ideas might have been criticized by many literary scholars, within literary discourse they are still an important and influential strategy to legitimize the value of literature, cf: Rigney, A., 'Teksten en Cultuurhistorische Context', pp. 295-331.

is almost automatically conflated with fiction. However, recently it seems that journalism and literature are drawing closer. A growing body of scholars points to a movement in both journalism and literature, in which journalists and literary writers borrow freely from each other in their mutual attempt to represent reality.[26]

> Writers, whether they have a background in fiction or non-fiction, appear to strive for reality, and they are looking for means to describe reality as adequately as possible. The one time these means can be found in the toolbox of the novelist, and the other in the toolbox of the journalist.[27]

Nevertheless, up until now there are important differences in discursive norms between journalism and literature, which revolve around the notion of referential truth and factual accuracy. Journalism is often presented as the mirror of reality. However, the acceptance of a journalistic truth claim depends not so much on factual accuracy as is rhetorically put forward, and it is certainly not the most important aspect in that decision process.

First of all, as scholars like Gaye Tuchman and Herbert Gans already established at the end of the 1970s, journalists do not passively report 'the facts', they interpret an event, and carefully select what they will report.[28] A news report is thus always and inherently the subjective interpretation of a journalist. From that perspective, a journalistic account is not true because it is the self-evident result of the specific reporting routines and textual forms being intrinsically used to capture reality. Rather, an interpretation is transformed into truth, because certain discursive strategies successfully convince the reader that journalism with its specific practices and forms is capable of mirroring reality adequately. Thus, it naturalizes the socially constructed nature of a journalistic text.[29] The preservation of the illusion of journalism as a mirror is of the utmost importance to the existence of journalism. Much more than is generally acknowledged, outside the scholarly field the acceptance of the truth claim relies on the prestige of the medium,

---

[26] Harbers, F. 'Defying Journalistic Performativity', pp. 141-163; Vaessens, T., 'Realiteitshonger: Arnon Grunberg en de (Non-)Fictie', in: *Tijdschrift voor Nederlandse Taal- en Letterkunde* 126 (2010), no. 3, pp. 306-326; Steensen, 'The Featurization of Journalism'.

[27] Vaessens, T., 'Realiteitshonger', p. 309.

[28] Cf. Tuchman, G., *Making News: A Study in the Construction of Reality* (New York, 1978); Gans, H., *Deciding What's News: A Study of CBS Evening News, NBC Nightly News, Newsweek and Time* (Evanston, 1979).

[29] Broersma, M., 'The Unbearable Limitations of Journalism', pp. 24-27.

the esteem of the journalists, and the accepted forms of presentation rather than on its actual factual accuracy.[30]

Contemporary journalistic discourse is still dominated by the notion of objectivity. Even if the impossibility of a strict conception of objective truth is accepted, a more pragmatic version of objectivity still underlies the dominant journalistic routines, and is translated in discursive norms like neutrality, balancing sides, and the detachment of the journalist. In general a journalist does not choose sides, consults multiple sources that shed light on different sides of the story, he or she writes from a third person perspective keeping himself outside of the text, and starts off with the main point of the story. These norms and corresponding forms, similar to the use of direct quotes, a composition following the inverted pyramid, and a depersonalized narrative perspective, are supposed to ensure an unambiguous and monolithic representation of reality.[31] Again, this latter aim is the opposite of literary discourse, in which complexity, ambivalence and reflexivity are among the most important criteria for a story.

The current debate about featurized journalism and literary journalism should be seen in the context of broader cultural developments, which are regarded as characteristic for postmodern – or late modern in the terms of certain scholars – society, which have also left their mark on journalism. In postmodern society notions like objectivity and impartiality have become suspect and oppositions between high and popular culture and between politics and issues concerning everyday life are being blurred.[32] As a result the trustworthiness of domains that base their authority on the ideal of an objective and neutral truth, like journalism and science, or those that rely on information from these two domains, like politics, seems to be less strong and stable than before. Although the general level of trust in these institutions is rather steady, Liesbet van Zoonen points to the complexity of such trust levels. For example, trust in the government is declining throughout Europe, but trust in democracy is fairly stable. Based on several examples in which institutional knowledge is openly challenged and put aside as just another opinion, Van Zoonen suggests that there are indeed signs that the level of trust in the government and the media is deteriorating.[33] She argues that the postmodern skepticism towards objective truth has undermined the exist-

---

[30] Broersma, M., 'Journalism as Performative Discourse: The Importance of Form and Style in Journalism', in: *Journalism and Meaning-making: Reading the Newspaper* (New York, 2010), pp. 15-35.

[31] Ward, S., *The Invention of Journalism Ethics: The Path to Objectivity and Beyond* (Montreal, 2005); Marcel Broersma, 'Journalism as a Performative Discourse', pp. 6-8.

[32] Cf. Conboy, M., *The Press and Popular Culture* (London, 2002), pp. 45-50.

[33] Cf. Van Zoonen, L. 'I-Pistemology', p. 60.

ence of mutual ground to make a consensual rational assessment of the 'correct' way to describe, interpret and organize society, which is often interpreted as a sign of declining democracy.[34]

Van Zoonen captures these developments with the term '*I*-Pistemology' pointing to the central role the personal, the individual has in the construction of knowledge and the representation of reality: "the self [has become] the source and arbiter of all truth."[35] Because of the deterioration of this mutual framework, individual convictions incited by and based on personal experiences and feelings have come to play a growing role in society. 'Truthiness', 'fact-free politics', 'post-fact society' are a few terms that have emerged to describe this development, mostly emphasizing its negative sides. Scholars like Anthony Giddens, Ulrich Beck and Van Zoonen argue that such developments do not necessarily mean a decline in democracy, but rather a reconceptualization of politics that is more in sync with the changing organization and values of society. They point to the narrow and conservative conception of politics and political issues as the institutionalized debate about issues concerning official policy, and they analyze how this notion has been opened up and merged with more personal information, private experiences and subjective approaches, which have been termed 'life politics'.[36]

These cultural developments can shed a more nuanced light on the ways featurized journalism can function, and it suggests that our postmodern society might offer a fertile ground for a broader valorization of featurized journalism in the newspaper.[37] It helps explain why the boundaries between traditional political coverage and human interest and lifestyle reporting are becoming increasingly vague and suggests that *I*-Pistemology means a stronger valorization of subjective and autobiographical forms of storytelling for which Jon Dovey reserved the term 'first person media'.[38]

---

[34] Cf. *Ibidem*, p. 60; Beck, U., 'The Reinvention of Politics: Towards a Theory of Reflexive Modernization', in: Beck, U., Giddens, A. and Lash, S., eds, *Reflexive Modernization: Politics Tradition and Aestetics in the Modern Social Order* (Stanford, 1994), pp. 1-55; Giddens, A., 'Living in the Post-Traditional Society', in: Beck, U., Giddens, A. and Lash, S., eds, *Reflexive Modernization. Politics Tradition and Aestetics in the Modern Social Order* (Stanford, 1994), pp. 56-109.
[35] Van Zoonen, 'I-Pistemology', p. 56-57.
[36] Cf. Bardoel, J., 'Het Einde van de Journalistiek?', pp. 360-366.
[37] Cf. Steensen, 'The Featurization of Journalism', p. 49-50.
[38] Cf. Van Zoonen, 'I-Pistemology', p. 60-61.

*Quantitatively Exploring the Role of Featurized Journalism in NRC Han-
delsblad*

To what extent featurized journalism actually plays a larger role in the daily
can be assessed by looking at the results of the content analysis of *NRC
Handelsblad* in 1985 and 2005. The characteristics of featurized journalism
and literary journalism relate to the level of the topics that are covered in a
daily and to the narrative techniques and structure of the articles, which is
expressed in the choice of genre.[39] In this chapter I therefore focus only on
these aspects. What is interesting and maybe somewhat surprising, is that
from a quantitative perspective there is no clear evidence for an increase of
featurized journalism within *NRC Handelsblad*. Looking at the share of
news topics focusing more on entertainment (human interest, lifestyle) and
'serious' news topics (politics, international relations) certain changes can
be seen between 1985 and 2005, but these correspond only partially to the
developments that can be related to featurized journalism (see fig. 1).

    The share of articles on politics increased a little. The share of news
about economics and international relations decreased somewhat, but the
most typical topics signaling the rise of featurized journalism do not seem
to have benefitted from this development. The importance of cultural news
increased somewhat in the paper. This category however consists of both
'high' and 'low' culture, but within *NRC* articles on culture deal for the
greatest part with classical high culture, like literature, classical music, and
theater, and is therefore not a very strong argument for the an increase of
featurized journalism. Although it could be argued that there is a slight decrease in traditional hard news topics like international relations and economy in favour of a stronger focus on culture, the choice of topics does not
reflect an increase of featurized journalism, as such. Moreover, the hallmark
topics of featurized journalism, namely human interest and lifestyle, do not
gain in prominence at all in the *NRC Handelsblad*.

    The same could be said for the choice in genre, in which case the only
difference that could suggest an increase of featurized journalism is the increase in the space devoted to interviews between 1985 and 2005. The
space devoted to reportages and columns or portraits however remained
steady (see fig. 2).

        On the side of the information genres only minor differences can
be discerned: the share of news reports increased slightly, whereas the
prominence of the analysis declined considerably. Still, generally speaking

---

[39] Steensen, 'The Featurization of Journalism', p. 50-55; Cf. Harbers, 'Defying
Journalistic Performativity'.

there is no real support for the claim that featurized journalism is assuming a more prominent position within the paper.

The most obvious explanation is that *NRC Handelsblad* has not changed its profile and stuck to the objectivity paradigm. However, such an answer might not tell the whole story. The media company which owns *NRC Handelsblad* did respond to the changing media landscape by launching *NRC Next* in 2006, its daily twin sister that was published in the morning instead of the afternoon. Although this paper also was described as a quality daily, it was explicitly more focused on trying to engage a new generation of readers, who were said to spend less time on reading the news and wanted more background information. Next to the traditional serious topics the paper focused more on culture and lifestyle, and the first responses indicated that it had a lighter touch than *NRC Handelsblad*.[40] It could be that *NRC Next* offers more space to featurized journalism so that *NRC Handelsblad* can maintain its quality profile, but more research is needed to confirm this suspicion.

Apart from that, I argue that while *NRC Handelsblad* appears not to be focusing a higher percentage of its content on featurized journalism, it does appear to be trying to publish more high-profile examples of featurized journalism, as former editor-in-chief Donker already indicated. One of the most telling examples of this is the reportage series Arnon Grunberg has contributed to *NRC Handelsblad*, which is part of the journalistic and literary discourse drawing closer.[41] Grunberg himself also pointed out the different approach of his pieces, in which he focuses much more on the human interest aspects of his topic:

> [I]t seems to me that mainstream journalism necessarily applies a strict definition of what is news. It is newsworthy when a roadside bomb explodes in Afghanistan, but it isn't newsworthy when a soldier chooses a pair of panties for his girlfriend. I do consider that news. Also, the added value resides in the way it is written down[.][42]

---

[40] Cf. Jensma, F., 'De Lezer Schrijft over de Introductie van NRC.Next, de Nieuwe Ochtendkrant', in: *NRC Handelsblad* (18-03-2006); Author unknown., 'Krant voor Nieuwe Nieuwsconsument', *NRC Handelsblad*, available from: http://vorige.nrc.nl/economie/article1869191.ece (15-08-2005).

[41] Other examples of a similar collaboration is the series 'Uit de stolp' in which literary authors shadowed politicians during the national elections, reportages written by the people behind the regular satirical cartoon 'Fokke en Sukke' or the use of their cartoons instead of pictures as Donker also pointed to in the first quote of this essay.

[42] Harbers, F., 'Between Fact and Fiction: Grunberg on His Literary Journalism', in: *Literary Journalism Studies* 2 (2010), no. 1, p. 76.

When Journalism Meets Literature: An Interesting Example

Grunberg's different approach has not gone unnoticed and has been characterized as an example of the changing norms within journalism discourse –
as well as within literary discourse for that matter. *NRC Handelsblad's* employment of this esteemed novelist and literary jack-of-all-trades can be
seen as interesting example of featurized journalism and offers therefore a
perfect opportunity to further examine this concept with regard to the relation between journalism and literature. As I will show, the cooperation attracted significant attention and inspired debate about trustworthiness and
truthfulness. These discussions often rested upon the institutional separation
of the two domains, which is traditionally so entrenched that the marriage of
Grunberg and *NRC* did not appear self-evident for either the newspaper or
the author. Although literary writers have remained within the ranks of the
newspapers, in general – apart from some notorious examples like Harry
Mulisch or Cees Nooteboom – they hardly ever enter the domain of news
reporting, which has everything to do with the rhetorical opposition between both practices. Since roughly the 1970s the column has always been
the domain of the literary writer, for it is a genre that is not strictly bound to
the dominant journalistic norms pertaining to factuality or impartiality that
govern news reporting.[43] It is therefore not surprising that a literary writer
performing the role of the reporter incited a critical response.

The tension between literature and journalism is reflected in Grunberg's journalistic work. In his first reportage series for which he was embedded with the Dutch army in Uruzgan, Afghanistan, he problematized his
own position as a reporter-novelist:

> I made this journey as an embedded journalist. What 'embedded' meant exactly
> remained to be seen, *and if I could be called a 'journalist' in the strict sense of
> the word was doubtful* [my italics, FH]. But just like 'safety situation,' 'journal-
> ist' is an elastic notion.

In this passage, and throughout the whole article series, Grunberg keeps reflecting on the relation between journalism and literature, suggesting an in-

---

[43] Cf. Wijfjes, H., *Journalistiek in Nederland: Beroep, Cultuur en Organisatie 1850-
2000* (Amsterdam, 2004), 338-340. Brems, H., *Alweer Vogels die Nesten Beginnen:
Geschiedenis van de Nederlandse Literatuur 1945-2005* (Amsterdam, 2006), pp.
381-384; Wijman, E., 'De Column als Literair Genre', in: *Bzzltetin* 17 (1989), no.
164, pp. 27-31; For a characterization of the column, see point 8 on the website of
the Dutch Association of Journalists: http://www.nvj.nl/ethiek/code-voor-de-
journalistiek.

tricate relation between both. In general, Grunberg deals with reality in a different way than is typical for journalism. His overt presence and personal observation form the heart of his reportage, and through the unremitting use of ironic reflection he keeps on highlighting the inherent subjectivity of the process of giving meaning to reality. As a result Grunberg undermines the basic performative truth claim of journalism, which I have analyzed in more detail elsewhere.[44] In the following I will therefore focus on the reasons behind this cooperation, and the way in which the daily and the novelist position themselves in this respect.

First, it is important to reflect on the reasons behind the collaboration of Arnon Grunberg and *NRC Handelsblad*. Of course, Grunberg had already worked as a columnist, so to a certain extent the choice for Grunberg instead of a different literary author was understandable. On the other hand, changes in the collaboration between freelance columnists and newspapers are quite common. So, the question remains: why was Grunberg in the eyes of *NRC* well suited to contribute reportages to the paper? From a commercial perspective this is quite clear, as Grunberg had since 1995 become a bestselling and a highly esteemed novelist, who evidently enjoys great popularity with the readership.[45] It is therefore highly likely that his articles were considered to attract readers, through which the sales revenue of *NRC* could be increased. This idea is supported by the way *NRC* advertised the first reportages Grunberg wrote for the paper in 2006. Preceding his opening reportage a full-page picture was published of Grunberg in military uniform, which announced the start of his reportage series further on in the newspaper. The emphasis of this 'teaser' is on the person who wrote the articles, rather than on the content of the articles themselves.

The logic behind the collaboration becomes more obvious by looking at the status of Grunberg and *NRC Handelsblad* and the respective audience they attract. The profiles of both the paper and the author correspond to some extent with one another. As indicated by his many literary prizes, Grunberg is widely acknowledged as an intellectual author, who writes profound literature in which he intelligently and thought-provokingly reflects on existential themes and issues. *NRC Handelsblad* is considered to be an intellectually oriented newspaper with nuanced and in-depth coverage of the world events and challenging reflective and analytic articles. Thus apart from the rhetorical opposition of both domains, Grunberg and *NRC* match in regards to their appeal to a certain readership.

---

[44] Harbers, 'Defying Journalistic Performativity'.

[45] This combination is rather rare as most books with high sales are suspect with regards to their literary quality. Grunberg has overcome this principle of 'reversed economy' and combines high sales with wide critical acclaim.

Between Priding and Disarming Grunberg's Reportage

Still, the tension between the two domains makes this collaboration a risky business as well. By publishing Grunberg's reportages *NRC*, to a certain extent, puts its trustworthiness at stake on which its status as leading quality daily is based. The newspaper implicitly acknowledges this, because they have adopted a few strategies in which they try to anticipate and deflect possible negative reactions on Grunberg's pieces. Whether Grunberg writes about his work as a chambermaid in a Swiss hotel or about international and politically controversial topics like the military missions in Afghanistan and Iraq, his accounts are mostly published within the cultural supplement or art section. These sections are generally filled with background stories about human interest or lifestyle, which are considered to be on the soft side of the journalistic spectrum with their connotation of superficiality. This defensive strategy, while insulating against critique of its 'news coverage', also means that Grunberg's work is diminished in terms of its prominence and authority as well. This is telling with regard to the way *NRC* regards these pieces.

In addition, *NRC* explicitly classifies Grunberg's pieces as columns, a genre in which the author is permitted the most freedom with regard to fact checking, fairness and integrating fictional elements.[46] This is striking, because the articles are generally – also by Grunberg himself – characterized as reportage. Calling Grunberg's articles columns suggests that the newspaper anticipated stories that deviated from the accepted journalistic norms with regard to news coverage might result in a possible negative reception by their readership. Grunberg himself seemed somewhat irritated by this hedging by the daily and implicitly argued that his accounts are at the least as truthful as those from regular foreign correspondents.

> [M]y articles [about the NATO mission in Afghanistan and Iraq, FH] were published in the Cultural Supplement of the *NRC* or in the art section. That is fine with me. But it is also a conscious choice of the newspaper to disarm the stories a little beforehand. It's as if they are trying to suggest that the articles in the foreign affairs section, mostly written by reporters located in Rotterdam, are closer to reality.[47]

Nevertheless, *NRC*'s anxiety about any negative responses was not unfounded, as proven by the multiple complaints *NRC* received about Grun-

---

[46] 'Ethiek: Code voor de Journalistiek', *Nederlandse Vereniging van Journalisten (NVJ)*, available from, http://www.nvj.nl/ethiek/code-voor-de-journalistiek (2008).
[47] Harbers, 'Between Fact and Fiction', p. 82.

berg's journalism, and which Grunberg himself also acknowledges.[48] The clever, but ambivalent way in which the deputy editor-in-chief Sjoerd de Jong defended the paper's decision to include work by Grunberg also shows the cautious attitude of *NRC* towards his reportages. It seems *NRC* also struggled with the way Grunberg's pieces fitted in with their journalistic profile.

In the first part of his defense De Jong justified Grunberg's articles by referring to the 'silly season' – those moments when politics is in recess – in which there is room for a 'lighthearted element' because of the relatively few newsworthy events in that period.[49] However, he added that although they regretted the discontent of some readers, the publication did deem such articles suitable for the front page, silly season or not.

> We obviously regret that not all our readers appreciate these pieces (yours truly personally finds them surely amusing), but we do not share the opinion that this series is altogether not worth a spot on the front page, summer or winter.[50]

De Jong then moved on to emphasize the merit of Grunberg's other insightful and compelling stories that have dealt with more serious topics, like the war in Afghanistan, or the captives in Guantanamo Bay. He closed his response by announcing that this series of articles by Grunberg would last for another week and tried to comfort any dissatisfaction of the readers by – again implicitly referring to the silly season – saying that 'like all summers this one will not last forever.'[51]

So, De Jong was aware of the deviant status of Grunberg's pieces. He implicitly also acknowledged the opposition between serious and more entertaining topics, but he presented both as an important part of newspaper journalism.

Truth and Trust

These issues with Grunberg's journalism are often discussed within the context of his capacity as a novelist and literary journalist. His alternative form of journalism and his status as a fictional author have infused doubt with regard to the factual accuracy of his reportages. For instance, in the following critique literary critic Max Pam praises Grunberg's accounts in terms of

---

[48] *Ibidem*, p. 77.
[49] De Jong, S., 'De krant Antwoordt', in: *NRC Handelsblad* (04-08-2007).
[50] *Ibidem*.
[51] *Ibidem*.

their literary quality, but doubts their accuracy and accordingly their journalistic veracity.

> That is why he often describes meticulously what he experiences, in which he
> focuses on small occurrences that are hardly worth the effort of writing them
> down. I do not believe that he actually transcribes all the conversations he has,
> but nevertheless everything he hears makes a lifelike impression. Possible that
> the author present us with more than just reality, but that is why he is an au-
> thor.[52]

Only a few critics reflect on the journalistic quality of the pieces, but when
they do, it is his originality and independent perspective that is mentioned
as a strongpoint.[53] These qualities are implicitly related to his position as a
literary author. Because of his literary status, Grunberg is believed to be
able to provide a highly personal perspective on reality that is generally not
permitted to reporters. Thomas Vaessens has also pointed to this form of
independence in his reflection on the relation between literature and journalism. As a journalist is part of a media system in which the media and
their objects of interest (politicians, spokespeople, the military) are entan-
gled in a long-term mutual dependence, they are to a certain extent bound to
a discourse that is the expression of their negotiation over information and
publicity. A literary author is not part of this co-dependence, and as a result
has more freedom in the choice of issues and the way he or she develops a
perspective on reality.[54]

Within the journalistic field Grunberg is thus treated as somewhat of an
outsider: a literary author who embarks on a domain that is largely alien and
whose allegiance is believed to lie primarily with the literary field. As a result the accuracy and veracity of his reportages is doubted by the readership.

An Alternative Way of Representing Reality

Grunberg objects to this image, but his statements about his reportages and
its relation with his literary work convey a somewhat ambivalent attitude
towards the journalistic discourse. On the one hand Grunberg presents himself as somebody who is dedicated to the veracity of his reportages. He emphasizes the importance of getting the facts right and providing the truth as
the *sine qua non* of the journalistic domain.

---

[52] Pam, M., 'Reizen met Grunberg', in: *HP/De Tijd* (13-02-2009).
[53] Pam, Vullings, Cloostermans
[54] Vaessens, T., 'Making Overtures: Literature and Journalism, 1968 and 2008', in:
Literary Journalism Studies 3 (2011), no. 2, pp. 55-72.

I would think it sad, no, appalling, if readers would believe that I visited Iraq or Guantánamo Bay to make up things. That the reality has its absurd aspects is not my fault. The fact that I see those aspects only speaks for my capacity to observe.[55]

He indicates both a responsibility towards his readership as well as to the people who figure in his reportages.

The moment I hand over an article to the newspaper and call it non-fiction, I have to justify to all the people who were willing to talk to me within the framework of the article in spite of the possible danger that my presence put them into. I have heard many people say that my accounts about Guantanamo Bay or Iraq were probably for the largest part invented. The people whom I talked to have to be able to retrace in the text what they have said. That is essential to me.[56]

In the same interview he formulates it even stronger and calls those people frauds who intentionally present and sell fiction as non-fiction.[57]

Yet, his adherence to the truth does not mean that he sees no connection between reality and fiction, or between journalism and literature. He emphasizes the intricate relation between reality and fiction, in which fiction is always in some way related to reality – not necessarily in a traditional fashion like in the realistic novel – and in which reality is influenced by fictional stories that function as a frame of reference to give meaning to experiences and subsequently influence our image of reality.[58] He, thus, implicitly criticizes a perspective in which fiction and reality are regarded as two entirely separate domains. He does maintain a distinction between fiction and reality, but he clearly sees a common ground between both domains, because of which he, as a literary author, is more than anybody capable of representing reality from that perspective.

As a result of his literary mindset, he has different goals and norms when writing his reportage. As I have shown before, Grunberg points to the discourse of journalism in which there exists rather standardized ideas about what constitutes traditional newsworthiness. He emphasizes the greater freedom he has in deciding what to include in his stories. Secondly, he also

---

[55] *Ibidem.*, p. 56.
[56] Goud, J., '"De Toekomst is Niets dan Leegte: Wat Zal Ik Eens Gaan Doen?" Een Gesprek met Arnon Grunberg', in: Goud, J., ed, *Het Leven Volgens Arnon Grunberg: De Wereld als Poppenkast* (Kampen, 2010), p. 145.
[57] *Ibidem*, p. 145.
[58] *Ibidem,* p. 142-143.

implicitly criticizes the depersonalization of modern mainstream journalism, and argues for a way of portraying reality in which, when relevant, the person who observes can be integrated in the story.

> I think you sometimes have to accept that your presence influences a situation. When I was in Afghanistan for the first time and the camp was besieged with a bunch of missiles, I would think it nuts not to write how I reacted to that.[59]

He thus makes a case for a form of reporting in which personal experience and emotion plays an important role. He presents this way of depicting reality in which 'everything that happens in [his] presence and that is interesting to [him] as newsworthy', as an alternative for mainstream journalism. He even argues that such an approach can come closer to reality than the accounts based on the discursive norms and practices of mainstream journalism revolving around objectivity.[60] Grunberg thus positions himself in a way in which he creates a discursive niche for himself by on the one hand emphasizing his dedication to the veracity of his accounts, but on the other hand claiming a different, more nuanced way of representing reality, which does more justice to reality. To a large extent his conception of journalism resembles the concept of featurized journalism.

Conclusion

In this essay I have analyzed the ways in which *NRC Handelsblad* has dealt with the increasing pressure of commercialization. By analyzing the development of their choice in topics and genres in 1985 and 2005 and by scrutinizing their collaboration with esteemed novelist Arnon Grunberg, I have shown that commercial pressures do not necessarily have to result in a stronger focus on 'soft news', but can manifest in other innovative forms of journalism, like literary journalism. This particular case shows how *NRC Handelsblad* presents Grunberg's literary journalism as a unique selling point, which is an addition to their more traditional repertoire. Both Grunberg and the paper acknowledge that his accounts show a deviant way of practicing journalism, but they both argues that it meets the standards of quality journalism.

Through this analysis I have also pointed out the shortcomings of the notion of tabloidization and argued that the 'featurized journalism' is a better, more neutral, term to capture the pluriform developments in journalism in the last decades. This different way of conceptualizing sheds a more nu-

---

[59] Harbers, 'Between Fact and Fiction', p. 81.
[60] *Ibidem,* p. 76-77.

anced light on the developments in journalism by offering room to see both the negative consequences as well as the opportunities featurized journalism has to offer. Featurized journalism thus should not be narrowed down to an increasing focus on celebrity news, superficial human-interest stories and lifestyle columns. Especially within the current age of *I*-Pistemology and life politics, in which the traditional oppositions of 'serious' and 'soft' journalism are dissolving, featurized journalism can offer discursive practices through which the reader can be simultaneously entertained, as well as informed about and engaged in our democratic society, and it is therefore both interesting from a commercial as well as a civic perspective.[61]

---

[61] Cf. Steensen, 'The Featurization of Journalism', p. 57-60.

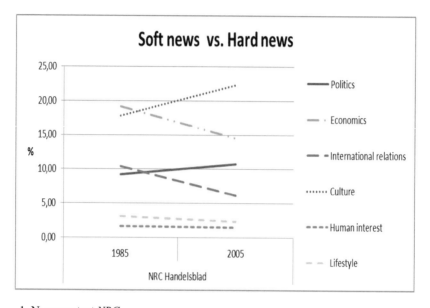

1. News content *NRC*

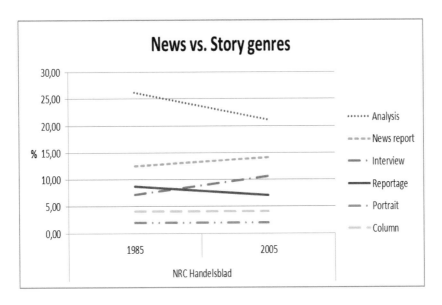

2. Genres in *NRC*

ALMOST LOST IN TRANSLATION

TALE OF AN UNTOLD TRADITION OF JOURNALISM

Gitte Meyer and Anker Brink Lund

This is a tale of an untold framework of thought about the mores and means of journalistic storytelling – a continental European '*Publizist*' tradition of journalism – which has been left largely untold by academics who tell stories about journalistic storytelling. Elements of this tradition appear rather frequently in journalism scholarship, framed as examples of immature modern journalism proper. However, viewed as a framework of thought that has a logic of its own, the tradition remains untold, which overlooks the important contribution it can make to the discourse on journalism. Increasingly, the established discourse on journalism tends to circle round a distinction between so-called traditional journalism and the supposedly diverse journalisms of the digital age. Thereby, the actual diversity of the former might easily be forgotten, and the development of the latter might become informed by assumptions that suit one dominant framework of thought on journalism, but ignore or misinterpret others. In effect, future journalism might become less diverse than many probably hope and expect.

The Northern-European *Publizist* tradition, the logic of which this essay attempts to unfold, has a contribution to make to the discourse on journalistic storytelling because it is rooted, in our interpretation, in a deep grammar of basic assumptions that differ significantly from the deep grammar of basic assumptions that characterize the currently dominant Anglo-American or Atlantic *Reporter* tradition of many schools. Our comparisons and discussions focus on that level of basic assumptions, which we take to be context-dependent, and which form the background also of political cultures and academic traditions.

The Publizist framework of thought relates to an intellectual and political tradition of journalism which has been thriving in particular, but not exclusively, in German-speaking and – in particular prior to the Second World War – Scandinavian-speaking countries.[1] It is marked by a good many concepts that do not translate easily (if at all) into English. Thus, for instance, the tradition is logically related to the concept of *Publizistik*, and that again

---

[1] Note that journalism in the Romance and Slavic languages are not included in our observations.

signifies contributions to the informal political institution of public discussion – *Öffentlichkeit* – and should not be confused with the English notion of the *publicist* as a propagandist or advertising agent. The tradition can be seen as an expression of and a response to political cultures that are based on multiple parties and organized interest groups, who regard compromise as a political virtue. Journalistic participation includes the identification of and enquiry into burning issues of public affairs, and the furthering of public exchanges between multiple and substantially different points of view on such issues.

While the Reporter tradition is well-equipped with academic attention, the Publizist tradition has been practised, rather than theorized or subjected to empirical study. In its own right, it is not a well-described tradition, and in theory it hardly exists. This essay, therefore, attempts to contribute to a theoretical reconstruction, thus preparing the ground for further enquiry and, hopefully, adding some otherwise neglected aspects to the current and future discourse on journalistic storytelling.

Distinct Frameworks of Thought on Journalism

The statement that journalists should 'speak the truth' is a platitude, unlikely to provoke any reflection or contradiction in everyday exchanges. It represents the firm, common ground of a universal ethos of journalism – or so it seems at first glance. At a closer look, however, the statement leaves ample room for interpretation. In fact, very different presuppositions may motivate the endorsement of the statement.

In one interpretation, to 'speak the truth' relates to a notion of universal and, thus, monistic truth as in religion and science – in the latter case twinned with technical rationality. Truth in this sense, and not least with the meaning of speaking truth to power, is essential to the Reporter framework of thought.

In another interpretation, to 'speak the truth' relates to a practical, worldly notion of truthfulness. The notion of *truthfulness,* rather than that of (universal) *truth*, is essential to the ethos of the Publizist tradition of journalism. That distinction is no mere quibbling, but may serve as a gateway to understanding Publizist ideals, norms and practices.

Using the well-known to throw light on the less well-known, we will compare the frameworks of thought that seem to be informing the Reporter and the Publizist traditions of journalism, respectively. Comparisons are made between the Reporter and the Publizist traditions of journalism as related, respectively, to the science and the humanist traditions of scholarship and, thus, even to different Enlightenment traditions.[2] A history of mutual animosity and conflict is recognized, and it is argued that the traditions can be seen as expressions of complementary frameworks of thought with possibilities for mutual learning. That, however, presupposes that the basic differences be acknowledged.

Against that background, the interplay between journalism scholarship and research on the one hand and journalistic practice on the other is discussed. The case is made that current scholarship and research may inadvertently, and in spite of a commitment to diversity, contribute to the disfigurement and gradual disintegration of the Publizist tradition of journalism.

The Anglo-American foundation of journalism studies may be leading to a dominance of a very specific paradigm that facilitates the understanding of the Reporter tradition, but prevents the understanding – to the point of making it invisible – of Publizist journalism. Not being seen means not being told, means moving even further into the sphere of ghosts. Thus, the force of untold academic tales about journalistic storytelling can be as fateful as that of untold journalistic stories and may alter the landscape of journalism. Scholarly *observers* of journalists and journalism *participate* in the field of journalistic practice. Therefore, there is a need to reconsider the interplay between, and the shared responsibility of, journalism scholars and journalistic practitioners in this shared field of practice.

The Reporter and the Notion of Universal Truth

The Anglo-American Reporter tradition, as it evolved in the early twentieth century, is widely taken to represent the epitome of modern journalism and has come to comprise a cluster of different schools.[3] As seen from within the tradition, the shared features of different schools may be hard to recognize. As seen from a distance, though, a shared framework of thought may become apparent. While recognizing that the Reporter tradition includes a good deal of diversity,[4] the following very brief analysis focuses on features

---

[2] Bahr, E., ed, *Was ist Aufklärung? Thesen und Definitionen* (Stuttgart, 2002); Jacob, M.C., *The Radical Enlightenment: Pantheists, Freemasons and Republicans* (Lafayette, LA, 2006); Porter, R., *Enlightenment: Britain and the Creation of the Modern World* (London, 2001).

[3] Schudson, M., *The Power of News* (London, 2000); Meyer, G. and Lund, A.B., 'Spiral of Cynicism: Are Media Researchers Mere Observers?' *Ethical Space: The International Journal of Communication Ethics* 5 (2008), no. 3, pp. 33-42.

[4] Williams, K., 'Anglo-American Journalism: The Historical Development of Practice, Style and Form', in: Broersma, M., ed, *Form and Style in Journalism: Europe-*

of the shared framework of the tradition that we consider to be crucial to a comparison with the Publizist tradition.

A notion of universal and impersonal truth constitutes the centerpiece of the reporter framework of thought. That makes science an obvious model and infuses the tradition with a striving for purity and a drift towards polarization, which has also been connected to the rise of monotheistic religion.[5] The idea of universal truth comes with a framework of assumed dichotomies, originating in truth vs. untruth or falsity or error, and moving on to observation vs. participation; description vs. normativity; objectivity vs. subjectivity; rationality vs. emotion; facts vs. value; the material vs. the spiritual; thought vs. action; science vs. politics; truth vs. power; top-down vs. bottom-up; unity vs. diversity; consensus vs. conflict; the elites vs. the masses; news vs. opinion; et cetera.

Recently, American journalism scholars have highlighted the hitherto unrecognized religious roots of American reporter values, and the dilemmas of American reporters have been related to 'a tension between profit and the prophetic voice in journalism'.[6] Less elegantly phrased, it seems a significant feature of, and a source of continuous tension within, the Reporter tradition that it is connected simultaneously to the marketplace and the sphere of production (the material), and also to absolute values that originate in religious thought (the spiritual) and appear to some extent in secularized versions in science. Along related lines, the public or citizenry may be perceived as consumers or as members of close communities of shared values.

Correspondingly, this tradition of many schools can be seen as expressing and responding to political cultures in which religious thought and values play a significant role in public and political life. Deeply committed to democracy and to science, those political cultures of two-party systems[7] display a distinct weariness towards politics and rhetoric as partisan phenomena of power-play and strife, and an acute awareness of the possible corrupting influences of social, economic and political interests and corruption of power-holders. Related features – such as a commitment to strict objectivity and a longing for consensus in the shape of truth(s) beyond dispute

---

an *Newspapers and the Representation of News, 1880-2005* (Leuven, 2007), pp. 1-26.

[5] Assmann, J., *The Price of Monotheism* (Stanford, CA, 2010).

[6] Nord, D.P., *Communities of Journalism: A History of American Newspapers and their Readers* (Chicago, 2001); Underwood, D., *From Yahveh to Yahoo: The Religious Roots of the Secular Press* (Chicago, 2008); Underwood, D., *From Yahveh to Yahoo*, p. 29.

[7] That such political systems are superiour to other varieties of democracy seems often to be taken for granted in journalism scholarship. See for instance Williams, K., 'Anglo-American Journalism', pp. 1-26.

– are prominent in the academic science tradition and in the Reporter tradition. The latter evolved in the wake of the American civil war in the nineteenth century, alongside the Progressive movement with its strong belief in science.[8] Along related lines, the academic science tradition was founded in the aftermath of the English civil wars in the seventeenth century.[9]

Generically, professional reporter values of objectivity, neutrality and impartiality are contrasted sharply with notions of partisanship, advocacy, activism, commentary and interpretation. Probably, the generic reporter would feel uneasy if designated a storyteller. Reporters are supposed to report on events and to do so as outside observers, eager to adopt methods and techniques that may support the standardization – the technical equivalent of universal truth – of journalistic descriptions of reality that everybody can rely upon. That can be linked to an overall aim of preventing conflicts between different points of view – 'the truth, beyond differences of opinion'.[10] It can even be seen as a social task, the task of creating social unity and consensus. Conflicts are supposed, also, to be two-sided, and the reporter should report from both sides. Apart from this, the generic reporter tasks, vis-à-vis political life, are limited to a watchdog function towards the powers that be.

There is space within this kind of framework for quite a lot of variation. Actually, the radically detached reporter, with his ideal of pure observation, came into being accompanied by partisan muckrakers, and the generic reporter has – not least during the most recent half century – generated offspring in the shape of alternative schools, based on alternative interpretations of the framework of dichotomies that served to define the reporter in the first place.[11] Most commonly, alternative schools appear to be founded on a normative inversion that reverses the attribution of value.[12] For example, instead of observation and objectivity, participation as advocacy, partisanship and subjectivity may be linked to truth – and perhaps even to the truth claim that the notion of truth represents a mere illusion, and that there is no other truth than power. Moreover, the view of the public as divided into the elites and the masses may inspire intellectually demanding and sentimentalist reporting styles, respectively.

Recently, approaches aimed at allowing different varieties of journalism to become visible in scholarly work have appeared and have included

---

[8] Cater, D., *The Fourth Branch of Government* (New York, 1959), p. 85.

[9] Shapin, S. and Schaffer, S., *Leviathan and the Air-pump: Hobbes, Boyle, and the Experimental Life* (Princeton, NJ, 1985), p. 76.

[10] Muhlmann, G., *A Political History of Journalism* (Cambridge, 2008), pp. 6,17.

[11] Underwood, *From Yahveh to Yahoo*.

[12] Assmann, *The Price of Monotheism*.

comparisons of such varieties with Anglo-American conventions and norms.[13] There is, however, a general tendency for assumptions, conceptual understandings and analytical approaches that originate in the Reporter framework of thought to be kept in place. In effect, the Reporter framework easily acquires the status of being the measure of all journalistic activities. Thereby, the ability to capture and understand the logic of other frameworks of thought on journalism may be hampered. That can be illustrated by the case of Publizist journalism.

The Publizist and the Demand for Truthfulness in Public Discussion

While the Reporter tradition has been connected to an Atlantic media model, the Publizist tradition of journalism can be placed within a North/Central European media modeland appears to have been thriving in particular, but not exclusively so, in German-speaking and – in particular prior to the Second World War – Scandinavian countries.[14] In our interpretation, it represents a framework of thought on journalism which was probably rather mainstream and taken for granted in North and Central Europe prior to the Second World War, but has never been spelled out as a framework of thought. In their practice, a good many journalists may still to some extent be tacitly informed by its logic, but as already mentioned, the tradition rarely appears as a distinct tradition in scholarly work and it hardly exists in theory. As a framework of thought it is, in other words, mute. A theoretical reconstruction is needed in order to make it speak.

Historically, public discussion between substantially different points of view (*Öffentlichkeit*) has been considered a pivotal institution of democracy by Scandinavian and German political thinkers.[15] Accordingly, it is the point of departure of the following step-wise and partial attempt to reconstruct the Publizist framework of thought that the institution of public dis-

---

[13] See for instance Broersma, M., 'Form, Style and Journalistic Strategies: An Introduction', in: *Form and Style in Journalism: European Newspapers and the Representation of News, 1880-2005* (Leuven, 2007), pp. ix-xxix; Hallin, D. and Mancini, P., *Comparing Media Systems: Three Models of Media and Politics* (Cambridge, 2004); Høyer, S., 'Rumours of Modernity: How American Journalism spread to Europe', in: Broersma, M., ed, *Form and Style in Journalism,* pp. 27-52; Muhlmann, *A Political History of Journalism.*

[14] Hallin and Mancini, *Comparing Media Systems.*

[15] Arendt, H., *Das Urteilen: Texte zu Kants Politische Philosophie*; Hallin, D. C. and Mancini, P., *Comparing Media Systems Beyond the Western World* (Cambridge, 2012); Habermas, J., *Strukturwandel der Öffentlichkeit* (Frankfurt am Main, 1962); Koch, H., *Hvad er Demokrati?* (Copenhagen, 1995).

cussion – rather than the notion of (universal) truth – constitutes its center-piece.

That, in turn, can be seen as a journalistic expression of and response to pluralistic political cultures which are based on multiple political parties and organizations, including a multitude of organized interest groups, in all walks of life. Within that kind of logic, compromise is taken to constitute a political virtue.[16] Accordingly, continuous discussion and negotiation be-tween multiple points of view is crucial to political life – a feature that may also originate in early modern traditions of literary debate.[17] Politics, thus, is taken to be participatory by definition, but the radicalism of English notions such as 'partisanship' and 'advocacy' – often applied by journalism schol-ars to elements of Publizist journalism – are not really compatible with the logic and cannot be translated into, for instance, the Scandinavian lan-guages.[18]

In current European scholarly work on journalism, references to the in-stitution of public discussion are actually quite frequent. At the same time, however, they also tend to seem oddly out of place, as if a piece from an-other puzzle had been inserted, but not successfully integrated, into the work.[19] The references leave the impression that public discussion, some-how, constitutes the *raison-d'être* of journalism. But from the context it is far from obvious why that should be the case.

Max Weber, who in 1919 described journalism as the epitome of a po-litical profession, provided a defining piece of that other puzzle.[20] At the same time, he linked politics to an ethic of responsibility for future action, as distinct from an ethic of ultimate ends, typical of religion.[21] Journalistic identification with the institution of public discussion makes sense if jour-nalism is taken to be part of political life – if journalists are taken to be par-ticipants (not to be confused with being partisans) rather than outside ob-servers.

Weber was not the only scholar of his time who took an interest in journalism. Actually, the Publizist tradition seems to have been matched, during the inter-war years of the German Weimar Republic, by a short-lived scholarly tradition of journalism and newspaper studies – *Zeitungswissen-*

---

[16] Gerhardt, V., *Partizipation: Das Prinzip der Politik* (Munich, 2007).
[17] Habermas, *Strukturwandel der Öffentlichkeit*; Safranski, R., *Goethe & Schiller: Geschichte einer Freundschaft* (Munich, 2009).
[18] Gerhardt, *Partizipation*; Meyer, G. and Lund, A.B., 'International Language Mon-ism and Homogenisation of Journalism', *Javnost — The Public* 15 (2008), no. 4, pp. 73-86.
[19] Meyer and Lund, *Spiral of Cynicism*.
[20] Weber, M., *Politik als Beruf* (Stuttgart, 1992), pp. 36-37.
[21] *Ibidem*, p. 70.

schaft – of a humanist vein. This was a scholarly approach marked by preoccupation in particular with questions relating to history and hermeneutics and congenial to the growing field of the humanities (*Geisteswissenschaften*) with their aim of 'understanding' (*verstehen*) as distinct from the natural scientific aim of providing causal and functional explanation.[22]

Thus, there is an obvious link to Renaissance humanism with its keen interest in human affairs, diversity, language, interpretation and exchange.[23] A consequent understanding of speech as the main cohesive factor of society and of truthfulness as the first command of public life can be found in Renaissance writings such as the essays of Michel de Montaigne, well-known for his skepticism with regard to universal truths in human affairs as well as for his combination of intellectual reflection and political practice.[24]

A Multitude of Perspectives

Another important contribution was made in 1929 by Siegfried Kracauer. He promoted an approach to journalism which might easily be misunderstood as a defence of eclecticism. Offering a critique of the journalistic ideal of reporting he proposed another approach to realism: a multitude of perspectives had to be included and put together, and the whole process should be supported by substantial reflection and interpretation.[25] Kracauer used the metaphor of a mosaic:

---

[22] Averbeck, S. and Kutsch, A., 'Thesen zur Geschichte der Zeitungs- und Publizistikwissenschaft 1900-1960', in: Duchkowitsch, W. et al., eds, *Die Spirale des Schweigens: Zum Umgang mit der Nationalsozialistischen Zeitungswissenschaft* (Berlin, 2004), pp. 55-66; Bohrmann, H., 'Als der Krieg zu Ende war: Von der Zeitungswissenschaft zur Publizistik', in: Duchkowitsch, W. et al., eds, *Die Spirale des Schweigens: Zum Umgang mit der Nationalsozialistischen Zeitungswissenschaft* (Berlin, 2004), pp. 97-122; Hardt, H., 'Am Vergessen scheitern: Essay zur historischen Identität der Publizistikwissenschaft, 1945-68', all in: Duchkowitsch, W. *et al.*, eds, *Die Spirale des Schweigens: Zum Umgang mit der Nationalsozialistischen Zeitungswissenschaft* (Münster, 2004), pp. 153-160; Schnädelbach, H., *Vernunft* (Stuttgart, 2007), p. 127.
[23] Kristeller, P.O., *Renaissance Thought: The Classic, Scholastic and Humanist Strains* (New York, 1961); Toulmin, S., *Cosmopolis: The Hidden Agenda of Modernity* (New York, 1990).
[24] De Montaigne, M., 'Wenn Man Einander des Lügens Bezichtigt', in: *Essais: Erste moderne Gesamtübersetzung von Hans Stilett. Vol II* (Frankfurt am Main, 2000), p. 508.
[25] More recently, David Hockney, the British painter, has presented a similar argumentation – not related to journalism, though, but to painting, in Hockney, D., *Secret Knowledge: Rediscovering the Lost Techniques of the Old Masters* (London, 2006).

Certainly, life must be observed in order for it to arise. However, it cannot be captured by the report's more or less haphazard sequence of observations. Rather, it is contained in the mosaic that can be put together from individual observations, guided by recognition of the substantial significance of those observations.[26]

Kracauer was a sociologist. He also practiced as a journalist. Initially, in 1929, he published his study of the white-collar workers – the source of the above quotation – as a series of articles in a newspaper, the *Frankfurter Zeitung*. He did so with the intention of stimulating public discussion.[27] To current readers he does not come through either as a scholar or as a journalist, but simply as an intellectual, committed to public discussion between substantially different points of view, and defying assumed dichotomies such as science vs. politics, or the elites vs. the masses.

After the Second World War independent intellectuals such as Hans Magnus Enzensberger carried on a similar approach to journalism. He described critical thoroughness as a journalistic virtue and saw the exchange between substantially different points of view as crucial to society. He also made a point of unfolding the Publizist notion of *Aktualität* – the counterpart of the Reporter tradition's notion of news. *Aktualität* is a thick concept, descriptive and normative at the same time.[28] It combines the identification of something as new (descriptive) with judgement on relevance (normative) and serves to identify burning issues that ought to be subjected to public scrutiny and exchange.[29] There is a concern, thus, with the conditions for collective action, rather than with (universal) truth. Like other thick concepts, the notion of *Aktualität* does not fit into the dichotomic scheme that forms the basis of the Reporter framework.

Thick concepts – truthfulness is another example – seem to be crucial to the Publizist mindset, but to the strictly analytical mind such concepts are likely to appear embarrassingly fuzzy and perhaps even irrational because of their blending of aspects, which in proper rational analysis ought to be kept radically separated. The prominence of thick thinking in the Publizist

---

[26] The original quotation reads: 'Gewiss muss das Leben beobachtet werden, damit sie erstehe. Keineswegs jedoch ist sie in der mehr oder minder zufälligen Beobachtungsfolge der Reportage enthalten, vielmehr steckt sie einzig und allein in dem Mosaik, das aus den einzelnen Beobachtungen auf Grund der Erkenntnis ihres Gehalts zusammengestiftet wird.', in Kracauer, S., *Die Angestellten* (Frankfurt am Main, 1929', p. 6. Above is our tentative translation.

[27] *Ibidem*, p. 8.

[28] Enzensberger, H.M., *Einzelheiten I: Bewusstseins-Industrie* (Frankfurt am Main, 1964); Williams, B., *Ethics and the Limits of Philosophy* (London, 1993).

[29] Meyer and Lund, 'International Language Monism'.

framework may make it incomprehensible from some scientific points of view. Actually, it may even result in it being recognized as no more than a mess: the combination, for instance, of a commitment to values of accuracy and thoroughness *and* a distinct dislike of standardization and techniques may to the scientist seem puzzling or downright illogical and erroneous.[30] Robert K. Merton was puzzled by a similar feature in European humanist scholars when, in 1949, he compared American mass communication research and European *Wissenssoziologie*. He took it to be a logical error.[31]

The clues we have gathered so far connect the Publizist framework or logic to a journalistic idea(l) of non-partisan participation in political life in the shape of public discussion between substantially different points of view. That again is connected to intellectual reflection and interpretation, to demands for truthfulness, critical thoroughness and the inclusion of a multitude of perspectives in journalistic storytelling about burning issues. Finally we have come across an affinity for thick concepts, which defy the conventional demand that descriptive and normative aspects be kept so radically separate as to make interpretation a suspicious activity.

The question that concerns us here does not relate to the possible merits or problems of journalism that may be based on such idea(l)s – which are, obviously, very demanding of journalists and their audiences, and, moreover, have been living in theoretical obscurity for decades. Rather, we are simply asking: does the above description constitute a distinct logic at all, or is it just a mess?

A logic may become apparent, we believe, if the classical notions of *praxis* and *phronesis* – practical reason – are introduced and used as stepping stones: The classical idea(l) of practical reasoning is actually an idea(l) of thick reasoning.

Practical Knowledge Pluralism

Plurality (of human beings and, consequently, of points of view) and uncertainty (with regard to the consequences of action) are main features of the classical, Aristotelian (and, thus, pre-monotheistic) approach to the world as the specifically human space, captured in the notion of *praxis*: the human world of limits, diversity and uncertainty.[32] Within this three-dimensional ontology, the world of human affairs is defined as a specifically human

---

[30] Enzensberger, *Einzelheiten*.

[31] Merton, R.K., *Social Theory and Social Structure* (New York, 1968), pp. 493-509.

[32] Arendt, H., 'Kultur und Politik', *Merkur: Deutsche Zeitschrift für Europäisches Denken* 130 (1958), no. 12, pp. 1122-1145; Arendt, H., *The Human Condition* (London, 1969).

sphere of speech and action – and not according to an assumed dichotomy of the material vs. the spiritual.

In this human sphere, as distinct from mechanical nature and the unlimited universe, human beings have only themselves, and their twin capacities for making and exchanging judgments, to rely on. Nothing is absolute. Everything human is limited in time, in space and because of the plurality of mankind. Human affairs are worldly affairs and must – as death is the only escape route from the world – be viewed from positions *in* the world. Action in the world depends on human judgment and exchange between different perspectives that enrich and delimit each other. Such positions and perspectives cannot be anything but personal. Accordingly, personal integrity and credibility are of utmost importance to dealings with human affairs.

Public and political life, essential activities in the world, depend on the exercise of the intellectual virtue of practical reason, *phronesis*; that is, the art of reasoning and judging on the conditions for proper and rightful action on a case-to-case basis.[33] *Phronetic* reasoning is thick reasoning. There is no assumption that (worldly) facts and values can or should be radically separated. Rather, the *phronetic* reasoner combines descriptive and normative aspects and considers thought and action to be interdependent.[34] Actually, the very ability to act is defined, as part of this logic, by the human capacity for thought and reasoning and is seen as a specifically human quality. Truthfulness, signifying at the same time the personal virtue of credibility (normative) and the feature of accuracy in an account (descriptive) can be seen as a precondition for the exercise of practical reason.

If the world of human affairs is taken to be many-sided and open-ended, then human action must be guided by the continuous exchange between different points of view. Public discussion between citizens, therefore, is the political mode and should be seen as a form of enquiry – the success of which is preconditioned by a critical audience.[35] Discussion and deliberation are, in other words, neither aimed at the creation of social intimacy, nor at achieving consensus in close and homogeneous communities; neither can the aims of discussion be reduced to mere negotiation between conflicting social interests nor to exchanges on purely moral values.[36] Ra-

---

[33] MacIntyre, A., *After Virtue: A Study in Moral Theory* (Notre Dame IN, 1984); Arendt, *The Human Condition*.

[34] This should not be confused with holism which is concerned with universal truths that encompass all dimensions of reality. Phronetic reasoning concerns only the world of human affairs.

[35] Crick, B., *In Defence of Politics* (New York, 2005); Aristotle, *Retorik* (Copenhagen, 2002).

[36] Dallmayr, F., 'Hermeneutics and Inter-Cultural Dialog: Linking Theory and Practice', *Ethics & Global Politics* 2 (2009), no. 1, pp. 23-39.

ther, public discussion is considered a mode of enquiry into actual conditions in the world, aimed at assessing the lay of the land and at probing into
political issues proper, as distinct from questions and problems relating to
nature or universal truth.

Within this framework of practical knowledge pluralism, that which is
considered genuinely public and shared *in* the world of human affairs is no
more and no less than the responsibility to continuously, truthfully and critically consider and discuss the possibilities for proper and rightful action.
Public discussion is considered pivotal to society because it is ascribed a
capacity for improving the understanding of the conditions for action in the
world as distinct from a capacity for uncovering universal truth(s) or solv-
ing technical problems. Pluralism is, at the same time, an idea about reality
(descriptive) and an ideal (normative) concerning the political living together of the diverse group of citizens who are bound together only by equal political responsibilities and rights and a shared capacity for thought, speech
and reasoning.

Journalism as Practical Reasoning

Against the backdrop of the classical notions of *praxis* and *phronesis*, seeming contradictions of the Publizist framework acquire a logic of their own.
The accuracy of journalistic stories and the personal integrity of journalists
are crucial to public discussion as enquiry into the possibilities for proper
action, related to burning issues of public affairs. Standardization, on the
other hand, might invalidate the *phronetic* abilities of journalists. Thereby it
would make the whole scheme fall apart.

Because of its affinity with public discussion, the Publizist framework
may easily be linked to ideas about *deliberative* democracy. The framework
does not, however, fit into mainstream deliberative theory, which tends to
relate deliberation to social aims of consensus and to be operating on the
assumed dichotomies of consensus vs. conflict, and unity vs. diversity.[37]
Instead, there is a commitment to exchanges between substantially different
points of view as a mode of practical, political enquiry which includes conflict *and* may support reasonable collective action and political compromise
from case to case.

The Publizist framework can also be linked to ideas about *participatory*
democracy, but is at the same time committed to intellectual exchanges. The
framework does not fit into interpretations which – on the basis of assumed
dichotomies of thought vs. action and the emotional vs. the intellectual –

---

[37] Mutz, D.C., *Hearing the Other Side: Deliberative vs. Participatory Democracy*
(New York, 2006).

take participation to signify the fervor, shouting, cheering et cetera of a group of people gathering around a common cause.[38]

Finally, the Publizist tradition may be described as a *critical* tradition. Except for the fact that the notion of critique, rather than being taken to signify thorough and many-faceted attention to substance, may be incorporated into a dichotomic scheme and narrowed down to signify mere negation of a dominant position.[39]

Summing up, the Publizist framework appears neither to be founded on the strong tension between the material and the spiritual nor on those other assumed dichotomies that seem so conspicuous in the Reporter framework. Rather, it can be characterized as a worldly framework of thought and assumptions, connecting journalism to civil society and the market-place and expressing and responding to pluralistic political cultures. It perceives the journalistic tasks to be at the same time intellectual and political, and stresses substance and personal abilities to discern rather than techniques, and reasonable participation rather than outside observation. It even adopts a task of realizing the potential for critical thought in the public; and if successful, it may, as a side-effect, contribute to a continuous, societal process of critical self-interpretation.

As a journalistic variety that circles the institution of public discussion rather than the notion of (universal) truth, the Publizist tradition makes sense when connected to the classical notion of practical reason as thick reasoning. The Publizist framework can be seen as a distinct framework of thought on journalism, which is substantially different from the Reporter framework.

That should not be taken to imply the existence of a Reporter vs. Publizist dichotomy. From a historical point of view, it would be fairly easy to trace and tell a story of mutual animosity between the kinds of thought and assumptions that the two traditions represent, and to connect that animosity to different enlightenment traditions and to a conflict between modern science and key aspects of Renaissance thought.[40]

From a logical point of view, however, dichotomies are not constituted by animosity and conflict, but by the fact that they represent two sides of one and the same coin. They are divided and connected by shared basic (and often tacit) assumptions. The Reporter and the Publizist framework, however, seem founded on basically different assumptions. In this case, thus, we are dealing with different coins. The classical notion of *praxis* may serve as a stepping-stone to understanding the Publizist tradition and the

---

[38] *Ibidem.*

[39] Marcuse, H., *One-Dimensional Man* (Boston, 1968).

[40] Toulmin, *Cosmopolis.*

thick concepts of that tradition. The Reporter tradition, on the other hand, makes sense when compared to the notion of *universal truth* and a conceptual framework of dichotomies.

The different frameworks are likely to come with different problems and possibilities – and with different understandings of seemingly shared notions and concepts – and the very difference between them is likely to constitute a source of conflict, but can also be seen as a possible source of mutual learning. The relationship between the frameworks might be seen as being of a complementary nature. That, however, would be preconditioned by the general acknowledgement that basically different frameworks of thought on journalism do, indeed, exist.

With respect to the Publizist logic, it would be preconditioned by the specific acknowledgement that it is a non-dichotomic logic and is likely to defeat attempts at analysis and categorization, which are based on dichotomic schemes. Observation vs. participation; unity vs. diversity; the individual vs. society; the elites vs. the masses; knowledge vs. opinion; intellectual vs. popular; science vs. politics and conflict vs. consensus are examples of assumed dichotomies that are likely to hamper the understanding of the Publizist framework of thought.

The Interplay of Academic and Journalistic Storytelling

The current separation of journalism scholarship and journalistic practice is an outcome of several historical processes. One such process can be related to real-life attempts to separate thought and action.

Looking sufficiently far back, the common roots of social science and journalism become apparent. Thus, the intellectual and political enlightenment movements of Europe in the seventeenth and eighteenth centuries were carried on by publicists, and some modern historians have chosen simply to define a whole lot of them as journalists.[41] The understanding of this early history of journalism – and its implications with respect to today's interplay between journalists and journalism scholars – is hampered by the standard dating of the birth of modern journalism in the 1830s. At that time, social scientists and journalists were parting company, and the classical understanding of practice as *praxis* had gone a long way towards succumbing to a technical understanding of practice as no more than the application of scientific knowledge.[42] The ground had been prepared for a hierarchic rela-

---

[41] Burke, P., *A Social History of Knowledge. From Gutenberg to Diderot* (Cambridge, 2000); Jacob, *The Radical Enlightenment*.
[42] Gadamer, H.-G., *Wahrheit und Methode* (Tübingen, 1975), p. 518.

tionship between journalists and future journalism scholars to appear as part of the natural order of things.

Roughly since the end of the Second World War, journalism and journalists have increasingly been made the objects of academic study and interpretation. The scholarly field of media and journalism studies has evolved into an academic authority which tells journalists who they are, what they are doing, how they are doing it, why they are doing it and, now and again, why they ought to do some things differently. To a large extent, a division of labor has evolved along the lines of a relationship between brain (academic study) and body (journalistic practice).

After 1945, it has been noted, a cultural re-orientation towards the Allies took place among journalists.[43] During the same period of time, the science tradition – alongside the English language and its concepts – has gained momentum in the academic world at large. It appears to have been forceful in particular within the growing area of communication research, including journalism studies. The contributions of Weber and Kracauer represent scholarly approaches to journalism that were largely left behind by academics after the Second World War.[44] Currently, therefore, the journalistic Reporter tradition – using science as the model and being well-furnished with concepts in English – is likely to be more easily understood by many journalism scholars and researchers than the Publizist tradition of journalism. That might lead to distorted academic representations of the latter tradition, affecting the practice of Publizist journalism adversely.

The idea of the researcher and, indeed, of the Reporter as a mere observer – marked by perfect objectivity – has been deconstructed in theory again and again for decades. Against this background, the argument seems uncontroversial that scholarly observation of journalism constitutes more than mere observation. Scholarly observation can be regarded as a variety of participation in a wide, but today seemingly unrecognized field of practice which includes journalists and journalism scholars. The scholar-cum-researcher is always also present and contributes to the field by way of educating, monitoring, interpreting and evaluating journalists and journalism.[45] Using the rhetoric of theoretical analysis and empirical study, journalism scholars tell stories about journalism, and their stories – as well as their untold tales – impact the reality of journalism.

---

[43] Broersma, 'Form, Style and Journalistic Strategies'.
[44] Averbeck and Kutsch, 'Thesen zur Geschichte'; Bohrmann, 'Als der Krieg zur Ende war'; Hardt, 'Am Vergessen scheitern'; Splichal, S., 'Why be Critical?', *Communication, Culture & Critique* 1 (2008), no. 1, pp. 20-30.
[45] Meyer and Lund, 'Spiral of Cynicism'.

However, while scholar-cum-researchers observe and analyze 'the gaze of the journalist', the presence of the second order gaze of the scholar-cum-researcher might easily be ignored. Even though the idea(l) of objectivity has been debunked in theory, it may still to some extent inform scientific methods which are designed to prevent normative judgments in academic researchers, and to support efforts aimed at pure description.[46] In so far as scientific observation is regarded as the opposite of participation, the attention of academic researchers may be diverted from those basic assumptions that inform their own gaze at journalism and journalists: Only participants who acknowledge themselves as participants have reason to scrutinize how they participate. Consequently, unspoken and unrecognized assumptions from scholarly frameworks of thought might be imposed on the object of study and inform the scholarly storytelling. To some extent, however, that may be prevented by efforts to actually reflect on such assumptions.

The Potential Paralysis of Publizist Journalism

In order to prompt such reflection, it may be useful to take a very brief look – at a very basic level – at the possible interplay between empirical journalism studies and Publizist journalism; using the scientific notion of 'social reality' as the point of departure.

As a rule, empirical social science produces social facts and is aimed at depicting 'social reality'. The notion can be seen as a kind of stand-in for (universal) truth. At the same time, 'social reality' seems to be defined by what may (and may not) be captured by empirical methods. The notion of 'illusions', then, signify all that cannot be captured by empirical methods. Accordingly, the notion of 'social reality' appears to form part of an assumed dichotomy of social reality vs. illusions.

The institution of public discussion, as discussed in the above, may not easily – if at all – be captured by empirical investigation and is at constant risk of being labeled an illusion.[47] A benign illusion perhaps, but an illusion nevertheless. Consequently, the kind of reasoning that underpins Publizist journalism is at constant risk of being labeled, by academic authorities, as the epitome of naivety and perhaps even romanticism. Other possible labels include elitism, partisanship or advocacy.

Such labeling may induce awkwardness in journalists. They may be prompted to exit Publizist practices and adapt to expectations that go more easily along with the dominant Reporter tradition. Adopting an unfamiliar framework of thought, some may even be pushed into extreme positions,

---

[46] Muhlmann, *A Political History of Journalism*.
[47] Meyer and Lund, 'International Language Monism'.

advocating for instance – more fiercely, perhaps, than any 'born' reporter – the equally untrustworthy alternatives of absolute objectivity or absolute subjectivity. Increased standardization and loss of diversity in journalism would be likely to be the cumulative result of many such processes.

We do not believe this to represent the only possible mode of interplay between empirical journalism studies and Publizist journalism. Rather, it can be used as a starting point for reconsidering the interplay of journalism research and scholarship on the one hand, and actual journalism on the other.

The Potential Recombination of Academic and Journalistic Storytelling

Journalism studies serve, among other things, a monitoring function. We have been arguing that there is no such thing as monitoring pure. The monitor is always also a co-producer. However, this should not be read as a prologue to the introduction of a new field of study and monitoring – the field of 'journalism studies studies', so to speak. That would never end. Monitors monitoring monitors would follow in an endless chain.

A more fertile approach might be to institutionalize habits of discussion on equal footing between journalism scholars and journalists, supported by increased scholarly awareness of and attention to different frameworks of thought on journalism. With regard to the Publizist tradition, for example, this would include attention to its ethos, to its early history and to the short-lived humanist tradition of journalism scholarship that evolved in the German Weimar Republic of the inter-war years.

As substantial discussion is vital to the Publizist tradition, the presentation of the outcomes of empirical studies as open-ended presentations for reflection and discussion within a shared field of practice would leave the Publizist framework intact *and* open to criticism. Moreover, other frameworks of thought on journalism might benefit and, indeed, become visible. Scholars might be provided with material for hitherto untold tales. The only precondition seems to be that scholars recognize themselves as observing participants or participating observers in a field of practice, which they share with journalists.

Not presented as views from nowhere, but as something that somebody has seen, and that may be well worth listening and responding to – as no more and no less than truthful stories to be reckoned with – empirical journalism studies may inspire reflection in journalists, while avoiding any push towards a de facto standardization of journalism. And that, in turn, might not only serve a purpose of maintaining diversity in journalism, but could also further the experience of shared responsibility for a shared field of practice.

The shared responsibility concerns the possibilities and limitations *of* and the challenges *to* journalism as part of the multiple varieties of public and political life in democratic societies. Journalists participate by way of journalistic storytelling. Journalism scholars participate by way of academic storytelling about journalism and journalists. The maintenance of diversity in journalism – whether digital or traditional – can be seen as one shared task, which may be obstructed by a radical separation of scholarship and research on the one hand, and actual journalism on the other.

Acknowledging and Maintaining Diversity

We have compared two frameworks of thought on journalism, equally context-dependent and historically rooted, but connected, in our interpretation, to different political cultures and academic traditions. One is the currently dominant framework of the Anglo-American Reporter tradition, the center-piece of which is a notion of universal truth. That, again, generates a rationalistic scheme of dichotomies such as observation vs. participation, consensus vs. conflict and unity vs. diversity. Another framework relates to the Northern-European Publizist tradition of journalism, the center-piece of which is the political institution of public discussion between substantially different points of view. That, again, makes sense if connected to classical Aristotelian thought about practical, political life and reasoning, linking public discussion to an idea(l) of practical knowledge pluralism in the world of human affairs.

Those two frameworks, we have argued, do not constitute a dichotomy. They have a history of mutual animosity and conflict, but are genuinely different. One is of a scientific vein. Another is political in the classical sense. Moreover, we have argued that the latter framework is an endangered variety of journalism, that it tends be overlooked and misinterpreted, and thus, to remain untold as a framework of thought in its own right in current scholarly work – which is a pity because it attends to problems that journalists and journalism scholars struggle with all the time. Those problems relate, in a variety of ways, to concerns about journalistic objectivity and participation.

The school of Public Journalism represents current attempts to deal with the problems and can be seen as a kind of hybrid between the Publizist and the Reporter frameworks. In our interpretation, thus, the school seems to be sharing the political strivings of the former framework and, at the same time, the basic assumptions and religious rootsof the latter.[48] Public Journalism has been related to a commitment to 'democratic participation and public debate' and to 'a sense of community defined by something

---

[48] Underwood, *From Yahveh to Yahoo.*

stronger than a mere aggregation of personal preferences and private interests'.[49] The struggle, however, to identify that stronger sense of community, appears to be connected to an assumed dichotomy of the individual vs. the community.[50] Siding, then, with the community, Public Journalism is directed onto a track that may easily lead to communitarianism, committed to dialogue and unity in closely-knit constituencies.

As a rule – admitting room for disagreement within the school or within related varieties such as Civic Journalism – a dichotomic scheme appears to be present. If compared to the generic reporter, however, the attribution of value seems frequently to have been reversed. For instance, not impersonal reporting but journalistic empathy is valued, and there seems to be a general assumption of altruism rather than egotism in citizens. There is an ideal of the journalist as a servant of the common good in communities that engage in dialogues which encompass citizens' troubles, joys and hopes, their wonder, imagination, vulnerability, ignorance and failure, all linked to aims of achieving mutual understanding: The ancient longing for consensus (as distinct from compromise from case to case) appears to have been maintained, but now seems to be connected to dialogue and social intimacy rather than to the abstract notion of universal truth.[51] There is, on the other hand, some ambiguity. Among the purposes of dialogues, thus, one may also encounter the aim of '[a]ir[ing] conflicting perspectives' – an aim that would be typical of a Publizist approach.[52]

The possible hybrid quality of the school of Public Journalism might make it an interesting case for exchanges between representatives of the Reporter and the Publizist traditions. Those frameworks, in turn, like all such frameworks of basic assumptions, tend to be invisible when viewed from within, but can be recognized and narrated as distinct logics when viewed from another position. Sharing the acknowledgement of basic diversity in journalism, representatives of the Reporter and the Publizist logic, respectively, may offer each other the service of distanced interpretation and critique and thereby contribute to the maintenance of actual diversity in future journalism.

---

[49] Glasser, T.L., 'Preface', in: *idem*, ed, *The Idea of Public Journalism* (New York, 1999), p. xxxi.

[50] Glasser, T.L., 'The Idea of Public Journalism', p. 14.

[51] Campbell, C.C., 'Journalism as a Democratic Art', in: Glasser, T.L., ed, *The Idea of Public Journalism* (New York, 1999), p. xiii.

[52] *Ibidem*, p. xxii.

NEW MEDIA TECHNOLOGIES AND THE DESIRE TO BROADCAST YOURSELF

Susan Aasman

Let's begin with three documentaries made by someone named Ed. The first one is *Harvest of Shame* made by the famous journalist Ed Murrow, reporting for CBS in 1960 on the poor condition of agricultural farm workers. Although Murrow placed himself in front of the camera, the goal of the documentary is to report on the social realities of those who suffer. Thirty years later, in 1990, the Dutch filmmaker Ed van der Elsken also put himself in front of the camera addressing the audience in the television documentary *Bye*. In this film the focus is not on the wrongs of the world: Van der Elsken reports to his viewers in a kind of confessional monologue about the terminal illness he himself is suffering from. Another 20 years later, a man named Ed Matos, seated himself in front of a webcam to broadcast his story on his struggle with cancer on YouTube. The reason, as he explained on the webpage: 'I made this video with the hope that it may help anyone out there from having to go through what I am trying to endure. I made it with nothing but love for all'.[1]

Although these three examples are rather randomly chosen, they do represent three different moments in the history of documentary and television journalism from the last fifty years. In their successive phases they illustrate two major transitions. The first transformation entails a shift from the engaged, objective journalistic documentary that came to prominence in the age of television to a more inward looking genre, exploring the inner world of the filmmaker. The second transition entails a shift from the professional filmmaker telling personal stories to the amateur claiming the same privilege by producing his own story and sharing it through new media platforms like YouTube.

Different media scholars have attempted to locate and explain these changes. Jon Dovey, for example, placed the first transformation in the 1990s of the previous century. He described how – at that period – a new regime of truth emerged, namely that of the foregrounding of individual

---

[1] Matos, E., "I Have Cancer", *YouTube* (2007), available from: http://www.youtube.com/watch?v=0Q0Jo7JfbfE.

truth at the expense of more general truth claims.[2] According to Dovey: 'subjective, autobiographical and confessional modes of expression (…) proliferated during the 1990s – across print journalism, literature, factual TV programming and digital media'.[3] In this period, it became almost a 'requirement' to produce subjective, intimate, exposing forms of self-expression. This preoccupation of the Self influenced media and arts profoundly. According to media scholars Minna Aslama and Mervi Pantti, the key attraction of this change is the 'disclosure of true emotions'.[4] If we look at the domain of documentary art, this new focus provoked a different understanding of the traditional objective documentary as fair and fact minded towards an appreciation of a more personal and subjective approach. It has changed the documentary as a cultural practice of professional filmmakers guiding us through the world into a genre for exploring one's inner world. Turning private trouble into public stories not only gradually became deeply embedded in popular culture as well, characterized by some as 'therapy culture' or 'confessional media' culture.[5]

This constant and 'incessant performance of intimacy' seems to have arrived at a new stage.[6] Nowadays, the focus on the self as a privileged domain for professionals has been challenged by a new group of filmmakers, namely the amateurs or do-it-yourself filmmakers. There was a time when it was impossible for an individual outside the media industry to distribute his or her own audio-visual story to a general audience. But in a very short time frame, if we take the beginning of web 2.0 in the early 2000s or perhaps even better the start of the video-sharing website YouTube in 2005 as a turning point, the practice to upload audio-visual content and share it with potentially everyone who is interested, has become fully embedded within the contemporary media landscape. The way video sharing websites have institutionalized themselves as global distribution platforms is almost beyond comprehension. According to YouTube's own statistics every single minute sixty hours of video are uploaded. This means that in just one month the amount of video production surpasses what the three major American television networks have produced in the past sixty years.[7] Some estimate

---

[2] Jon Dovey, *Freakshow:First Person Media and Factual Television* (London, 2000), p. 25.

[3] *Ibidem.*, p. 1.

[4] Aslama, M. and Pantti, M., 'Talking Alone: Reality TV, Emotions and Authenticity', in: *European Journal of Cultural Studies* 9 (2006), no. 2, pp. 167-184.

[5] Furedi, F., *Therapy Culture: Cultivating Vulnerability in an Uncertain Age* (London, 2003)

[6] Dovey, *Freakshow*, p. 26.

[7] 'Statistics', *YouTube*, available from: http://www.youtube.com/t/press_statistics.

that 80 percent of this content is user generated material.[8] By now, YouTube claims to have 800 million users and argues that its significance as a news site has grown accordingly: 'For years, YouTube has been the global living room – today it's becoming a global newsroom'.[9]

However accurate these figures are, it is safe to conclude that we are witnessing a period that has user-generated content at the heart of contemporary media production. Making a picture or a video has become a fully integrated practice in our daily life. When something special happens, when people witness something important or funny, they take out their cameras, mobile phones, iPads or whatever other device they have, and shoot and share. The easiest explanation for this phenomenon is simply that it is technically possible to do so. The emergence of web 2.0 provided a switch to a model of two-way media, thanks to new means of distribution that delivered the basic technological prerequisite for a truly interactive media practice. For the first time in the history of mass media, the growing means for distribution altered the power of licensed broadcast institutions. It can be seen as a form of true democratization: in principle every citizen can participate. With the arrival of this 'grassroots' cultural production as media scholar Henry Jenkins named it, we face the appearance of a radical alternative to dominant media content.[10]

It's not too difficult to see that the rise of alternative media production and alternative media distribution has problematized the concept of professional documentary filmmaking. In this chapter I will trace the recent developments of people taking up the camera to report on themselves as part of an on-going and complex historical process. Ideas and ideals of self-expression, participation and democratization did not emerge with the arrival of the internet. It is probably the other way around. My thesis is that these developments are part of a rather slow change that emerged in the 1960s, grew stronger in the 1970s, before finally becoming mainstream just before the internet really took off in the 1990s. Both transformations – from objective to personal film making and from professional filmmakers to amateurs – are very much interconnected, as they are part of some other changes such as the arrival of new media like television, the internet and new consumer technologies like the video or camcorder, but also broader

---

[8] Wesch, M., 'Digital Ethnography: YouTube statistics', *YouTube*, available from: http://mediatedcultures.net/smatterings/youtube-statistics/.

[9] 'Broadcasting Ourselves: The Official YouTube Blog', *YouTube*, available from: http://youtube-global.blogspot.nl/.

[10] Jenkins, H., *Convergence Culture: Where Old and New Media Collide* (New York, 2008).

cultural changes that took place, like the growing appreciation of media-tions of the self and everyday life.

Turning the Camera: A Slow Change Coming

When former radio journalist Edward R. Murrow turned in to television in 1951 as his main platform, he continued his already distinguished career as a reporter in a new setting. In the next decade he would contribute consider-ably to broadcast journalism's development. *Harvest of Shame* was his last CBS documentary, made in close association with his co-director and pro-ducer Fred Friendly, before he resigned in 1961 from CBS. Murrow left a legacy that stayed and even grew long after his death in 1965. According to Michael Dillon he gradually turned into 'an omnipotent and omniscient dis-penser of journalistic justice, almost a Christ figure.'[11] Others depicted him as the electronic media's first hero: 'Murrow is undoubtedly the first hero in the history of American broadcasting, a distinguished reporter who forever set the industry gold standard through his unparalleled courage, integrity and newsgathering excellence'.[12] Murrow combined journalistic on-the-spot newsreel coverage and a more distinct documentary approach in the famous news show *See It Now*, followed by *CBS Reports* in the late fifties and early sixties.[13] Many of these television documentaries were appreciated as a new genre that brought important topics, with the purpose to inform, to instruct and to change.[14]

There were critical notes as well. Some critics suggested that these TV reportages did not bring enough emotion and contained a certain neglect of the everyday human drama. They lacked the ordinary 'real' life. As the film critic Arthur Barron wrote: 'As for me, I'd like a little less information and a lot more feeling. I think we know enough facts: what we don't know is how to feel, to identify with others'.[15] This complaint may seem rather out-dated now. For many critics television has become the prime medium for showing feelings and emotions. In the words of media scholar Mini White:

[11] Dillon, M., 'Ethics in Black and White', in: Good, H., ed, *Ethics in Black and White* (New York, 2007), p. 112.

[12] Quoted in: Strout, L.N., 'The Edward R. Murrow of Docudramas and Documen-tary', *Media History Monographs* 12 (2010), no. 1, pp. 1-21. And see also: *Galacy Cinima*, http://www.mygalaxycinema.com/harvestofdignity.php.

[13] Barsam, R., *Nonfiction Film: A Critical History* (Indiana, 1992), p. 344.

[14] Barron, A., 'Toward New Goals in Documentary', in: Jacobs, L., eds, *The Docu-mentary Tradition* (New York, 1971), pp. 494-499.

[15] *Ibidem*, p. 497.

'television is a therapy machine'.[16]   But in the early sixties documentary had to find its place as a genre within a new media landscape that saw a very quick rise of television as the dominant platform for news and information. Murrow and other reporters and documentary filmmakers had to re-define the more traditional film documentary. They had to deal with the transformation from a cinematic scale to the small screen of the television set. Furthermore, on almost every level (production, distribution and screening) the film documentary had to adjust to a potentially bigger audience, new technologies, new aesthetics and new formats. Eventually there emerged a strong attention for the everyday and the ordinary in a wide variety of non-fiction and new formats such as talk shows. According to John Ellis, television became the prime witness of social historical reality.[17]

One of the more remarkable new aspects of documentary filmmaking in the age of television was the extensive use of interviews. Because of a much greater ease of applying synchronous sound, documentary could record people talking about their own experience. Media historian Eric Barnouw pointed out the difference with earlier documentary film, which was very much a silent genre. In post-production sound and voice were added, usually in the form of a voice over. This post-production method made those 'non-talking people (...) puppets, manipulated in the editing'.[18] The new sound recording technology though, brought spontaneously talking people on the television screen. But it had, according to Barnouw, an unforeseen effect: 'In a sense they [talking people] began to take control away from the director. It was to these people – including people whom the audience had not counted as part of their world – that viewers were reacting'.[19]

It was not just this foregrounding of the ordinary man that became so prominent on the small screen, but also a growing visibility of private life of the filmmaker himself telling his personal story. Gradually, documentary filmmakers turned to a more personal approach that included a much more autobiographical perspective; they chose to make their own lives as the prime topic, challenging the private/public divide. However, it took a while before this was fully accepted on television. When, for instance, in 1963 the Dutch documentary filmmaker Ed van der Elsken made his documentary *Welcome to life dear, dear little one* about his life in Amsterdam, and more in particularly about the birth of his son, critics were shocked when it was

---

[16] White, M., 'Television, Therapy and the Social Subject; Or, The TV Therapy Machine', in: Friedman, J., eds, *Reality Squared: Televisual Discourse on the Real* (New Brunswick, 2002), pp. 313-321.
[17] Ellis, J., *Documentary: Witness and Self-Revelation* (New York, 2012), p. 17.
[18] Barnouw, E., *Documentary: A History of Non-Fiction Film* (Oxford, 1993), p. 234.
[19] *Ibidem*, p. 235.

broadcasted on national television.[20] They resisted the idea of bringing elements from the private sphere into the public domain. They thought it was
too much like a home movie and therefore 'too personal' for a public medium like television.

That is an interesting conclusion and quite ironic too, since many
scholars interpreted television as the key mass medium that contributed
greatly in disclosing the private realm, or as Liesbeth van Zoonen wrote:
'We rediscover on television what has become ever more invisible around
us, the private life of ordinary people (…)'.[21] According to Van Zoonen, the
division between public and private rests on a fairly recent historical dichotomy between the rational and restraint – being the public world of men
– versus the emotional and spontaneous – being the private world of wom-
en. Van Zoonen emphasizes how this 19th century construction was never
fully accepted. She connects the rapid rise of reality TV programs like *Big
Brother* to a strong resistance against this dichotomy. The strong desire to
look behind the curtains resulted in a growing appreciation of people who
dared to make their private lives public as in a deliberate attempt to 'throw
off the bourgeois bodice of the public-private divide'.[22] Van Zoonen's explanation for this collapse of the public and private through endless proliferation of talk shows and reality TV formats is that popular culture was able
to fill the vacuum that art had not been able to bridge. Art, as Van Zoonen
argues, is always about the exceptional and never about the everyday and
the ordinary.[23]

Van Zoonen might be right in her analysis of the historical dichotomy,
the resistance against it and the desire to overcome the gap. She is also
pointing to the right direction when she emphasizes the role of popular culture in this process. But I think she underestimates the role of art in her explanation. Within documentary history we can find many examples of
filmmakers trying to bridge that gap. Van der Elsken for instance, did not
go for the exceptional. On the contrary, he saw his movie as an experiment
in how to represent ordinary everyday life in a non-fiction form. Ed van der
Elsken was not the only one experimenting with this public/private divide;
there were other filmmakers who explored new ways of crossing the line
between life and art. Especially filmmakers who participated in the under-
ground film movement in New York, like Stan Brakhage or Jonas Mekas,

---

[20] *Welcome to Life, Dear Little One* (1963), broadcast: January 15, 1964, 16 mm.
black-white with sound, partially post-synchronised, running time: 36' 00" (EYE
Institute).
[21] Van Zoonen, L., 'Desire and Resistance: Big Brother and the Recognition of Everyday Life', in: *Media, Society, Culture* 23 (2001), p. 672.
[22] *Ibidem,* p. 672.
[23] *Ibidem,* p. 672.

took up the camera and recorded their own lives. Brakhage, for instance, made the film *Window Water Baby Moving* in 1958 in which he recorded his pregnant wife and the birth of their child. The film was considered controversial because of its explicit images. However, over the years it would turn into a landmark documentary, because it broke new ground in exploring life on film. Brakhage could exhibit his films only at art festivals and other small marginal circuits, whereas Van der Elsken was able to find a more general audience through public television. In that sense, the latter was ahead of his time.

Technology played a role here as many of these filmmakers turned to cheap consumer film technology, like the semi-professional format of 16 mm or the smaller 8 mm camera. They believed that the use of such domesticated technology would be able to fulfill the need for a more personal approach as it could enable them to focus on their own, immediate world. Some of these filmmakers tried alternative cinematic styles that – as film historian Jim Lane noticed – resisted a 'realist mode of representation' by experimenting with form and content even to the point of abstract images of domestic life.[24] A next step was a shift from a focus on the everyday and the personal towards a more inward perspective. Lane, and not only he, connects this move to a more general turn towards subjectivity and experience in the late sixties and early seventies. There was a growing emphasize on self-reflection, self-realization and/or self-fulfillment of the individual.[25] This clearly had political connotations as well: self-realization became a new kind of radical politics. As many philosophers of the day liked to explain: radical social change could only be reached through radical personal change. That change could only be processed through a thorough exploration of the self-consciousness.[26]

Amateur and semi-professional film technology, but also new video technology that was launched in the late sixties, thus seemed to be the right tool at the right moment. In fact, these technologies were reviewed as excellent machines to perform self-reflection. They were relatively cheap, easy to handle and portable. Especially the arrival of the Sony Portapack video camera attracted new kind of users that liked the idea of the features that this new technology offered. For instance, the ease of using synchronous sound brought human speech to the fore. You could talk to the camera and have a monologue, or you could record a dialogue. It made film making much more self-reflective and stimulated the autobiographical approach.

---

[24] Lane, J., *The Autobiographical Documentary in America* (London, 2002), p. 13.

[25] *Ibidem*, p. 20.

[26] See for instance: Hill, C., *Rewind: Video Art and Alternative Media in the United States, 1968-1980* (Video Data Bank, 2008).

Just as interesting was the possibility for instant feedback as video did not have to be developed like film. Because of this there was no delay in watching the images. Shooting and viewing were no longer separated – both materially and temporally.[27] This instant possibility for viewing without any intermediaries, such as technicians, offered also more room for an intimate and confessional attitude. When Stan Brakhage in 1958 sent his film reels for the documentary *Window Water Baby Moving* to the Kodak plant to be processed, Kodak sent a note to Brakhage: 'Sign this at the bottom, and we will destroy this film; otherwise, we will turn it over to police.' Only after some efforts, Brakhage received his material back.[28] With video this interference was no longer necessary and thus the filmmaker gained a much higher degree of autonomy. Another aspect of the video camera was its capacity to record in real time stimulating new ways of exploring everyday events.

Some of the filmmakers who picked up the cameras and turned it 180 degrees were politically very active and took part in new social movements that wanted to address issues of gender, sexuality, race and class, taking personal issues as political issues. Michael Renov signaled that 'much current autobiography has been produced at the margins of commercial culture by feminists, gays, people of color, and mavericks of every stripe'.[29] Exploring yourself in order to construct your identity became central to western culture. According to Keith Beattie this new acceptance, or even a sense of urgency of taking a more subjective and personal view, caused a significant revision of the more traditional objective documentary practice.[30]

Another way to explain this tendency is to understand this move towards self-revelation as a form of post-objectivism and postmodernism questioning the grand narrative, and more specific the fundamental questioning of what 'the real' constitutes. Post-structuralism doubted the idea of absolute truth and thus also doubted reality as something that can be observed through a camera. As Jim Lane writes: 'By shifting away from the promise of the immediate truth of direct cinema, autobiographical documentaries acknowledge the problem of grand model of reference.'[31] There is an unavoidable subjectivity in every documentary. The acknowledgment of this principal idea about documentary gave way to a more self-reflexive style and method. Already at the time of Direct Cinema and its presumed

---

[27] Renov, M., 'Video Confessions', in: Renov, M and Suderburg, S., eds, *Resolutions: Contemporary Video Practices* (Minneapolis, 1996), p. 84.
[28] MacDonald, S., *A Critical Cinema 4: Interviews with Independent Filmmakers* (Berkeley, 2005), pp. 64-66.
[29] Renov, M., *The Subject of Documentary* (Minneapolis, 2004), p. xvii.
[30] Beattie, K., *Documentary Screens* (London, 2004), p.105.
[31] Lane, J., *The Autobiographical Documentary in America* (London, 2002).

objectivity when observing and recording reality, filmmakers like Jean Rouch in France experimented with new methods in the new documentary movement called Cinema Verité. Rouch sought for a method of filmmaking that would not mask the process of film making, but rather show it to the viewers and thus make them aware that documentary is a construction of reality. It was an important step in the development of a different discourse on documentary, one that no longer emphasized the indexical, rational reference to reality, but rather the subjective, localized individual experience of reality.[32]

What happened initially within a limited circle of artists and activists, gradually became mainstream in the eighties and even more so in the nineties. In the United States television programs such as PBS's *POV* (Point of View) (1988-present) strived for 'putting a human face on contemporary social issues'. PBS favoured this in many of their documentaries, as Patricia Aufderheide notes, utilising middleclass professional filmmakers who pointed the camera on a medical crisis like AIDS, Alzheimer's disease, brain damage, bulimia, mental illness or a family crisis.[33] More than once, such portraits were self-portraits. First person cinema became an important genre: in the early 1990s most requests for public funding of documentaries were for first person or personal essays.[34] It is in that particular historical period that scholars like Bill Nichols signaled how the word documentary no longer suggested 'fullness, and completion, knowledge and fact, explanations of the social world and its motivating mechanisms. More recently, though, documentary has come to suggest incompleteness and uncertainty, recollection and impression, images of personal worlds and their subjective construction'.[35] The quick rise of reality television paralleled this development in certain ways. In many reality soaps the audience could see a complex mix of raw, authentic private lives that were heavily scripted and edited at the same time. Film historian Id Bondebjerg is right when he notes that 'there is a significant historical conjunction of the interest for the subjective and intimate in art cinema documentaries and in reality TV: they are two trends of the same historical flow of new tendencies.'[36] According to

---

[32] See for instance Nichols, B., *Representing Reality: Issues and Concepts in Documentary* (Bloomington, 1991); Nichols, B., *Introduction to Documentary* (Bloomington, 2001).

[33] Aufderheide, P., 'Public Intimacy: The Development of First-Person Documentary', *Afterimage* 25 (1997), no. 1, pp. 16-18.

[34] Beattie, *Documentary Screens*, p. 119.

[35] Bill Nichols, *Blurred boundaries. Questions of meaning in contemporary culture* (Bloomington and Indianapolis 1994), p. 1.

[36] Bondebjerg, I., 'The Social and the Subjective Look: Documentaries and Reflexive Modernity', *Paper presented at the Australian International Documentary*

Bondbjerg there is a clear blurring of the boundaries between art and journalism, or between subjective expressions with highly developed aesthetic
and rhetorical forms, and factual and objective forms with a just functional
and invisible aesthetic in a shared search for getting closer to the private
lives dominated the cultural field.[37] So, when Ed van der Elsken turned the
camera again – as he had done so in the early sixties – on himself in 1990 in
his film Bye, television audiences had both in content and approach grown
accustomed to a focus on the private realm. As said before, in 1961 the reception had been critical to his rather intimate self-portrait. It was seen as
something 'not-done'. But thirty years later, television had turned into a
confessional medium. Talk shows, reality shows and human-interest reportages explored the private feelings and thoughts of individuals. Television
makers had acquired the skill to turn personal drama into universal stories a
general audience could identify with. This is also what happens in the film
Bye wherein Van der Elsken reflects on his illness. He is suffering from
prostate cancer and he knows his time is limited. For him it had become
quite natural to take up the camera to share this with his audience, because
he had done so at every important moment of his life. In this self-portrait,
he explains to the viewer in all of its painful and sometimes even graphic
detail what is going on. Although the images Van der Elsken provided were
sometimes shocking, using black and white video shots of himself stark na-
ked, including full frontal shots of his genitals in order to explain his viewers how the operation would take place. Seeing and hearing Van der Elsken
talking about his illness, showing his emotions without any hesitation
moved the audience. While his Welcome to life, my dear one, broadcasted
some three decades earlier, had received bad press because he turned the
camera on himself, by 1990 critics no longer thought such an approach was
'too personal'. On the contrary, Bye was praised because it was 'so personal'. This shift in perception is interesting, since it was not Van der Elsken
who had changed that much, but the audience its appreciation of the personal and private had altered gradually.

In Front and Behind the Camera: Do-it-Yourself

It is November 2007 when Ed Matos, a middle-aged man living in the United States, uploads his first video on YouTube. At the beginning of this nine
minute video, Matos installs himself in front of a webcam camera situated

---

Conference, available from:
http://www.modinet.dk/pdf/WorkingPapers/The_Social_and_the_Subjective_Look.`
pdf (2003).
[37] *Ibidem.*

in his bedroom and introduces himself with the words: 'Hello, my name is Ed Matos and I have cancer. I'm not really sure why I am making this video. I am not an actor, I am not a video buff...'.[38] A month later, he creates a follow up video in which he gives an update of his illness. He is sure he will die, and so he ends the video by blessing his viewers and then waves his hand, saying goodbye. For all the differences in style, length, and performance between the shy and inexperienced Ed Matos and the flamboyant Ed van der Elsken, there is a remarkable similarity between these two portraits. They both start in the same manner: seating themselves in front of the camera, explaining their purpose to the viewer. They both report on their experiences and in the process they create a strong sense of intimacy with their audience by glancing directly in the camera, leaving out any aesthetic overdo.

However, there is also an interesting difference. Ed van der Elsken knew exactly why he was making his documentary. He considered it to be quite logical to share his life with others, to document the intimate details about his life, his body, his friendships and relationships. He was an artist, after all. Ed Matos is less secure on the how and why of making his video. He seems to question if he, as just a user, as an amateur or average consumer, has the right to tell his story and share it with a general audience. On the other hand, he takes the opportunity to speak for himself.

This is one of the central problems many professional documentary filmmakers have struggled with: whom are they 'Speaking for, Speaking about, Speaking with, or Speaking alongside', as the American anthropologist Jay Ruby phrased it in an article in which he discussed this issue extensively.[39] According to Ruby, questions of voice, authority, and authorship have always been a serious concern among documentary filmmakers. They struggle with the issue 'who can represent someone else'.[40] Already at the start of documentary history, filmmakers actively sought collaboration from those who they were filming. The famous film director Robert Flaherty, for example, collaborated very closely with Nanook, the protagonist of his documentary *Nanook of the North* (1921) and the leader of the Inuit tribe that Flaherty was documenting. Nanook assisted in planning the shooting and evaluating the footage, and also helped to handle the equipment. Although it is possible to draw a line from Flaherty's working methods to today's participatory ideals of film making, it was Flaherty who remained the sole au-

---

[38] Matos, video 'I Have Cancer'.
[39] Ruby, J., 'Speaking For, Speaking About, Speaking With, or Speaking Alongside – an Anthropological and Documentary Dilemma', in: *Visual Anthropology Review* 7 (1991), p. 50.
[40] *Ibidem.*, p. 50.

thor. He held on to the right to represent, because as Ruby explains, documentary is not only an art form but also in essence a social service and a political act. In general, 'it is assumed that this task is best accomplished by
having professional filmmakers employ their technical skills, artistic sensi-
tivity, and insight to reveal the "reality" of others'.[41]

But attempts throughout documentary history demonstrate different
models of filmmaking that would share authorial authority between
filmmakers and subjects. In 1969 the Canadian government funded the
Challenge for Change program that strived for the use of film and video as a
catalyst for social change. The film *You are on Indian Land*, for example,
was about Indians, but also (partly) made by Indians who were trained in
using a camera. However, as anthropologist and filmmaker Sol Worth critically remarked, despite the cooperation, the film remains a white middle
class liberal product. Worth himself tried to explore 'subject-generated'
filmmaking when he and his college John Adair in 1966 went to the Navajo
Indians, an American tribe that had no experience with cinema or television.
The local youth got amateur film cameras and received some training in
filming and editing. Afterwards, they made seven films.[42] Worth and Adair
used these films to obtain insight in how people structure their own reality.

This anthropological innovation in documentary filmmaking became
quite influential and many anthropologists turned to comparable documentary projects. It spawned a heightened interest in the amateur as producer of
filmic content, and it stimulated a utopian idealism that one day – if the
technology and the techniques of filmmaking became accessible to everyone – it could establish a real shift of empowerment. No longer would the
professional be speaking for or about or with, but alongside. Or as anthropologist and filmmaker Jean Rouch hoped for in 1974:

> And tomorrow? Tomorrow will be the time of colour Video Portapacks, video
> editing, of instant replay ('instant feedback'). The dreams of (…) a camera that
> can so totally participate that it will pass automatically into the hands of those
> who were, always in front of the lens.[43]

This rhetoric was very much part of the discourse of the late sixties and early seventies. It fitted the critical opposition to the assumed monopoly of
mass media institutions. 'People are the information' was the slogan that a

---

[41] *Ibidem.*, p. 51.

[42] Adair, J. and Worthy, S., *Through Navajo Eyes: An Exploration in Film Communication and Anthropology* (Albuquerque, NM, 1972); See also: Sol Worth's home
page: http://astro.temple.edu/~ruby/wava/worth/worth.html, (last visited 13-04-
2013).

[43] Quoted in Ruby, 'Speaking for', p. 57.

New York artists' project used as its guideline in their People's Video Theater: 'Everybody could do it and everybody should do it. That was the mandate – pick it up, it's there. Like the power to vote – vote, take responsibility. Make it and see it.'[44] What is remarkable is that much of the optimism about a media revolution was that these activists thought that people only had to wait for the right material conditions. They believed that new media technology, like video, could provoke a more democratic media practice.[45] One of the most fascinating quotes from this era is the prediction made by Sol Worth in 1968:

> Imagine a world where symbolic forms created by one inhabitant are instantaneously available to all other inhabitants; a place where 'knowing others' means only that others know us, and we know them through the images we all create about ourselves and our world, as we see it, feel it, and choose to make it available to a massive communication network, slavering and hungry for images to fill the capacity of its coaxial cables.
>
> (…)
>
> Imagine a place where other cultures...are available to all; a place where almost anyone...can produce verbal and visual images, where individual or groups can edit, arrange, and rearrange the visualization of their outer and inner worlds, and, a place where these movies, TVs. … can be instantaneously available to anyone who chooses to look.... Imagine this place, for it is where we are at now.[46]

It reads like a prediction of the YouTube era. Since the rise of the internet, and more in particular the emergence of what has been labeled web 2.0, users are indeed able to contribute their own text, pictures and video content. Ever since the start of the interactive video-sharing platform YouTube in 2005, users have done so in overwhelming numbers. Some have labeled this enormous rise of the amateur as a 'pro-am revolution' indicating a diminishing of the difference between the professional and the amateur. And this user-generated content is not restricted to the traditional topics of the classical home movie genre that preferred happy moments of family life. Amateur broadcast is about everything. Think of a topic and it is on YouTube: drunken mums, pets, football games, tsunamis, war, sex, parties, new phones, new cars, new child, first steps and cancer. The sentence 'I have cancer' in the YouTube search engine delivers 485,000 hits, and certainly

---

[44] Chris Hill, *Rewind*, p. 12

[45] *Ibidem*, p. 17.

[46] Worth, S., 'Toward An Anthropological Politics of Symbolic Form', in: Gross, L., ed, *Studying Visual Communication* (Philadelphia, 1981), pp. 85-86.

half of them are do-it-yourself videos made by ordinary people telling about the fact that they have cancer, how they deal with it, or how they look back on it. They are ordinary people like Ed Matos who mostly carefully and sometimes hesitantly take their place in this network of stories and images, giving their unique view of their world, while sharing such a do-it-yourself practice with many others.

Between Sol Worth's dream of a nearby future and today's everyday practice lies not just a growing acceptance of the voice of the amateur, but also evolving technology. The history of amateur film started with the material history of film itself. At the end of the nineteenth century when film cameras were invented, there were non-professionals immediately experimenting, appropriating and remodeling the standard theatrical film format of 35mm that was too costly for individual amateur use. Amateur film really took off in the 1920s when companies like Eastman Kodak introduced the cheaper and easier to use 16mm film format and the French company Pathé marketed the even smaller and cheaper 9.5 mm film. Gradually there emerged an amateur film practice that predominantly was seen as a private practice exercised strictly within the domestic sphere.

As a new ritual that celebrated domestic happiness, home movie making was booming in the 1930s. After the Second World War, when Kodak and other companies launched Super-8 with easy-load cartridges, amateur filmmaking became an even more popular hobby. At the same time, within the field of documentary, it remained a marginal practice. Recording your family life with consumer technology and without professional skills could hardly compete with professional use of equipment to document the world. Only at particular moments was there a cross-over, for instance when social activists attracted attention with their films or when the local amateur filmmaker not just documented his family but also chronicled the lives of his community. Others stumbled into world history, like Abraham Zapruder who in 1963 recorded the shooting of President Kennedy in Dallas with his 8mm Bell & Howell camera.

In the late 1960s and early 1970s new technologies like the Video Portapack were quickly embraced by new emerging groups who felt marginalized by the traditional media and were searching for new opportunities to give them access to media. According to media scholars like Deirdre Boyle, the portable video camera launched an independent television movement in the United States. This recording system has the great advantage that it was easier to handle and enabled the use of synchronous sound. Besides that, it was far cheaper. Social activists and artists alike appreciated video making as a radical cultural tool that could provide a more democratic media system, a serious alternative to the dominant broadcasting companies.[47] They could make themselves visible and audible. Local communities, women, ethnic groups and homosexuals took up the camera as a form of social activism.

Still, the early video systems were relatively expensive and the equipment was rather heavy compared to home movie equipment.[48] In the 1980s smaller and cheaper equipment was launched like VHS video and the camcorder. Only in the 1990s when digital camcorders were introduced did the breakthrough of amateur filmmaking as an everyday practice seemed possible. Even more so, with the arrival of camera phones in the early 21st century, equipment became small, cheap and easy to handle. Recording became just as easy as taking up a pen. When the internet began to facilitate easy uploading of video footage, Sol Worth's words about a massive communication network making images instantaneously available, did eventually come true.

In the meantime, not just the internet but also television had already opened up to amateur imagery. A famous example is the BBC television series *Video Diaries* that was broadcasted in the early nineties in the UK. This program opened itself up to the non-professional. Out of an initiative by David Attenborough, who favored what he called 'access television, the network started experimenting with community programs in the early seventies, eventually leading to programs like *Video Diaries*. The average and not so average viewer could send in home videos. A viewer who was interested to participate in the program was loaned a video camera, received some instructions and was allowed to shoot anything he or she considered important. Consequently, the material was edited in close collaboration with the diarist. It brought about new ways of storytelling: that of first-person monologues in a direct-to camera style and also new topics like gays coming out of the closet, and people telling about child abuse. After some years the program evolved to another innovative program called *Video Nation*, which was able to give television access to ordinary people.[49] Besides these kinds of open access programs that brought non-professional or amateur images on the national screen, there emerged other genres as well, such as the funniest home movies shows that showed homemade slapstick. It brought the intentional private home mode to the public screen. Through these immensely popular video slapstick programs, audiences became fa-

---

[47] Chris Hill , *Rewind,* p. 5.

[48] See for an account, Willett, R., 'In the Frame: Mapping Camcorder Cults', in: Buckingham, D., and Willet, R., eds, *Video Cultures: Media Technology and Everyday Creativity* (London, 2009), pp. 1-23.

[49] Henderson, J., 'Handing Over Control? Access, 'Ordinary People' and Video Nation', in: Buckingham, D. and Willet, R., eds, *Video Cultures: Media Technology and Everyday Creativity* (New York, 2009), pp. 152-171.

miliar with the do-it-yourself as something that could fit a mass medium like television.[50]

The effect of the availability and visibility of amateur video has been, according to Jon Dovey, that we can see a certain sense of 'amateurishness' as 'guarantor of truth' in the sense of being 'unmediated' raw data'.[51] We have come to appreciate the non-professional as something trustworthy and more truthful. We judge technical low grade and stylistic informal images against the familiar framework of the home movie and home video as being private and authentic. We experience them as intimate and embodied – we can feel the presence of the filmmaker handling his handheld camera – and thus subjective views on the world. It is as the avant-garde filmmaker Brakhage already said in the early seventies:

> [I] have come to be called a 'professional,' an 'artist' and an 'amateur.' Of those three terms—'amateur'— is the one I am truly most honored by. Why have they come to make 'amateur' mean: 'inexperienced,' 'clumsy,' 'dull,' or even 'dangerous'? It is because an amateur is one who really lives his life—not one who simply 'performs his duty'—and as such he experiences his work while he's working—rather than going to school to learn his work so he can spend the rest of his life just doing it dutifully.[52]

From Home Movie to Social Media

From the early beginning of film there has been a clear linkage between documentary film and ideals of democracy. Grierson already advocated the non-fiction genre documentary as the privileged media format in capturing the life as lived. Almost a hundred years later, media scholar John Corner suggested that recent developments in media culture have led to a kind of post-documentary culture wherein the traditional documentary has to deal with a whole new set of practices, forms and functions which 'greatly expanded the range of popular images from the real'.[53] More importantly, what used to be a documentary project that was part of a larger vision for civic enlightenment and democracy, has now become a democratic practice

---

[50] Dovey, *Freakshow*, p. 58.

[51] *Ibidem*, p. 64.

[52] Brakhage, S., 'In Defence of Amateur', (1971), reprinted in: Brakhage, S., ed, *Essential Brakhage: Selected Writings on Filmmaking* (Kingston, 2001).

[53] Corner, J., 'Documentary in a Post-Documentary Culture: A Note on Forms and Their Functions", available from:
http://www.lboro.ac.uk/research/changing.media/index.html (2000).
See also: 'Afterword. Framing the New', in: Holmes, S. and Jermyn, D., eds, *Understanding Reality Television* (London, 2004), pp. 290-299.

itself with the emergence of Web 2.0. That the internet was able to align to this documentary project of democratization of self-expression, is not so surprising. Already in the seventies, in the early days of the computer countercultural ideology of self-expression and do-it-yourself went hand-in-hand with ideals of the computer as an instrument of liberation. It became the basis as well of the construction of the world wide web, and later web 2.0 in terms of interactivity, participation, two-sided communication.[54]

The fascinating subtitle of YouTube with its call to 'Broadcast Yourself' seems to have become the ultimate realization of this process in bringing a certain degree of democratization to the telling of stories. The radical aspect is that it transports the confessional mode from the domain of arts into the domain of the amateur and along the way brought the performance of intimacy back home. Where filmmakers like van der Elsken adapted the intimate and confessional of the private sphere, as it has become a social norm and cultural convention it has been appropriated by the Ed Matos's of the web. This online user-generated content has now become a challenge to media studies in many respects. One of them is the understanding of the why. Why do people share with total strangers their most intimate details? Media scholar David Gauntlet explored exactly this question and interviewed many users who gave different but overlapping motivations: they varied from the desire to share thoughts, to chronicle their existence, be an active participant on the web, be a producer and not just a consumer, to collaborate with others or to have the urge of being heard.[55] His final conclusion is that to many users, 'making is connecting'.

This interpretation seems to fit Ed Matos' intention. If we return to Ed Matos one more time: he really felt connected because a few weeks after his first video he produced a second one after some encouraging reactions to his debut. People who watched his video wrote some sympathetic reactions on YouTube.[56] Not long after he had uploaded the second video he died, but his widow kept the videos online and kept communicating with people who responded to the videos. By now, after almost six years, the statistics show that there have been 11,000 viewers for the first one and more than 3000 for the second video. It received 290 comments – some before and most after his death. He was able to express his own voice.

One of the more fascinating changes over the last decades has been the inversion of public and private followed by the collapse of professional and amateur. Public documentary went private, shifting its goal to look at the

---

[54] Van Dijck, J., *The Culture of Connectivity: A Critical History of Social Media* (New York, 2013), p.10.

[55] Gauntlet, D., *Making is Connecting* (London, 2011), pp.100-101.

[56] Matos, video 'I Have Cancer'.

world towards a more inward perspective. The reverse also happened: the private becoming public with the home movie being broadcasted on the internet. Gradually this development became part of a general cultural transformation that saw this practice as something embedded in our everyday life. Now, anyone can claim space and voice in the public arena, sharing the intimate and the everyday with whoever wants to listen or watch. Right now we are in the middle of a reconfiguration of this development, again, because as scholars like José van Dijck critically analyses, many of these platforms like YouTube do not 'simply channel' but program with a specific objective. As van Dijck explains: 'Whereas before, websites were generally operated as *conduits* for social activity, the new platforms increasingly turn these conduits into applied services, rendering the internet easier to use but more difficult to tinker with.'[57] But we don't yet know what it will mean to the future of audio-visual practices of self-expression. So, when Michael Renov describes our contemporary media culture as a mass medium of intimacy, he seems to point to documenting our life as a vital expression of agency: 'We are not only what we do in a world of images: we are also what we show ourselves to be'.[58] That is not something that is easily given up.

---

[57] Van Dijck, *The Culture of Connectivity*, p. 6.
[58] Renov, *The Subject of Documentary*, p. 53.

Part II

———

SENSATIONAL STORIES

CELEBRITY NEWS JOURNALISM

THE STORYTELLING INJUNCTION

Annik Dubied and Magali Dubey[1]

In the last decade, there has been a steady quantitative expansion of celebrity news content in general-interest newspapers in French-speaking countries in Europe. This phenomenon is part of a more general 'proliferation of celebrity across the media since the 1980s.'[2] It is occurring in a context where daily and weekly publications, whether regional or 'quality' press, publish this form of content despite its bad reputation, whereas, prior to this expansion, it was confined to either the specialized or the popular press. While the celebrity theme has caught on to an international scientific and academic community, whose collected studies and reflections have recently opened up an emerging field of Celebrity Studies, there are yet few empirical analyses in the field.[3] We go even further and suggest that there is also a need for studies of celebrity content as news, which it turns out to be in most cases.

In this chapter, we employ a case study on the French-speaking part of Switzerland to analyze celebrity news as a form of journalism, considering the subject to be highly relevant to many recent challenges in that field.[4] We aim to analyze the impact of a shift in content, be it in journalistic practices or journalists' perception of their professional identity, based on the observation that celebrity news is increasingly present in general interest newspapers. Indeed, one might ask what kind of news could better embody the taste for the spectacular, for the personal and private, for the endless embroidery of information not to mention its consequences, if it weren't for celebrity news? What other kind of news focuses so heavily on a private individual, raising a legal issue concerning the right to privacy? What other

[1] Warm thanks to Leah Kimber for the translation.
[2] Turner, G., 'The Mass Production of Celebrity: "Celetoïds", Reality TV and the "Demotic turn"', *International Journal of Cultural Studies* 9 (2006), no. 2, p. 153.
[3] Holmes, S. and Redmond, S., *Framing Celebrity: New Directions in Celebrity Culture* (London, 2006); Marshall, P. D., *Celebrity and Power* (London, 1997); Ferris, K., 'The Sociology of Celebrity', *Sociology Compass* 1 (2007), pp. 371-384.
[4] Research PP00P1 124806, funded by the Swiss National Science Foundation (SNF). See: http://www.unige.ch/ses/socio/annikdubied.html "Recherches".

type of content so brazenly highlights the ethical tensions that surround trying to address the economic constraints that are ever-present in journalistic
routines?

With this in mind, we conducted a series of in-depth, individual interviews with journalists working on celebrity news.[5] Celebrity news seems to
lie at the core of many contemporary debates around journalism. Its characteristics challenges the limits of news and journalism, be it between news
and entertainment or news and advertisement. It also challenges the limits
between facts and fiction, as well as the legal and ethical limits within the
field. This marginal genre therefore questions the way a journalist defines
his work, the way he defines himself within his professional field, and the
common values he shares with his colleagues.

While practices in the field of celebrity news are defined by journalistic
conventions, they also seem to go beyond, by experimenting around those
conventions. More specifically, there seems to be an injunction to 'storytelling' (defined by Salmon as a utilitarian use of narrative) in the routines of
this genre; telling (never-ending) stories seems to benefit all stakeholders in
the star system, and many journalists implicitly recognize that they willing-
ly elaborate stories suggested by their sources or favored by their superiors.[6]
However, this storytelling injunction is not always compatible with the specific requests of traditional journalism. Journalistic routines of celebrity
news are therefore exemplary case studies for those who wish to understand
the contemporary changes in journalism. In this regard, celebrity news
seems to offer a fruitful path to identifying emerging trends in the sociology
of journalism. To our knowledge, celebrity news has hitherto rarely been
studied in this way.[7]

Identities and Values

Our objective is to have a better understanding of how celebrity news and
its recent expansion have challenged journalistic routines. What are the possible shifts within the profession? What are the various issues journalists
face regarding their professional identity? In other words, how do journalists define themselves with respect to this shift? Does the genre portray an
aspect of their professional identity? And if so, in what way?

---

[5] Interviews conducted with journalists working in the field of celebrity news in
popular, regional and free daily newspapers and in various magazines, all edited in
the French-speaking part of Switzerland.
[6] Salmon, C., *Storytelling: Bewitching the Modern Mind* (London, 2010).
[7] A special issue of *Journalism. Theory, Practice and Criticism* on the subject, edited by Thomas Hanitzsch and Annik Dubied, is currently in preparation and will be
published in 2013.

These are the questions that must be addressed when analyzing the profession and its definition. The issues at stake were tackled and commented upon by journalists we met during our fieldwork. Indeed, analyzing their narratives allowed us to pinpoint the core of their profession. They explained the challenges they face reconciling such a hybrid genre that includes traditional values of journalism.

Research makes it possible to emphasize the values that journalists share or do not share, and the skills they claim to grasp. Based on our analysis, it seems that celebrity news journalists consider themselves as journalists, in their own right, bearing in mind that they work on celebrity news. Traditional journalistic values are claimed, including factuality, objectivity, relevance, timeliness and public interest.[8] However, journalists share their doubts about being able to respect those fundamental values in their practices (the relevance and the public's interest in particular). In the same way, journalists tend to boast about a number of greater skills they grasp such as using digital media, the ability of storytelling as well as writing about trivia, in spite of the fact that they implicitly use writing and structuring skills to distance themselves from their topic. These contradictions and debates along with the traditional conceptions of journalism prove that writing celebrity news challenges the profession of journalism and points it towards the fundamental shifts and definition within the field.

In this context, storytelling appears to be a key issue, the 'result of a [specific] interdependent system' in the field of celebrity news journalism.[9] It is frequently referred to as the result of constraints imposed on journalists as well as a 'natural propensity' for writing celebrity news. Indeed, narratives are known to reach the core of individuals – their dreams, their life experience – and to trigger deep emotions. These are precisely the qualities that are wanted in such a genre, which ultimately focuses on the individual and the sensational.

What Journalists Say: Constraints and Skills

We conducted the analysis of journalistic routines from a strongly qualitative approach. Indeed, we carried out in-depth and comprehensive interviews through 'work-narratives', whereby we accessed the selected journalists' rationales and representations with a thematic content analysis, which

[8] Neveu, E., *Sociologie du Journalisme* (Paris, 2001); Hanitzsch, T., 'Deconstructing Journalism Culture: Toward a Universal Theory', *Communication Theory* 17 (2007), pp. 367-385.
[9] Neveu, *Sociologie du Journalisme*, p. 62; Benson, R. and Neveu, E., *Bourdieu and the Journalistic Field* (Cambridge, 2005).

considered the importance of a theme by the number of times it was mentioned in the interviews.[10] The interviews encouraged the narrative of professional 'sequences' of journalists, who told us how they work in their daily professional life, how they came to write about celebrity news, and how
they turn pieces of information into interesting and pertinent stories.[11] We
encouraged them to give us examples and anecdotes, and asked them to detail information related to topics such as skills, constraints, objectives,
changes as well as the relationships at stake in their job.

As with any other qualitative methodological procedure, this research
does not intend to be representative, but nonetheless allows us to confront
current assumptions and pre-existing theory. Talking about their respective
routines when it comes to celebrity news reports, journalists who accepted
the invitation to participate in our survey discussed certain privileged subjects. As a result, content analysis offers an accurate synthesis of the way
professionals present their work in celebrity news when they are asked to
talk about it (see fig. 1).

Two main conclusions can be drawn from our results. First, celebrity
news routines as described by our participants seem to echo McNair's description of social determinants of journalism.[12] The general results of the
content analysis confirm that constraints and pressure account for at least
one-third of what journalists talked to us about (28 percent) although they
were not specifically highlighting those elements. In addition to those central elements, journalists also emphasized sources (8 percent), relationships
between journalists and celebrities (14%), and mentioned a few elements of
the context (5 percent). According to them, the elements presented as constraints lead to storytelling. A second important observation appears in the
categories of 'skills' (24 percent) and 'definition of celebrity news' (15 percent), which illustrates the hybrid nature of celebrity news as an amalgam of
fact and fiction, and the skills that producing this type of journalism requires. In sum, it appears that skills are also a 'natural' driving force to storytelling. In the following section, we discuss these results.

---

[10] "Logiques D'action" in French. ; Bertaux, D., *L'enquête et ses Méthodes: Le Récit
de Vie* (Paris, 2005); About 450 pages transcribed, coded through the CAQDAS At-
las.ti in 1536 segments and 7 main categories (see figure 1).
[11] We conducted 20 interviews with journalists working in different types of written
media (magazine, popular, free, reference, regional) and with different socio-
professional backgrounds (nine women, eleven men, every hierarchical position,
from trainee to section editor, aged 27 to 55) to get the broadest range of practices
and specialties possible.
[12] McNair, B., *The Sociology of Journalism* (London, 2008), p. 14.

Hierarchical Constraints and the Public

Between one-third and one-half of the accounts we collected are directly related to issues of job constraints. As a result, these factors weigh heavily on routines and even more so, are in contradiction with the traditional values promoted by the profession. The reason for this is that irreconcilable tensions arise between the journalists' own sense of ethical values and the necessity to fill the celebrity news section with spicy stories. Respondents also placed emphasis on the scanty financial resources devoted to celebrity news in the French-speaking part of Switzerland, which causes journalists to rely on second-hand sources.

Like their colleagues, celebrity news journalists claim to be subjected to hierarchical and economic pressures in order to improve newspaper sales and global performance. If we are to believe our informants, celebrity news sections are the best way to ensure financial goals are achieved. Undoubtedly, many assert that celebrity news sections were created specifically to improve sales figures. The following excerpt is a good illustration.[13] It describes the migration of this kind of content into general-interest newspapers and the reasons for it:

> *Journalist*: I think that until now there wasn't any because of the respect for private life and that … there will be more and more of it, yeah. …At the moment, not for electoral reasons or … politics, but only for … let's be honest, the media's thirst for money.[14]

Most journalists found it difficult to come to terms with this migration and its causes. They emphasized that this is the result of the pressure of advertising, which implies a problematic relationship between journalists and the need to advertise:

> *Journalist*: We are products, I mean, to them it's a product and a product has to attract advertising. For instance, we had 'Music' pages with interviews of music stars every week. It was cancelled. Why? Because music doesn't attract enough publicity. So the newspaper is made in such a way that …this is anonymous. OK?

---

[13] All the interviewees were made anonymous and masculine. The description of some of the situations has been simplified in order to make it impossible to identify the journalists.

[14] All following excerpts of interviews are translated by the authors from the original French texts.

> *Interviewer*: Yes, yes, absolutely
> *Journalist*: ...because it is true. In a way the paper is built around advertising. And I think ...yes, it's unfortunate.

We observed a form of reluctance of the journalists to talk about this; a reluctance, which can only partially be explained by their desire not to get into trouble. It is also attributable to every journalist's recognition that 'refusing to confuse the profession of journalism with other activities such as advertising, espionage or police work, [to avoid] conflict of interests' is a fundamental ethical requirement in their profession — even identified as one of the three essential duties of journalism by Grevisse, who compared western national and international ethical codes.[15] Finally, if the insistence on constraints and pressure recalls that journalists are not autonomous individuals who can work freely in the 'liberal profession of news', it is also obviously part of a 'rhetorical justification' heard from journalists who maintain an ambiguous relationship with the disreputable aspect of their job.[16]

Indeed, the journalists we interviewed often proved to be quite critical about the work they produce. According to them, there are 'good quality' and 'poor quality' celebrity news. Once again, most claim that pressure and technical constraints allow them to produce only 'poor quality' celebrity news. However, not surprisingly, their superiors seem to be satisfied with what they write.

> *Journalist*: Just today I wrote 200 words on Britney Spears because I know people are waiting for this news. But quite frankly I could have gladly done without it.

For instance, they emphasized that the most celebrity news sections created over the course of their professional careers had been initiated in reaction to a loss of readership. But they also see celebrity news sections, especially when promoted by the marketing department, as means to avoid losing precious advertising revenue. In fact, a newspaper simply sells better if lighter, entertaining news is added to the more serious content. The same type of argument can be found in Mark Deuze's interviews with tabloid reporters: 'Just negative news does not work, people want to have a bit of fun

---

[15] 'Le refus de la confusion du métier de journaliste avec d'autres activités relevant de la publicité, de tâches d'espionnage ou de police, ou encore de la confusion d'intérêts.' (Authors' translation); Grevisse, B., 'Le Journalisme Gagné par la Peoplisation: Identités Professionnelles, Déontologie et Culture de la Dérision', *Communication* 27 (2009), no.1, pp. 179.

[16] Neveu, *Sociologie du Journalisme*, p. 43.

reading as well'.[17] In other words, 'people' (the reader) want celebrity news – they want to be entertained. This validates the 'rhetorical justification' mentioned above, although others, such as Le Bohec, consider it as a professional myth.[18] Some consider it as a myth precisely because it substantiates the idea that some sort of demand precedes supply – and therefore justifies its (poor) quality.

Again, if we are to believe our participants, these constraints implicitly tend to favor embroidering stories; celebrity is indeed known as a good ingredient for narratives, and the pressure upon the readers and the editors are said to encourage journalists to make their copy spicy, 'like in the movies'.

Sources as Constraints

In this context, all the parties actively contribute to maintaining the tension of the narrative (stars and PR managers, editors and journalists, audiences). A sports star was presented by a journalist as 'extraordinary' because she had many lovers in a short period of time, to the point where even the traditional media did not resist the temptation to comment on her 'soap opera'. Another star was presented as 'a caricature, … a junkie' because he was suspected of being able 'to sell his (sick) mother' to get coverage, accepting every proposal and sometimes even phoning journalists himself to inform about his latest adventures. In this case, star-figures act as a very efficient leitmotiv ('fil rouge'[19]), to the point of risking an 'overdose':

> *Journalist*: You need to be careful, because there is a risk of overdose, at the end you are fed up with always seeing the same persons. You need to take care of about three or four stars … [who are always contacting you].

This blatant conniving is often augmented by gifts and counter-gifts.[20]

> *Journalist*: [I] try to … 'celebritize' locals a bit, with their agreement. Because, since this is a small country, if you write about them in the celebrity news section without their okay … well, you lose your contacts and since it's a small country, well …

---

[17] Deuze, M., 'Popular Journalism and Professional Ideology: Tabloid Reporters and Editors Speak Out', *Media, Culture & Society* 27 (2005), no. 6, p. 869.
[18] Le Bohec, J., *Les Mythes Professionnels des Journalistes* (Paris, 2000), p. 210ss.
[19] Reuter, Y., 'Le Personnage', *Cahiers de Recherches en Didactique du Français* 1 (1987), p. 9ss.
[20] In French: 'système de don et de contre-don.'

This may sometimes make routines easier, but complicates them at the same time, giving rise to a number of ethical and concrete dilemmas: journalists know more than they publish, and some kind of negotiation often occurs between celebrities and journalists.[21] The latter phenomenon has also been observed elsewhere, but the personal relationships between journalists and celebrities in the French-speaking part of Switzerland makes this tension even more acute.

> *Journalist*: Well that's always very annoying. Because if a local celebrity tells me "I'm telling you, but I don't want it published", in that case I have a very strict code of ethics and I won't publish it, that's for sure. But on the other hand I sometimes tell them "ok, but your next mission, your next holiday, your next child or your next wedding, that's in [our magazine]."

As usual, the need to preserve one's network is of course important. However, the counter-argument (I want the 'series' to continue, and we have to work on it together) seems somehow legitimate: the storytelling here is presented as a common objective that is implicitly accepted. Celebrity news stories need a new spin every day and every stakeholder is expected to take part in its dynamic. As Richard Dyer asserts, the star system implies a convergence of the interests between all its stakeholders.[22]

> *Journalist*: There is a kind of unreported alliance, an unacknowledged collusion; I don't know how it happens. ... You come into the circle, and I think this means you want to be in.

In this case, the wording seems to reveal a very widespread state of mind that is somewhat surprising in a journalistic context.

The Narrative Advantages from a Scoop

The way in which journalists handle scoops in the field (one of the three main components of 'constraints') is also linked to both pressures and storytelling (see fig. 2). Scoops are a matter of professional pride, but also represent one of the constraints imposed on journalists in order to increase sales performance.[23] The excerpt below illustrates vividly the tension between ethics and the success of having found a scoop:

---

[21] Deuze, 'Popular Journalism', pp. 869-870.

[22] Dyer, R. *Heavenly Bodies: Film Stars and Society* (London, 2003).

[23] Another 'myth' in the professional culture, according to Le Bohec (p. 287ss), because journalists believe in it without thinking about its relevance.

Journalist: We didn't have any problem with lawyers; we didn't go to court because [the star] told me [she was getting married to another star]. She told me I could write about it; she just told me "Don't make a headline out of it." And it was on the headline banner, the headline, on a full page … anyway. Well, I didn't feel too good. I felt very bad and I withheld some of it. Or rather, I felt cornered and my boss told me, "You're being unprofessional." And I said, "Well, I can't do anything about it."

The rationale behind this excerpt makes the tension between scoop and ethics very explicit. On the one hand, the tension derives from individual performance motives where the journalist is 'proud of his scoop'. Thanks to him the newspaper is 'the first' to reveal the information. On the other hand, the tension derives from collective performance motives to the point where his editor-in-chief considers his hesitations as being 'unprofessional'. In this case, the journalist also emphasizes the fact that he was forced to write what he did. Hence the tension that arises from the journalist's need to preserve his network as well as the trust celebrities have in him (he offers a champagne bottle to make amends, and uses of the word 'betrayal' to qualify his attitude).

Even if our informants do not say it explicitly, a scoop is conducive to developing a narrative. Surprise effects and sudden changes from happiness to unhappiness (as in Aristotle's *Poetics*) are 'narratogenic'.[24] In a genre sometimes defined by our informants in a more positive light, as favoring the human side and the ability to listen, the empathy for individual life stories is taken into account whereas elsewhere it might have been considered as irrelevant:

Journalist: What attracted me to artists … to people who all of a sudden have to matter … beside their private lives, is (having) a public life. That's really interesting: what do they keep private? And what part of their private lives do they put in their public lives and all that? Because they're still human beings. … What interested me, what always interested me more, is what people are, not what they do. I love people, I love people, I don't know, I'm not exploiting people's weakness, I can't tell you. … I love life stories and … I just love it.

Here, the 'rhetorical justification' meets what Denis Ruellan calls an 'upstream rhetoric', stressing the fact that celebrity news, such as crime news,

---

[24] Dubied, A., 'Catalyse et Parenthèse Enchantée: Quand le Fait Divers Rencontre la Politique-people', *Le Temps des Médias* 10 (2008), pp. 142-155.

is focused on either individuals or specific cases.[25] And narratives happen to be specifically linked to human interests and individual stories.[26]

Managing PR Sources: A Professional Skill

Skills are the second most important aspect (24% of 1536) when journalists identify the main issues of their professional routine in connection with celebrity news. A first mention of these skills is linked to the prevalent 'professionalizing' of journalists' sources: here, professionalizing implies going through public relations advisors and the additional risk a journalist takes if he relies only on pre-packaged speeches and stories (see fig. 3).

> *Journalist*: The first time it was in Como and I didn't understand the rules of the game. So I tried to get hold of [the actors of *The Bold and the Beautiful*] just like that, but it was very difficult. It was only afterwards that I understood it was the PR chief who was managing absolutely everything. So I went to see him and the second time I even brought him a box of chocolates. The second time was in Venice and it was like a dream. I could sit on the set, on my little chair and they brought me the chocolates! [laugh]. What more could I want?

The traditional corollary to the professionalization of sources is their active collaboration with journalists:

> *Journalist*: You can ask [some celebrities] any question and they'll answer it. I think they use it to give another image ... more glamorous. ... Yeah, they make a living out of it, but some of them understood the system well ... Some of them are more reluctant and some of them really know how to use it.

The excerpts above suggest that an active approach for collecting sources actually works, especially when it comes to storytelling. At the same time, this reinforces the constraints mentioned above. Various stakeholders (producers, stars, TV channels, etc.) want newspapers to talk about their product, i.e. to help build their media agenda. They therefore use a well-known strategy – a reward/punishment system – with their networks. And they offer pre-packaged ('preconfigured') narrative material (scoops, breaking

---

[25] 'rhétorique de l'amont' (Authors' translation); Ruellan, D., *Le Professionnalisme du Flou: Identité et Savoir-faire des Journalistes Français* (Grenoble, 1993), p. 173ss.

[26] Ricoeur, P., *Time and Narrative* (Chicago, 1984).

news, exclusives, etc.) for storytelling, which is known to have the ability to influence the media agenda.[27]

The Revolution of the Internet and the Irony

The situation described above shows a journalist dealing with his primary sources in the field. However, that does not seem to be the most common procedure in the French-speaking part of Switzerland. Most journalists we interviewed stressed the fact that they mostly worked with second-hand sources. There seems to be a very clear tendency towards 'sitting/armchair journalism' (journalisme assis), which implies no field work, nor cross-checking sources and few investigative efforts.[28] The question of truthfulness, another fundamental ethical requirement for journalists, therefore arises.[29] The quest for truth traditionally goes along with cross-checking one's sources, which appears to be mostly second-hand in the case of Swiss-French celebrity news journalists. News dispatches from agencies and news found on specialized websites are basic to most professional routines in celebrity news. The following except illustrates the phenomenon:

> *Journalist*: Well, it depends. If it's information about Swiss celebrities, we generally get first-hand sources, especially from the [local television]; in general, we get it directly. If it's information about international celebrities, French or … well, for American celebrities, the internet really revolutionized the way in which we work because what did we do before? We're a small newspaper compared to magazines like *Paris Match* and others … Well, we used to "harvest." We used to look at all the newspapers, pick out the news and rewrite them in our own style. … And now there's the internet, for everything that comes from the US. In any case, well, there are websites on celebrities, so it's absolutely fantastic. So when it's my turn to write on celebrities (actually I don't do it anymore since I have a lot of other things to do), but if all of a sudden I have to step in for someone and write about celebrities, I go on these websites.

In this long excerpt, the 'source' is not the celebrity itself, nor is it a witness, nor someone involved in the facts, but a celebrity news website which is probably not even managed by professional journalists. Roughly speaking (since we do not claim to describe routines of all the celebrity news journalists), we can say that, according to our informants, direct sources represent

---

[27] *Ibidem*; Salmon, *Storytelling*.
[28] Neveu, *Sociologie du Journalisme*, p. 47.
[29] Grevisse, 'Le Journalisme', p. 179.

only one-third of celebrity news. The rest is found and cross-checked on the web.

In this context, writing skills appear to be the best way for an interviewer to distinguish himself and to take a step back from the topics he is writing about. Many of our informants stressed the fact that there are two highly important skills celebrity news journalists should have. The first skill is writing and the ability to find the best possible vantage point from which to write a story that will stand out. The second is the ability to obtain professional satisfaction without compromising their ethical need to be truthful. Similar conclusions were drawn from another study, based on discourse analysis of celebrity news.[30] The use of irony allows journalists of more authoritative news media to set themselves apart from their counterparts in the specialized press and from the subject itself, which is sometimes not even considered to be proper journalism:

> *Journalist*: To write celebrity news, huh, in the pages of [a popular newspaper], when you turn the pages of this thing, reading stuff about American [celebrities], and just by making too much noise about it, I think … that's not really journalism. No.

In this case, the statements we recorded focus for the most part on the distinction between 'good quality' and 'poor quality' celebrity news (15% of 1536). This attempt to simultaneously legitimize and to criticize the subject may seem strange. It is as if our informants wanted to be the only ones to say the worst things about celebrity news. Thus they are led to emphasize on their clear sightedness and the distance they adopt to their topic, as mentioned above.

Contrary to the reporting of facts, the emphasis on structuring skills and on expressing subjectivity allows celebrity news to be considered closer to journalistic commentary. This situation seems to suit our respondents. They choose either humor or criticism to get distance from their stories. Sometimes, they even choose to intervene in the 'facts' they are mentioning by expressing value judgments about what is happening to one celebrity or another.

> *Interviewer*: OK, which professional skills or qualities did you need [to write celebrity news]?

---

[30] Rais, C., 'Presse et Événement People: Une Subjectivité qui S'affiche', *Recherches en Communication* 26 (2007), pp. 225-241.

Journalist: Style … it was style. We would obtain information through agencies and celebrity websites … and then we'd re-write it, arrange it, we were not inventing, we were not telling lies, but we were arranging it to make it funny.

In a sense, they act as if they, the journalists, and the readers as well 'knew' the celebrity as a friend. This way, they assume they have the right to judge a celebrity's love life, or to make fun of his or her figure when the celebrity is on the beach, for example. While this may imply a so-called proximity with the star, this type of information also seems to respond to a certain need whether it be real or imaginary ('Do we really care about that?'). More and more, journalists tend to question the ever-growing importance and the need for celebrity news making in general interest newspapers in which we can also find special reports. These elements need to be questioned, especially in a country such as Switzerland, where there is no tradition in terms of celebrity gossip and where famous people come to live in the country in order to preserve their anonymity. In other words, they explicitly question the relevance and timeliness of this genre.

'Writing about Nothing'

Photographs are always the core of any event; they are the most important ingredient for celebrity news. Our informants assert that in order to be good at writing celebrity news, you have to be able to 'write about nothing', almost *ex-nihilo*. In other words, their work often consists in 'organizing trivial things into a hierarchy' and 'embellishing' stories based on rumors:

> *Journalist*: In celebrity news, rumors are information … I would say that it is so even more [than] in other sections. So is the fact that we pass off rumors as facts … We must be very watchful over the words we use.

This excerpt shows how difficult it is to work with second-hand sources and shows the distance induced by the practice of 'armchair journalism', as well as the constraints on performance mentioned above.

Here, the storytelling is highly questionable. Previous studies on discourse confirm that celebrity news is written according to a specific narrative matrix.[31] As Ricoeur explains it, such narratives 'claim to be true' (by using names, dates, pictures), even though they are using strategies associated with fiction (suspense, sudden changes of events, description of the

---

[31] Dubied, A., 'L'information People, Entre Rhétorique du cas Particulier et Récit de l'intimité', *Communication* 27 (2009), no. 1, pp. 54-65.

characters' moods, etc.).[32] Narratively speaking, the hybrid character of celebrity news might partially explain the success it encounters, as well as the
problems that arise on the public level. In fact, our informants claim that in
order to produce the best celebrity stories, they have to be able to embellish
the material with little tidbits, facts they cannot check, images that replace
information, or material which has been previously written by authoritative
figures. At the same time, they also claim to be journalists in their own
right.

> *Journalist*: Paparazzi will suddenly take pictures of her, we'll talk about her
> weight, about her feet, her hair, her tattoo, anything, but without saying any-
> thing about her career. It's a new level in celebrity news: the only thing they
> need to do is simply 'to be', never mind what they do.

In this contradictory context, the storytelling practice is justified through an
explicit distance to the genre.

Of course, 'armchair journalism' also affects the financial success of
newspaper publishers. Journalists can be made to work at a lower cost since
all they need is access to the internet and a good command of foreign lan-
guages:

> *Journalist*: How many times, huh, have I tried to check information on the in-
> ternet, on English websites, on Italian websites ... I find it's a great advantage
> to be multilingual because nowadays everything's on the internet so you have
> to know how to find your information on it.

Not only does 'armchair journalism' save money, it also saves time. News
is produced at a faster rate. The excerpt, concerning the French celebrity
couple mentioned above, also highlights the fundamental importance of
'time'.[33] Stress and pressure was felt among journalists in the newsroom.
They had to publish the sensational news of the wedding as soon as possible
to beat the competition.

Conclusion

Factors such as economic pressure, a shift in the professionalization and the
use of sources due to the web revolution, pressure from the sources themselves, particularly when celebrity news relates to politics, all contribute to

---

[32] Ricoeur, *Time and Narrative*.

[33] Grevisse, B., *Le Temps des Journalistes: Essai de Narratologie Médiatique* (Louvain-la-Neuve, 1997).

challenge the professional integrity of journalists working in this particular field. Mentioning different types of regulation operating within it, our participants clearly wish to define themselves as professional journalists. However, they systematically set themselves apart from it by adopting a somewhat cynical view. Quite lucidly they see their type of news as being affect-affected by a conflation of interests: those of the stars themselves, those of their 'employers', those of the newspapers which talk about them — a conflation born of the Hollywood star system.

It is interesting to note that celebrity news journalists, who work around a genre that has expanded in the last couple of years, emphasize that they have specific writing skills in terms of subjectivity and storytelling. Indeed they implicitly legitimize their work by mentioning the use of some characteristics, which are fundamental values of narrative journalism. Indeed, narrative journalism gives priority to thick narratives, where the emphasis is put on details. In other words, the 'voice', the style, the implication and the details lie at the core of this genre. However, implicitly wanting to stick closely to this genre, celebrity news journalists are hindered by a number of elements which have been presented above: they do not take part in field-work, their experience is not the core of their narrative, and they often face deontological limits that are particularly important to narrative journalists.[34]

Celebrity news reflects the contemporary propensity to talk about private issues in the public sphere as well as mutating modes in public deliberation.[35] In this domain celebrity news journalists seem to be ahead of their colleagues. The difficulties they meet are of the same kind as those encountered by the rest of the profession; however, they experience them in an exacerbated and particularly virulent form. Their type of news stands out due to characteristics such as excess and ethical dilemmas and thus celebrity news journalists find themselves in the front line of an evolving profession. In this type of news reporting, the marketing of information, its sensational nature, its personalization, the vulnerability to pressure and the dependence on technological growth, all these factors combine and reinforce each other, making this journalistic category at times into a kind of laboratory of the profession.

The blurred boundaries of the profession of journalism may lead some to think that celebrity news is only a small part of its routine, marginal to the profession and therefore that it only exists by default.[36] Instead, shouldn't we consider that 'celebrity news contaminates the whole present

---

[34] Lallemand, A., *Journalisme Narratif en Pratique* (Bruxelles, 2011), p. 209.
[35] Mehl, D., 'La "Vie Publique Privée"', *Hermès* 13-14 (1994), pp. 13-14; Marshall, P. D., *Celebrity and Power* (London, 1997).
[36] Ruellan., *Le Professionnalisme.*

information logic', and that – to paraphrase Zelizer – it is time to start 'taking [celebrity] journalism seriously', journalistically and academically speaking?[37] This is precisely the point made in this chapter: we do not defend or condemn the genre, nor do we congratulate or wish to lecture those who practice it. Instead, we undertook empirical studies, detailing its development, in order to move beyond a purely superficial analysis.

---

[37] Grevisse., 'Le Journalisme', p. 180; Zelizer, B., *Taking Journalism Seriously* (Thousand Oaks, 2004).

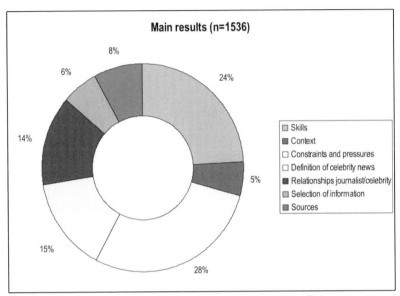

1. Key Job-Related Themes Noted by 'Celebrity News' Journalists

ANNIK DUBIED AND MAGALI DUBEY

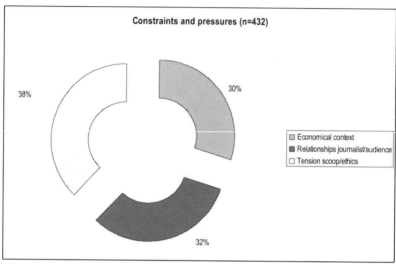

2. Key Constraints and Pressures Identified

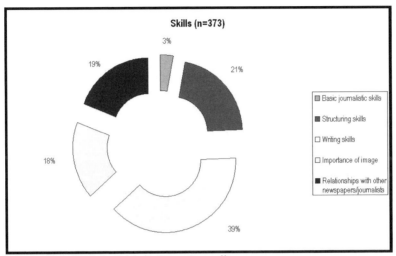

3. Journalistic Skills in Celebrity News Journalism

NARRATIVE MEDIA CONSTRUCTION OF FALLEN HEROES

THE CASES OF TOM BOONEN AND TIGER WOODS

Tim Hoebeke, Annelore Deprez, and Karin Raeymaeckers

Within journalism studies, myth and storytelling are regularly used concepts.[1] Most scholars fall back on either an existential narrative condition or a more pragmatic evolutionary frame to label journalists as storytellers. From the first point of view, Barthes states that 'narrative is present in every age, in every place, in every society.'[2] This idea is central for the narrative paradigm, which claims that every journalist is in essence a storyteller. 'Storytelling will never be in crisis (even if individual storytellers are), because storytelling is an essential part of what makes us human.'[3] As our logic and reason are captured not only within a rational paradigm, but also within a more all-encompassing narrative paradigm, it is no surprise that journalists construct news as stories.[4]

There is also a more pragmatic way of looking at journalists as storytellers, dictated by historical evolution. From this angle, journalists are considered to be the contemporary continuation of storytellers in oral traditions. This bardic function of oral storytellers and troubadours evolved with the invention of print into modern mass circulated newspapers.[5]

Journalists as modern bardic storytellers are active constructors of reality. 'We turn nature to culture as we talk and write and narrate it.'[6] During this process of news writing, journalists tend to revert to formulaic patterns similar to mythological tales. Jack Lule even states that 'daily news is the

---

[1] Bird, S.E. and Dardenne, R.W., 'Myth, Chronicle and Story: Exploring the Narrative Qualities of News', in: Berkowitz, D., ed, *Social Meanings of News: A Text-Reader* (Thousand Oaks, CA, 1997), pp. 333-350; Bird, S.E. and Dardenne, R.W., 'Rethinking News and Myth as Storytelling', in: Wahl-Jorgensen, K. and Hanitzsch, T., eds, *The Handbook of Journalism Studies* (New York, 2009), pp. 205-217; Zelizer, B., *Taking Journalism Seriously: News and the Academy* (Thousand Oaks, CA, 2004).
[2] For Barthes, see Wright, B., 'The Hero in Popular Stories', *Journal of Popular Film & Television* 32 (2005), p. 146.
[3] Lule, J., *Daily News, Eternal Stories: The Mythological Role of Journalism* (New York, 2001), p. 4.
[4] Fisher, W.R., 'The Narrative Paradigm - in the Beginning', *Journal of Communication* 35 (1985), pp. 74-89.
[5] Aitchison, J., *The Word Weavers: Newshounds and Wordsmiths* (New York, 2007); Hartley, J., *Understanding News* (London, 1983), pp. 102-106.
[6] Schudson, M., *The Power of News* (Cambridge, 1995), p. 52.

primary vehicle for myth in our time.'[7] Myth is both a contextual story and an archetypal narration, so it can be expressed in different ways and remains the same.[8]

News and myth are so closely intertwined because they both narrate resonant dramas which the storytellers 'know how to tell and audiences know how to decode.'[9] News and myth represent central social values by telling stories with more or less fixed sequences. One of the more common myths is the hero myth. 'The hero is integral to the culture of a society – that is, to the beliefs, values, and goals of a society – because the hero is integral to storytelling, the essence of culture.'[10]

The Construction of Heroes Within Journalism

Heroes are a product of communication, which means that real persons only provide us with the rough material for heroism. It is during processes of narrativization that heroes emerge.[11] Mass media serve as one of the main communicators of heroism; they 'serve as the primary vehicles through which we learn of the extraordinary accomplishments, courage, and deeds of cultural heroes and the faults and ignominious deeds of villains and fools.'[12] This is why Hook considers contemporary heroes as 'synthetic products', stating that 'whoever controls the microphones and printing presses can make or unmake beliefs overnight.'[13]

If mass media are our contemporary storytellers, telling stories closely linked with hero myths, it is of course of vital importance to delineate the hero concept. Heroes are defined in countless ways, but most definitions focus on three main features: narrative sequentiality; social values; and two status elements (heroes as role models and heroes as celebrities). Susan Drucker and Robert Cathcart touch upon some of these features by stating that heroes are men and women who 'transcend ordinary human qualities and embody the divine, the ideal, the quest, the courageous, the virtuous

---

[7] Lule, *Daily News, Eternal Stories*, p. 19.

[8] Lozano, E., 'The Force of Myth on Popular Narratives: The Case of Melodramatic Serials', *Communication Theory* 2 (1992), pp. 207-220.

[9] Berkowitz, D., 'The Ironic Hero of Virginia Tech: Healing Trauma through Mythical Narrative and Collective Memory', *Journalism* 11 (2010), p. 645.

[10] Wright, 'The Hero in Popular Stories', p. 146.

[11] Strate, L., 'Heroes and/as Communication', in: Drucker, S.J. and Gumpert, G., eds, *Heroes in a Global World* (Cresskill, 2008), pp. 19-45.

[12] Vande Berg, L., 'The Sports Hero Meets Mediated Celebrityhood', in: Wenner, L.A., ed, *MediaSport* (London, 1998), p. 152.

[13] For Hook, see Smith, G., 'The Sport Hero: An Endangered Species', *Quest* 19 (1973), pp. 59-70.

and the superior.'[14] With the addition of the celebrity status of contemporary heroes, this will form the basis of this research (see fig. 1).[15]

Social Values

While storytellers recount their stories, heroes are laden with moral and social values. This occurrence reflects one of the main functions of myth: the moral tale its tellers want to spread. Heroes are perfect hosts of social values such as virtue, sacrifice, courage, discipline, and perseverance.[16] According to Orrin Klapp, heroes evoke 'the appropriate attitudes and behavior.'[17] Whereas the narrative storyline of archetypal myths such as the hero is supposed to be universal, these social values are cultural.[18]

Status Elements: Role Models and Celebrities

Because heroes are presented as carriers of social values, they can be considered as role models. 'Heroes symbolize something greater than attaining wealth and fame, performing death-defying acts, or acquiring media-promoted status. They reflect our values, our ideals, our dreams.'[19] Heroes are both, on both an individual and collective level, ideal representations. On a collective level, heroes are the embodiment of our ideals, individuals to whom a society can look up to. Different authors focus on this collective level following from Klapp, who states that, 'the hero in social life is thus essentially more than a person; he is an ideal image, a legend, a symbol.'[20]

---

[14] Drucker, S.J. and Cathcart, R.S., 'The Hero as a Communication Phenomenon', in: Drucker, S.J. and Cathcart, R.S., eds, *American Heroes in a Media Age* (Cresskill, 1994), p. 1.

[15] Boorstin, D.J., *The Image: A Guide to Pseudo-Events in America* (New York, 1992); Drucker, S.J., 'The Mediated Sports Hero', in: Drucker, S.J. and Gumpert, G., eds, *Heroes in a Global World* (Cresskill,, 2008), pp. 415-432; Gumpert, G., 'The Wrinkle Theory: The Deconsecration of the Hero', in: Drucker, S.J. and Gumpert, G., eds, *Heroes in a Global World* (Cresskill, 2008), pp. 129-147; Sanchez, T.R., 'It's Time Again for Heroes - Or Were They Ever Gone?', *The Social Studies* 92 (2000), pp. 58-61.

[16] E.g. Gumpert, 'The Wrinkle Theory'.

[17] Klapp, O.E., 'The Creation of Popular Heroes', *The American Journal of Sociology* 54 (1948), p. 135.

[18] Duffy, S., 'Heroes in a Global World', in: Drucker, S.J. and Gumpert, G., eds, *Heroes in a Global World* (Cresskill, 2008), pp. 205-225.

[19] Sanchez, 'It's Time Again for Heroes', p. 61.

[20] Parry, K.D., 'Search for the Hero: An Investigation into the Sports Heroes of British Sports Fans', *Sport in Society* 12 (2009), pp. 212-226; Smith, 'The Sport Hero';

On the other hand, heroes are also role models on an individual level, because they represent our ideal selves.[21] This individual level accentuates the importance of introspection, which can lead to self-observation, identification, and imitation.[22] Although the concept of heroes can be ambiguous, heroes have always existed as a standard against which to measure ourselves.[23]

Still, heroes are not fixed during time; they evolve through social processes and their evolution is closely linked with technological progress.[24] In this light, many authors discuss the celebrity factor of contemporary heroes. Concerning this 'celebrification' process of heroes, two lines of reasoning have developed.[25] The first mindset proclaims the end of heroism in favor of celebrities. This insight is inspired by Daniel Boorstin. He claims that contemporary heroes are 'human pseudo-events' who lack every form of greatness, which defines traditional heroes.[26] For the other group, heroes are still present in modern societies, but have transformed and now are also celebrities.[27] As fame is a condition for heroism, this fame is spread by mass media.[28] One might say that every contemporary hero is also a celebrity, while at the same time, not every celebrity is a hero. Adrian North et al. and Joshua Shuart make it clear that heroes have produced ideas or objects of lasting importance, while the only condition for celebrities is their fame.[29]

Vande Berg, 'The Sports Hero Meets Mediated Celebrityhood'; Klapp, 'The Creation of Popular Heroes', p. 135.

[21] Strate, 'Heroes and/as Communication'.

[22] E.g. Hirschman, E.C., 'The Interplay Between Archetypes and Autobiography in Mass Media Preferences', *Advances in Consumer Research* 31 (2004), pp. 168-173; Klapp, O.E., 'Heroes, Villains and Fools, as Agents of Social Control', *American Sociological Review* 19 (1954), pp. 56-62; Zehnder, S.P. and Calvert, S.L., 'Between the Hero and the Shadow: Developmental Differences in Adolescents' Perceptions and Understanding of Mythic Themes in Film', *Journal of Communication Inquiry* 28 (2004), pp. 122-137.

[23] Sanchez, 'It's Time Again for Heroes'.

[24] Dean, J., 'U.S. and European Heroism Compared', in: Drucker, S.J. and Gumpert, G., eds, *Heroes in a Global World* (Cresskill, 2008), pp. 19-45; Strate, 'Heroes and/as Communication'.

[25] Drucker, 'The Mediated Sports Hero'.

[26] Boorstin, 'The Image'; see also: Drucker, 'The Mediated Sports Hero'.

[27] E.g. Vande Berg, 'The Sports Hero Meets Mediated Celebrityhood'.

[28] Cathcart, R.S., 'From Hero to Celebrity: The Media Connection', in: Drucker, S.J. and Cathcart, R.S., eds, *American Heroes in a Media Age* (Cresskill, 1994), pp. 36-46.

[29] North, A.C., Bland, V. and Ellis, N., 'Distinguishing Heroes from Celebrities', *British Journal of Psychology* 96 (2005), pp. 39-52; Shuart, J., 'Heroes in Sport: Assessing Celebrity Endorser Effectiveness', *International Journal of Sports Marketing & Sponsorship* 8 (2007), pp. 126-141.

Still, there is a certain blurring of the boundaries between heroes and celebrities, 'in which the heroic has become entertaining and the ideal is reduced to fame and fortune.'[30] However, Shuart shows that there is still a fair distinction between celebrities and heroes, because of the greater identification factor of heroes, their bigger influence on society and the values they represent.[31] Celebrities have commercial value and are prone to commodification, but a combination of celebrity with heroism has an even larger commercial impact.

Narrative Sequentiality

Joseph Campbell is one of the principal authors to describe the hero narrative, which he called 'monomyth'.[32] 'The standard path of the mythological adventure of the hero is a magnification of the formula represented in the rite of passage, the nuclear unit of the monomyth: separation – initiation – return.'[33] This is the archetypal hero journey, which means that the sequences of the story transgress temporal and cultural barriers. More recent scholars inspired by the work of Campbell are Peter Williams and Jack Lule.[34] While the former reduces the hero myth to two main elements (the journey outward and the trip back), the latter expands it to four elements: humble descent, the quest, triumph and return.

To investigate the hero narrative (see fig. 1), we synthesize the hero narrative as described by these three authors. We discern three major phases in the hero narrative, beginning with the rise of the hero, followed by his temporary fall from grace and concluding with his resurrection. During the first phase, the rise of the hero, we deduce four narrative sequences: (1) the hero emerges from a humble origin; (2) he has to go on a journey or a quest; (3) on his journey, he meets different obstacles and ordeals, which he has to conquer; and (4) he has to gain important victories over these obstacles. As heroes are not perfect, they sometimes face defeat or give in to certain temptations. This is the temporary fall from grace of heroes, during which they can be portrayed by the media as archetypal tricksters. The rise and fall of the hero is followed by the third phase, the resurrection of the hero. This third phase comprises three main narrative sequences: (1) heroes get a chance to explain or defend their mistakes; (2) this penance is publicly ac-

---

[30] Sanchez, 'It's Time Again for Heroes', p. 59.

[31] Shuart, 'Heroes in Sport'.

[32] Campbell, J., *The Hero with a Thousand Faces* (London, 1993).

[33] *Ibidem*, p. 23.

[34] Williams, P., *The Sports Immortals: Deifying the American Athlete* (Bowling Green, 1994); Lule, 'Daily News, Eternal Stories'.

cepted; and (3) finally their media coverage turns positive again and the hero reclaims his status.

It is clear that there is a general consensus regarding heroes as role models, closely linked with the social values they represent. But of course, such status is accompanied by obligations. Garry Smith states that the behavior of heroes as social models should be consistent and superior to other members of society.[35] If heroes fail to meet these demands, they become role models in reverse and fall from grace. Heroes are not infallible and sometimes yield to temptations. They have to conquer many obstacles on their quest for success, and sometimes these obstacles take the upper hand.

During their fall from grace, heroes can be portrayed as archetypal tricksters.[36] Carl Jung, who introduced the term 'archetype', focuses on the contrasting character of the trickster 'a bestial and divine being.'[37] Along this line of thought, Helen Lock describes the trickster as the archetypal boundary-crosser, citing Lewis Hyde that the, 'trickster is the mythic embodiment of ambiguity and ambivalence, doubleness and duplicity, contradiction and paradox.'[38] As Lule explains, the trickster archetype can be subdivided into two main categories: the savage and the victim.[39] While being portrayed as a savage person 'driven by physical appetites, lust and desire [who] has no control over his impulses', he is at the same time a victim and an unfinished person.[40]

True heroes eventually overcome their obstacles and temptations and are welcomed back as more experienced individuals. A temporary flawed status as a vulnerable hero, a sudden fall from grace, does not necessarily imply the end to the hero status.[41] By conquering their obstacles, heroes can confirm and reinforce this status. Heroes gain lasting fame by performing valuable deeds, but they gain an even more heroic status by winning the struggle against their own desires.[42]

---

[35] Smith, 'The Sport Hero'.

[36] Hoebeke, T., Deprez, A. and Raeymaeckers, K., 'Heroes in the Sports Pages: The Troubled Road to Victory for Belgian Cyclist Tom Boonen', *Journalism Studies* 12 (2011), pp. 658-672.

[37] For Jung, see O'Donnell, M., 'Preposterous Trickster: Myth, News, the Law and John Marsden', *Media and Arts Law Review* 8 (2003), p. 295.

[38] For Hyde, see Lock, H., 'Transformations of the Trickster', *Southern Cross Review*, available from: http://www.southerncrossreview.org/18/trickster.htm (2002).

[39] Lule, 'Daily News, Eternal Stories'.

[40] *Ibidem,* p. 124.

[41] O'Donnell, 'Preposterous Trickster', p. 298.

[42] Duffy, 'Heroes in a Global World'.

Sport Journalism as a Breeding Ground for Heroism

One of the most prominent platforms for contemporary heroism is delivered by the field of sports.[43] According to Garry Whannel, sports events are susceptible to narrativization because of their inherent hermeneutic codes.[44] The domination of star athletes within sport journalism makes them the carriers of this narrativization process. One of the central narratives within sport journalism is the hero narrative because the life and career of athletes evoke heroic stories comparable to archetypal hero myths. Sport heroes also serve as our contemporary role models and are expected to live up to this status.[45] Being a sport hero implies more than mere athletic skills or making money hand over fist. A society wants heroes who reinforce its social values.[46] Although Harris shows that personal competences are more important than social values, most authors claim that sport heroes need to combine extraordinary achievements and athletic skills with social values.[47] Nick Trujillo and Leah Vande Berg mention such values in reference with sports as 'achievement, hard work, discipline, teamwork, loyalty, and tradition.'[48]

Because of the growing impact of professionalism, commercialism and the mass media, sport has become more and more business and entertainment. This trend is reflected by sport heroes who are molded by the mass media as celebrities. Athletes have become commodities and an increasing focus on their salaries, marketability, and private life, combined with growing media attention, are obvious manifestations of this 'celebrification' process.[49] Although this evolution makes Susan Drucker decide that contemporary sport heroes are flawed pseudo-heroes, we join Vande Berg by stating that 'as a result of contemporary media, today's heroes inevitably become celebrities as well as heroes.'[50]

Globalization has had a major impact on the ubiquity of celebrities, and without dwelling upon these much debated terms, as this is not the focus of

---

[43] Vande Berg, 'The Sports Hero Meets Mediated Celebrityhood'.

[44] Whannel, G., *Media Sport Stars: Masculinities and Moralities* (London, 2002), p. 54.

[45] Drucker, 'The Mediated Sports Hero'.

[46] Parry, 'Search for the Hero'.

[47] For Harris, see Vande Berg, 'The Sports Hero Meets Mediated Celebrityhood'; e.g. Smith, 'The Sport Hero'; Vande Berg, 'The Sports Hero Meets Mediated Celebrityhood'.

[48] Trujillo, N. and Vande Berg, L., 'From Wild Western Prodigy to Ageless Wonder: The Mediated Evolution of Nolan Ryan', in: Drucker, S.J. and Cathcart, R.S., eds, *American Heroes in a Media Age* (Cresskill, 1994), p. 222.

[49] Drucker, S.J. and Gumpert, G., *Heroes in a Global World* (Cresskill, 2008).

[50] Drucker, 'The Mediated Sports Hero'; Vande Berg, 'The Sports Hero Meets Mediated Celebrityhood', p. 139.

our research, it is still fruitful to mention that sports in general and sport heroes in particular also seem to be prey to these globalizing trends.[51] Different authors have shown that local and national sport stars increasingly have to deal with international competition, also in regards to the public's selection of heroes.[52] On the other hand, there is also a contradicting power at work within sport, as it is a platform for nationalism.[53] These two seemingly conflicting forces justify the comparison we make in this chapter between a national and an international sport hero with comparable career histories, which sheds new light on this debate.

The Cases of Tiger Woods and Tom Boonen

As we have indicated, sport journalism is one of the most prominent domains for heroism and mythic storytelling. In this chapter we draw a comparison between a national and an international sport hero, the Belgian cyclist Tom Boonen and the American golfer Tiger Woods, in order to explain myth at work in the Belgian sports press.

Tom Boonen is a Belgian cyclist whose career has had many highlights (e.g. world champion, Belgian champion and many UCI World Tour victories), but also many low points (predominantly related to private affairs like his amorous vicissitudes, reckless driving behavior, and drug abuse). Tiger Woods, on the other hand, travelled a journey which was practically flawless for the first 15 years of his career (i.e. record-breaking achievements, a role model for ethnic minorities, especially in the United States, and an immaculate family life.) A major sex scandal, however, put things in a different light. Because both athletes were involved in media scandals, these two

---

[51] Harvey, J. and Houle, F., 'Sport, World Economy, Global Culture, and New Social Movements', *Sociology of Sport Journal* 11 (1994), pp. 337-355; Houlihan, B., 'Homogenization, Americanization, and Creolization of Sport: Varieties of Globalization', *Sociology of Sport Journal* 11 (1994), pp. 356-375; Maguire, J., 'Sport and Globalization', in: Coakley, J. and Dunning, E., eds, *Handbook of Sports Studies* (London, 2000), pp. 356-369; Melnick, M.J. and Jackson, S.J., 'Globalization American-Style and Reference Idol Selection', *International Review for the Sociology of Sport* 37 (2002), pp. 429-448.

[52] Falcous, M. and Maguire, J. 'Globetrotters and Local Heroes? Labor Migration, Basketball, and Local Identities', *Sociology of Sport Journal* 22 (2005), pp. 137-157; Melnick and Jackson, 'Globalization American-style and Reference Idol Selection', pp. 429-448.

[53] Jarvie, G. and Reid, I.A., 'Sport, Nationalism and Culture in Scotland', *The Sports Historian* 19 (1999), pp. 97-124; Rowe, D., 'Sport and the Repudiation of the Global', *International Review for the Sociology of Sport* 38 (2003), pp. 281-294; Rowe, D., McKay, J., and Miller, T., 'Come Together: Sport, Nationalism, and the Media', in: Wenner L.A., ed, *MediaSport* (London, 1998), pp. 119-133.

cases are comparable. The temporary fall from grace of the hero and its aftermath also summons an analogy with the common scandal script used by the media: 'accusation or revelation, broadcast, denial and/or confession – and frequently, a comeback or attempted comeback.'[54]

Researchers have already demonstrated the media construction of these figures. Recent research shows the existence of the hero myth in the media portrayal of Tom Boonen in the Belgian press and could clearly identify the presence of the hero myth.[55] Vande Berg, on the other hand, has shown how the media portrayal of Tiger Woods indicates a return to traditional heroism.[56] However, recent shifts in this portrayal can be expected after the sex scandal was uncovered at the end of 2009.

Comparing a Belgian sport hero with an American sport hero in the Belgian press can add some new insights to the discussion on globalization of athlete heroes. These two cases provide us with the opportunity to see if the storytelling function of journalists in this digital age is reduced to the creation of celebrities as 'pseudo-heroes' or whether journalists are still able to claim their function as creators of heroes in their retelling of the archetypal hero myth.

Methodology

Within this framework, we analyze the sports related news in two popular Flemish newspapers: *Het Nieuwsblad* and *Het Laatste Nieuws*. These two newspapers have the highest circulation in Flanders and are broadly based, which is a precondition for myth to function. Because they are both well-known for their sports section, they are the two of the most appropriate newspapers to study myth at work in Flemish newspapers. In the case of Tom Boonen, we analyzed one year by selecting three periods: we started with his second victory in the classic race Paris-Roubaix (04-12-2008 until 04-16-2008), then focused on the period in which he tested positive for drug abuse (06-10-2008 until 06-16-2008), and finally we analyzed the period of his third victory in Paris-Roubaix (04-11-2009 until 04-15-2009). For the analysis of the narrative media representation of Tiger Woods, we opted to analyze two years (2009-2010), without purposive sampling techniques because of the smaller number of articles. In the middle of these two years, Woods' sex scandal broke (the first rumors emerged on 11-27-2009). In to-

---

[54] Gamson, J., 'Normal Sins: Sex Scandal Narratives as Institutional Morality Tales', *Social Problems* 48 (2001), p. 186.

[55] Hoebeke, Deprez and Raeymaeckers, 'Heroes in the Sports Pages'.

[56] Vande Berg, 'The Sports Hero Meets Mediated Celebrityhood'.

tal we analyzed 157 articles focusing on Tom Boonen and 214 articles focusing on Tiger Woods.

Results

The Narrative Sequences of the Hero Journey

During the first phase of the hero journey, the story of Tom Boonen focuses on the humble origins. Even though he now lives in Monaco, Boonen is cited as saying: 'I am and I will stay a boy from La Campania [the region of his birthplace].' Residents of his hometown were often quoted and the little village was also seen as a '*pars pro toto*', representing the Flemish people. By emphasizing his hometown during the drug-period, newspapers contrasted his lifestyle with 'home-town values'; in a lesser way, they also focused on his simple family and his old life. In the case of Tiger Woods, on the other hand, there was hardly any mention of a humble origin or a difficult childhood.

The second phase, the quest, was twofold for Boonen. First, competitive expectations for the future were imposed concerning record-breaking goals. Second, comparisons were made with legendary predecessors, in whose footsteps he was destined to follow, showing the process of mythmaking fully at work. Tiger Woods' development into a hero was also portrayed dually. First, Woods was portrayed as a child prodigy whose exceptional talent was described as 'otherworldly'. His father saw in him 'the chosen one' and a 'Messiah', and Tiger Woods himself was quoted after winning his first Major title as saying: 'I am predestined.' Second, comparisons were also made with legendary predecessors. Woods was compared to Senna, Merckx, Jordan, Ali and even Boonen: 'athletes who have a touch more than others.'

On their quests, heroes have to overcome various obstacles in their paths. Tom Boonen had to conquer both competitive and non-competitive obstacles. The most important competitive obstacles were, of course, his adversaries, but injuries, pile-ups and doping were also mentioned. In a lesser way, the pressure imposed by the media and racing fatigue also arose as possible obstacles. Amongst alcohol abuse, reckless driving behavior, an affair with a 16-year old girl, his move to Monaco, his relationship split, wild parties, his 'weakness' for the other sex, and the fame, his main non-competitive obstacle was his drug abuse. Readers were warned that drugs and sportsmanship were not complementary ('He who snorts cocaine on a daily basis, can scarcely succeed as top class sportsman.')

The obstacles Tiger Woods has to conquer almost exclusively exist on a non-competitive level, except for a knee injury and his adversaries. Of course, there was a huge focus on his extramarital affairs and his mistresses, which were also shown to be incompatible with competitive successes: 'Experience shows that sportsmen underachieve when they do not have a safe haven. Look at Tiger Woods. Suddenly, he can't golf anymore, now it is leaked how he cheated on his wife for years.' As the story unfolded, the press started talking more and more about sex addiction. Another addiction surfaced too, because various sources claimed that Woods was addicted to drugs. One journalist heaped his obstacles together as hubris, portraying Woods as a true Icarus burning his wings by flying too close to the sun:

> Hubris or overconfidence became a leitmotiv in his life as the absolute number one of the noble sport of golf and by extension the worldwide sports. Untouchable was he who seemingly could permit himself everything and who had in every American city one or more beauties to have it off with.

Heroes have to obtain important victories and, in the case of Tom Boonen, this meant winning Paris-Roubaix for the second and third time. In Tiger Woods' case, we did not find any important victories during our two-year selection. However, although Woods did not win a Major in 2009, he did win six PGA tournaments, which made 2009 his third most lucrative year for prize money. In 2010 Woods did not win any tournaments, so logically there were no victories to report. Belgian readers only learned about his achievements in retrospect and without getting into much detail in many portrayals such as 'the greatest golfer ever' or even 'the greatest sportsman ever.' The Belgian press also referred many times to his number one position in the world ranking.

When heroes yield to temptation or are unable to conquer an obstacle, they fall from grace and can be temporarily portrayed as tricksters, who are savages and victims at the same time. When Tom Boonen was caught for cocaine abuse, the press described him as someone who wears a mask, a *persona non grata*, even a plague sufferer. This change in language provides a clear sign that the hero has fallen from grace.

Boonen's mishaps were contextualized as a series of mistakes, cited chronologies as a form of condemnation. Newspapers referred to past problems and showed that Boonen's drug abuse was not a solitary incident, but rather an exponent of a series of mistakes. His deeds also had an impact on his surroundings; we learned that Boonen caused damage to his family and friends, his team, his sponsor, cycling in general, and his fans. Boonen was also portrayed as dumb and naïve ('Dumber than the asphalt he's driving on'), and as a highly sexed person unable to control his own impulses, considering his relationship with a sixteen-year-old girl and being described as a 'debauchee'.

On the other hand, Boonen was also portrayed as a victim of external conditions. These external conditions can be summed up as: his young age, pressure, fame, wealth and his fast transition from a simple boy to a super-star. His status as an athlete, society in general, the media, hypocrisy and bad friends were also cited as external conditions causing his lapses. The press also pointed to the lack of counseling and guidance. This need for more guidance is imperative, because Boonen was portrayed as an imma-ture person: 'A child of almost 28 years old.'

The newspapers seized the opportunity to contextualize his drug abuse as a social problem. And for the press, 'this is a case out of a society broken adrift that transcends the sport.' Central to the story was the infiltration of drugs in celebrity culture and sport culture, while the problem of doping in the world of sports received much less attention. This again shows that Boonen's problems were considered to be non-competitive. When Boonen returned at the pinnacle of his game, the press radically changed its dis-course and kept silent about his mistakes. This indicates that the press for-gave Boonen's mistakes and that his fall from grace was temporary.

This was not the case for Tiger Woods. He was also portrayed as a trickster, but unlike Tom Boonen's case, the press kept mentioning his mis-takes. The lack of a major victory after the scandal is a prime explanation for this. Woods was portrayed more as a savage than as a victim, which can also have an influence.

The media did not list any previous mistakes in the case of Tiger Woods, except for the serial-like intricacies concerning his mistresses. The contrary is true: Tiger Woods had the image of 'the perfect son-in-law' with a happy family life. The glaring contrast between his assumed irreproacha-ble life and his actual conduct made Woods' fall from grace immediate. His affairs had an impact both on himself and on his surroundings. The conse-quences for him were numerous: first of all, it meant the end of his mar-riage; but it also meant damage to his image, sponsors who dropped their endorsements, downheartedness and weak results. His behavior also had a negative impact on others: his wife, his children, his mother-in-law, his sport, his sponsors, and even his mistresses were all cited as being victims of Woods' reckless behavior. The following quotation sums it up: 'But what do you do when your extensively documented adultery did not only hurt your mother, woman and children, but also cost your sponsors lots of mon-ey, damaged your sport and disillusioned little children?' As tricksters lack self-control and are impulsive characters, Woods is portrayed as person with 'irrepressible urges' who is 'fluttering around cheerfully for years.' In a lesser way, he is also portrayed as a naïve and dumb individual. Woods himself described it very concisely, hinting at the mask he was wearing, the lack of self-control, the damage he inflicted on others and his naiveté: 'I had the feeling I could do everything – and hurt many people with my behavior. I was living a lie. I wanted to stop, but I couldn't. It was terrible.' In a lesser way, Tiger Woods was sometimes portrayed as a victim of his own fame and a lack of guidance: 'Tiger had no one around to point him to his responsibilities.' His status as an athlete and other conditions such as male testosterone, male problems with monogamy, his genes, and the pressure were also mentioned to give him some excuses. Tiger Woods was also portrayed as a man-child, 'this is the behavior of a three year old who temporarily escapes the parental attention and grabs undisciplined in the closet for sweets.'

When heroes see the error of their ways, they get a chance to publicly defend or explain their mistakes. In a public statement, Boonen asked for forgiveness concerning his drug abuse. However, some criticized the content of his speech and others reacted quite negatively. His public apology was also described as an orchestrated publicity stunt, 'part of a legal strategy.' There were positive reactions as well: 'At his press conference you could tell from the expression on his face that he felt sorry.' His confession was considered to be the starting point of his comeback: 'That Tom Boonen showed regret, can be a sign that he has taken the first step to recovery.'

Tiger Woods made a commensurable public apology, but hesitated much longer. It took Woods more than two months to make a public apology (except for two short statements on his website). Journalists were complaining about his silence and publicity agents advised him to make a public apology ('If he wants to repolish his heavily damaged image, he has to make a public apology.') Just like Boonen's apology, there were advocates for, and opponents of the way it was handled. Advocates applauded the content of the speech, but opponents found it 'overdirected', banal in regards to content, lacking emotion and not credible. He was also reproached for being too submissive ('Golfer and skirt-chaser Tiger Woods set a new standard yesterday on CNN for public penance. He groveled and kept on groveling.') There was also a hint that his apology had another, more hidden motive: 'His sponsors think that's very important.' Still, despite the criticism Tiger Woods had to endure, a communication expert said that 'if he disappears now for a little while, he can later make a glorious comeback.'

Despite some criticism of his apology, Boonen's penance was rather quickly accepted. Competitive achievements were not needed for him to be excused. Two main factors emerged: (1) the press had already judged and disciplined him and there was no need for further punishment ('A sanction? Tom Boonen has already suffered enough, his case is already conducted in the press'); and (2) Boonen's fans said they had not lost faith and wanted to be there for him ('We keep on supporting him. We give him a second chance').

These two factors were not readily present in the Tiger Woods case. The press did mention the huge media attention, but because of the distance of the scandal, the Belgian media did not feel responsible. Because of the minor interest in golf and the relative distance of the Tiger Woods scandal, there were no fans cited. Still, the press did mention the applause Woods got for his comeback. It is remarkable also that his sponsors Nike and Tag Heuer were cited, as a sign that the turbulence was over.

After having been forgiven, Boonen began winning important races. Again, his achievements were compared to legendary predecessors. The link was made between a renewed focus in his professional life and his competitive victory. 'He got himself back on track and came back as a chastened cycler who knows how to appreciate a victory.' For the press, 'this was again the real Boonen.' Interestingly, when Tom Boonen won his second victory in Paris-Roubaix, the press described this victory also as his big comeback, after two years without a significant victory. The media applauded Tom Boonen for his reunion with his girlfriend and linked these events to each other. 'Suddenly, Boonen is back in a flow of positive news, the picture around him complete again: as a top class athlete, a popular world star, an ideal son-in-law'.

This was never the case for Tiger Woods. The marriage did not stand, he did not regain his old level of golf and he lost his number one position. For the press, this was clearly the direct result of his extramarital affairs. 'He is paying his various non-competitive problems cash now'. There were hints, though, that the press was ready to welcome him back, judging by the following quotation referring to the first performance of his comeback: 'The sport icon who is damaged by sex scandals made in the Master tournament of Augusta, the first major of the season, an impressive comeback.' Because of the scandal, Woods also tumbled from the list of most influential American sportsmen. However, he maintained his position as the absolute number one on a financial level.

Social Values of the Hero

Heroes exhibit positive features and radiate social values. Particularly for athletes, they divide into physical or mental characteristics. Tom Boonen himself, his competitors, and journalists emphasized his physical strength. In a 'survival of the strongest' during his second victory in Paris-Roubaix, his rivals were quoted as saying that that they stumbled across a Tom Boonen 'strong as a lion'. During his third victory in Paris-Roubaix, his physical strength was even more accentuated and he was described as 'a paragon of power', or 'muscleman Boonen'. His physical power was also a reason for assuming that Boonen was not a drug addict. 'Boonen a drug ad-

dict? Probably not, or else he would not succeed competitively as he is doing now.' His ability to suffer is another element, but was almost exclusively emphasized during his third victory in Paris-Roubaix: 'it had cost him
blood, sweat, and tears.' His mental assets also played an important part.
Boonen was a team player with a sense of perspective who could cope with
pressure. Boonen was also portrayed as a smart, self-assured, and composed
person, with tremendous will power and perseverance. Additionally, he was
depicted as spontaneous, immune to stress, sympathetic, determined, a leader, sober-minded, caring, realistic and combative.

In the case of Tiger Woods, there is only one central social value: the
importance of family. Before the sex scandal, the press showed the first
photos of his son Sam Alexis together with the Woods family. After the
scandal broke out, the emphasis was still on family values. 'Holding the
family together means everything for him', a friend of the couple was quoted. Once the divorce was definitive, the press noted: 'Tiger Woods and his
wife have done everything to keep the children away from the stress of their
divorce.' The readers also sporadically learnt about Woods' Buddhism and
his charity work. On a competitive level, there are few values mentioned.
Physical values are lacking, and his mental assets are also barely mentioned,
except for his winning spirit, his ambition to push beyond frontiers and his
team spirit. This can partly be explained because of his bad results after the
sex scandal; but before the scandal, there was also scarcely any mention of
sport-related values. The low interest for golf in Belgium and the Belgian
media is probably the underlying reason.

Status Elements: Modern Heroes as Celebrities

Contemporary heroes are also celebrities. This is true for Tom Boonen, who
became a true star in Belgium. Newspaper articles focused on his private
life and he was literally called a celebrity. That Boonen transcends his status
as a sportsman becomes evident when we learn about his commercial activities, his 'godparenthood' of a charity organization and his own comic strip.
Most of the discussion concerning his private life occurred during the week
his drug abuse was revealed when everything from his drug problems to his
nightlife and his love life were heavily discussed. The disregard for his private life during his third victory in Paris-Roubaix is extremely revealing. To
repair the hero myth, his private life was cast aside and only his competitive
achievements were mentioned. As indicated earlier, his private life is not
compatible with his competitive life, so journalists paid it no attention. This
clearly shows myth at work in a very significant manner. The focus on his
private life during the second period is also very revealing of how the press

interpreted his drug abuse. Although there were dissenting voices, his co-caine abuse was considered a problem located within his private sphere.

Just like Tom Boonen, Tiger Woods transcends his status as a sports-man, but to such an extent that the reason for his fame almost evaporates. The press often described Tiger Woods as a 'golf champion', 'best golfer ever' or 'golf star', but few articles really explain why he is or was the best. Most articles focused on his private life because of the scandal, but before the scandal broke out, few articles focused on his competitive results. Woods became a regular in the Belgian press because of the scandal, not because of his achievements. As a consequence, Tiger Woods is treated more as a celebrity. The press zoomed in on different non-competitive as-pects of his life, whether related with the scandal or not: his revenues, his sponsor deals, his (impending) divorce, his wife and children, his mistress-es, and his sexual behavior.

Status Elements: Heroes as Role Models

Besides celebrities, heroes are also role models. With Tom Boonen, the press focused on his exemplary role during the period of his drug abuse and some articles suggested that people could learn from his mistakes. Boonen was also reminded by the press of his obligations as a role model. 'Tom Boonen is a great champion, but a great champion also has an exemplary role.' The study's analysis makes it clear that he had an exemplary role to-wards two groups: the youth and the Flemish people. Youth were affected the most by his cocaine exploits. One journalist asked himself 'as a father, what are you going to tell your son who has a poster of Tom Boonen in his bedroom?' On another level, Boonen was also a role model for the Flemish people, as cycling is a true national sport in Belgium. Accordingly, a Dutch journalist is quoted as saying: 'The Church, the King... They don't count for you. You only have bicycle racing.'

Contrasted with cycling, golf is not a particularly important sport in Belgium and still has an elitist aura. Tiger Woods is clearly the personifica-tion of golf, but because of a lack of resonance with golf in the Flemish so-ciety, he is not really a role model. Once, IOC-chairman Jacques Rogge was quoted as reminding Tiger Woods of his duties: 'We ask our athletes to be an example for the youth and clearly that is not the case with Woods.' Un-like the case of Boonen, the press did not remind Woods of his obligations as a role model. After the sex scandal, Tiger Woods did become a sort of role model in reverse, especially concerning adultery and sex addiction. His story became the reason for the press to discuss these topics and compare it with other sportsmen, such as Belgian cyclo-cross racer Niels Albert and

English football players such as John Terry, Ashley Cole, and Wayne Rooney, who were also mired in sex scandals.

Discussion and Conclusion

Theories concerning heroes and the hero myth focus on three main characteristics: narrative structure, social values and positive features, and two status elements (role model and celebrity). We translated these three into a hero grid, in which the narrative sequences are for their part again subdivided into three main phases: the rise of the hero, the temporary fall from grace (trickster), and the resurrection.

This hero grid was applied to discern the presence of a heroic narrative in the coverage of Tom Boonen and Tiger Woods. The cases were comparable because previous research showed their heroic capacities and because both were caught in the middle of a media scandal. As Archetti claims: 'the fall of an idol breaks the fiction of the life and transforms it into a public spectacle.'[57]

In the case of Tom Boonen, the journalistic story was synchronous with the archetypal hero narrative, going on an archetypal hero journey, and meanwhile representing both competitive as non-competitive values, being a role model and a celebrity figure. The coverage of Tiger Woods, on the other hand, was less suited for the hero narrative, although his course of life took the same turn as Boonen's. Both his obstacles as his mentioned successes relegated to his private life. The narrative concerning Tiger Woods seemed more closely related to a celebrity caught in a media scandal than the hero narrative.[58] This is also reflected in the other elements of the hero narrative. The social values Tiger Woods represents were reduced to one major value: the importance of family. Ironically, this is also the one value he broke and which was the cause of the media scandal. This lack of attributed social values also hints at the fact that Tiger Woods is not considered a role model. Although he is portrayed as the embodiment of golf, there are no clear-cut signs that he is regarded as a role model. Again, the geographical distance and the minor interest for golf in Belgium are the most obvious reasons. However, his celebrity status is very much present. Non-competitive subjects drew more attention than his competitive performances. All this leads to the conclusion that Tiger Woods, more than being a top athlete, was recognized as a celebrity in the Belgian press.

---

[57] Archetti, E.P., 'The Spectacle of a Heroic Life: The Case of Diego Maradona', in: Andrews, D.L. & Jackson S.J., eds, *Sport Stars: The Cultural Politics of Sporting Celebrity* (New York, 2001), p. 161.
[58] Gamson, 'Normal Sins', p. 186.

Why then is there a distinction in media portrayal between these two comparable cases, and is Tom Boonen more likely to be a hero than Tiger Woods? The answer to this question is twofold. First of all, Tiger Woods has not make a major comeback thus far, playing on a lesser level than before the scandal, while Tom Boonen returned stronger than before. This made it difficult for the press to reinstate Tiger Woods as a hero. Second, there is the lack of resonance in the case of Tiger Woods. The game of golf receives minimal attention in the Belgian press (in contrast with cycling), so the competitive victories of Tiger Woods do not really resonate with the Belgian public. Tiger Woods did not really fall from grace as a hero because, before the scandal, his conquest did not receive the resonance necessary for heroes. Although American researchers prove Tiger Woods to be a hero, this is not the case in Belgium. Globalizing trends within the field of sports show to be fruitful as far as celebrities are concerned, but heroes lean much more on their cultural resonance. Heroes are universal and all cultures have their heroes, but the particular heroes do vary over culture and time. This is obviously the case for Tom Boonen and Tiger Woods: the first one was portrayed as a true hero, while the latter was depicted as a celebrity caught in a media scandal. Coverage of Tiger Woods proves the point Boorstin and Drucker are making on modern heroes as 'pseudo-heroes', but the case of Tom Boonen shows that journalists still contribute to the retelling of the age-old hero story, even now in this heyday for celebrities.[59]

---

[59] Boorstin, *The Image*; Drucker, 'The Mediated Sports Hero'.

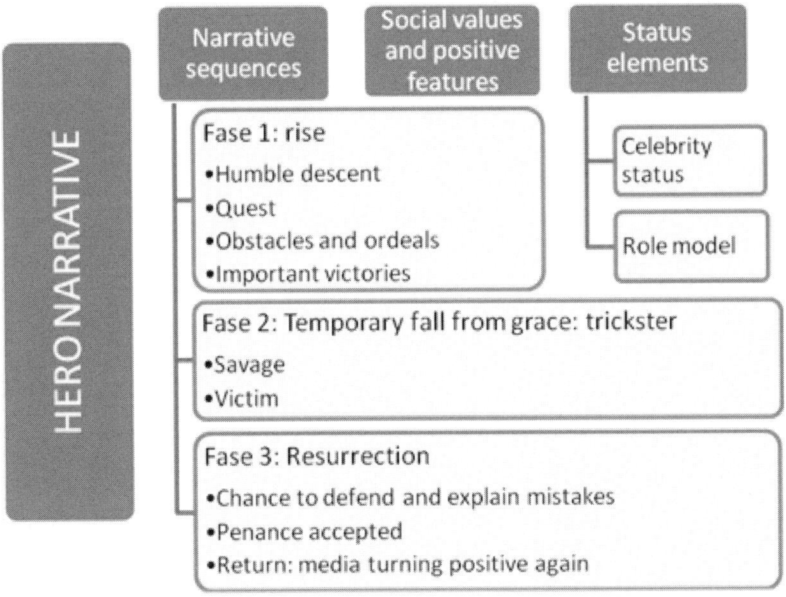

1. The Hero Narrative

'DESIGN IS CONTENT'[1]

ON TABLOIDIZATION OF FRENCH QUALITY NEWSPAPER JOURNALISM

Nicolas Hubé[2]

Introduction

During the second half of the 1990s the first page of French daily newspapers *truly* became the front page for most of them, i.e. not only reflecting the selected reality by journalists but also becoming the central feature of a newspaper's design and identity. This is the result of a long process of 'professionalization', which began in the 1970s. Traditionally, the different sections of the paper did not really exist yet and politics, economics, general information and sport were in competition for newspaper space. Papers were organized in a vertical layout until the end of the 1970s. However, the reconstruction of the social environment, as well as of politics, were amongst a number of elements that encouraged editors to provide a better 'constructed', 'clearer' journalistic product. The gradual specialization of political journalists, for example, was concomitant with the appearance of rhetoric of 'critical expertise', and of 'society' services, which divided politics into big policy issues while political correspondents began to focus on political parties and the declarations made by political actors.[3] This institutionalization of 'society' pages or sections owes a lot to the weekly *Nouvel Observateur*, to the alternative press (and particularly *Libération*), to newspapers of the new 'left' and to the spirit of a *newsjournalism à la française*, and also to the emergence of television news, a form of journalism that was

[1] *Le Monde*, Le nouveau "*Le Monde*", Acte 2, Internal document, June 1996, p. 11.
[2] The author would like to thank Emma Gormley and Kemo Simone for their help in the translation of a first draft of the paper.
[3] For the most typical examples: *Libération* in the 1970s and then again in the middle of the 1980s, *Le Monde* in 1978, *L'Humanité* in 1982, the *Figaro* in 1983, *France Soir* in 1988; Hubé, N. and Kaciaf, N., 'Les Pages Société... ou les Pages Politiques en Creux', in: Chupin, I. and Nollet, J., eds, *Les Frontières Journalistiques* (Paris, 2005), pp. 189-211.; Kaciaf, N., 'La Mort du Séancier. Les Transformations Contemporaines des Comptes-Rendus Parlementaires dans les Quotidiens Français', in: Ringoot, R. and Utard J.-M., eds, *Genres journalistiques. Savoirs et Savoir-Faire* (Paris, 2009), pp. 83-100.

'new, interrogative, explicative, non-institutional, full of surveys and eye-witness accounts.'[4] The strong interdependence of newspapers within a centralized journalistic field tends to force editors to follow each others innovations, when they seemed to be somewhat successful. This process is further facilitated by an increasing mobility of journalists between newspapers.[5]

In the 1980s, publishers started to slowly re-launch their papers. *Libération* initiated these changes with the launch of *Libé II* on May 12th, 1981. *Le Monde* launched a new design in September 1989 just a few weeks before *Le Parisien* changed theirs in October. In 1992, the regional newspaper *L'Alsace* also started promoting design by changing their type of rotary press. But these modifications were still graphically marginal (except for those of *Libération*) whereas those that took place after 1995 gave a new meaning to front page, content and form. A new process of commercialization of French press has begun, which this chapter will explore.

During this period of change, which began around 1995, many French papers tried to adapt elements of their design, launching different products and attempting to 're-brand' their product. *Libération* attempted an ambitious change on the 26th of September 1994 with the launch of *Libé III* that aimed to excel in all aspects of journalistic coverage, but abandoned this approach a few months later on the 30th of January 1995. *Le Monde* launched a new daily newspaper on the 9th of January 1995. *Le Figaro* changed its makeover for its November 29th 1999 edition and *L'Alsace* did so to on January 1st, 2000. The process of adaptation persisted and accelerated. *Le Monde* redefined its makeover on January 14th, 2002; *Libération* on the 13th of October 2003. *Le Monde*, *Le Figaro*, *Le Parisien* and the *Tribune* modified theirs between the autumn of 2005 and the beginning of 2006. Other daily newspapers like the regional *Le Progrès* or the national *La Croix* followed these examples. These transitions were rooted in a commercial logic, an adjustment to the readership's presumed 'expectations' that had become the norm. Now, every daily newspaper that seeks to multiply its readers is developing a so-called 'new formula' (as was the case with *Nord Eclair* and the *Figaro* who altered their approach to publishing in September 2009).

I would like to emphasize that the 1990s were a turning point for French quality dailies in terms of importing a new *marketing* ideology in French journalism that still continues today. The recommendations put forth

---

[4] Brusini, H. and James, F., *Voir la Vérité: le Journalisme de Télévision* (Paris, 1982), p. 37; Pinto, L., *L'intelligence en Action: le Nouvel Observateur* (Paris, 1984).
[5] Marchetti, D. and Ruellan, D., *Devenir Journaliste. Sociologie de l'entrée sur le Marché du Travail* (Paris, 2001).

in the *Etats généraux de la Presse* in 2009 – a national consultation of all press actors initiated by President Sarkozy in order to re-think French press laws and financial sustainability – demonstrated this by advocating for layout reforms. It is no longer possible for editors to think about winning new readers without design changes, although all papers are continuing their revenue losses.[6] In fact, the dramatic economic situation of the daily press helps justify the process of *tabloizidation*in the French press during this period.[7] This process is particularly effective because it was born over a period of significant revenue losses, which began in the early 1980s (see graphic 1). In the second half of the 1990s these reforms appeared to yield positive results, legitimizing these reforms, a trend which lasted until around 2000. When free papers *Métro* and *20 Minutes* were launched in 2002, it borrowed upon the more successful transformations in editorial structures, design formulas, and personnel already established. Its success and the easy switch of the French press to online products was made possible by the spectacular change in the way French journalism tells the news (see fig. 1).[8]

This process began in the second half of the 1990s after 15 years of hesitations and losses in revenue. The changes concerning the front page have to be analyzed as manifestations of a structural change of the French journalistic field, which was confronted with both an economic and professional crisis, coupled with a more and more research-oriented stance of product performance since the early 90s. In fact, the front page is a strategic editorial tool, reflecting the most important events of the previous day and journalism's approach to these events.[9] Here, front pages are giving 'added value' to daily newspapers. They are no longer created with the aim of transmitting information but are rather presented in a way where the news is supposed to appeal to the reader, like many magazines have been doing a

---

[6] In fact, one conclusion in the Green Paper of the *Etats généraux de la presse* insists on 'editing' (in English) to 'save' publications. At the same time, they advocate additional alternatives solutions such as the rebirth of field journalism or the necessity to appeal to industry captains to finance their newspapers.

[7] Esser, F., 'Tabloidization of News: a Comparative Analysis of Anglo-American and German Press Journalism', *European Journal of Communication* 14 (1999), pp. 291-324.

[8] Benson R. et al., 'Media Systems Online and Off: Comparing the Form of News in the United States, Denmark, and France', *Journal of Communication* 62 (2012), pp. 21–38; Chupin, I., Hubé, N. and Kaciaf, N., *Histoire Politique et Économique des Médias en France* (Paris, 2012), pp. 90-110.

[9] Rupar, V., 'Journalism, Political Change and Front-Page Design: A Case Study of the Belgrade Daily Politika', in: Broersma, M., ed, *Form and Style in Journalism. European Newspapers and the Representation of News 1880-2005* (Leuven, 2007), p. 201.

decade before. Stories have now to be set for the readers' attention and no longer *mainly* for their newsworthiness. It is an inversion of priorities between audience and political orientation of news. This change goes beyond the front page design: the sequencing and the categorisation of information, service restructuring and the introduction of 'opening' pages-acting as sections' front-pages are also part of these shifts. Similar to the processes described by Kevin Barnhurst and John Nerone about design changes in the American press in the 1920s, by Marcel Broersma for the Dutch press during the 20th century or by Verica Rupar for the Serbian *Politika's* front-pages, the performative force of this new *marketing* discourse is due to the fact that layout changes in newspaper are also organizational changes explained by economic transformations, which transform the French journalistic field.[10]

New Discourse, New Practices: A Structural Change

The economic crisis that has hit French newspapers since the 1980s has had a structural impact on the centralized French journalistic field. It is structured by an intense competition for sales – which provide the major source of revenues rather than advertising – in a centralized, concentrated national journalistic field. It provides a 'significant push for sensationalistic, scandal-driven news' and a decrease in newspapers' political leanings.[11] At the same time, it provokes a radical change in press design. It tends to divert press managers' attention: from the citizen-reader towards a consumer-one. The diagnostic seems simple: before informing, papers should be attractive for a broader audience. The 'traditional reader' is no longer assumed to be 'attached' to their newspaper but expects journalists to 'convince' and to catch them.

This is where the front page plays a major role by publishing news in new forms and writing formats and thus contributing to the propagation of a 'communication journalism', which has as some of its characteristics: a

---

[10] *Ibidem*; Broersma, M., 'Visual strategies. Dutch Newspaper Design between Text and Image 1900-2000', in: *idem.*, ed, *Form and Style in Journalism. European Newspapers and the Representation of News 1880-2005* (Leuven, 2007), pp. 177-198; Nerone, J. and Barnhurst, K.G., 'Visual Mapping and Cultural Authority: Design Changes in U.S. Newspapers, 1920-1940', *Journal of Communication* 45 (1995), pp. 9-43.

[11] Benson, R., 'La Fin du Monde. Tradition and Change in the French Press', *French Politics, Culture and Society* 22 (2004), p. 120; Marchetti, D., 'The Revelations of Investigative Journalism in France', *Global Media and Communication* 5 (2009), pp. 353-388; Juhem, P., 'Alternances Politiques et Transformations du Champ de l'information en France après 1981', *Politix* 56 (2001), pp. 185-208.

growing attention of targeting audiences; blurred boundaries between professional, citizen and deliberative journalisms and corporate communication; and the strengthening of 'complicity' and 'intersubjectivity' between journalists and their public.[12] In newspaper articles and press releases, journalists constantly repeat that newspapers aim 'to be as close to the reader as possible' and that 'they are not at all undergoing a revolution but instead an important evolution that will allow them to better live up to the expectations of their readership, who have been taking a certain interest in new domains lately.'[13] The global trend of these changes seems to confirm Daniel Hallin and Paolo Mancini's hypothesis: the progressive harmonization of European press in direction of the liberal model.[14] I would like to emphasize that this has less to do with an 'Americanization' of the French press – defined as an external factor – than as a response to the need for commercialization of newspapers, in order to come through the economic crisis. In other words, this is an internal transformation of French journalistic field.

Moreover the process is a structural one where form and style are compounded with organizational changes. This ideological change of journalists' views on public expectations have to be simultaneously analyzed with the changes of social structures and cultural forms of French journalism, as well as the complex interplay between these three mezzo-levels (organization, professional groups and ideology).[15] These changes are established by journalistic staff with various social characteristics *and* – that's new – by non-journalistic staff (managers, graphic designers and art directors). It also brings new methods of rationalization of journalistic practices. Competing newspapers in the centralistic field will tend to 'imitate' each other given the fact that they will be obliged to adapt to new economic orders and to size up the importance of sales in kiosks (particularly in Paris). Journalistic staff as well as the non-journalistic staff are more mobile and move from newspaper to newspaper. Each time, they bring with them new methods and practices they have learnt from journalism schools or from the rival papers.[16] The new layouts are different ways of handling news. With this new discourse on graphic design and modernity, the former way of organizing

---

[12] Brin, C., Charron, J. and De Bonville, J., eds, *Nature et Transformation du Journalisme: Théorie et Recherches Empiriques* (Laval, 2004).
[13] *Le Figaro Économie*, 'Le Figaro, a Newspaper that is Attentive to its Readers' Expectations', November 11, 1999, p. VIII.
[14] Hallin, D. C. and Mancini, P., *Comparing Media Systems Beyond the Western World* (Cambridge 2012), pp. 251-295.
[15] Benson, R. and Neveu, E., 'Introduction: Field Theory as a Work in Progress', in: *idem.*, eds, *Bourdieu and the Journalistic Field* (Cambridge, 2005), pp. 12-16.
[16] Hubé, N., *Décrocher la 'Une'. Le Choix des Titres de Première Page de la Presse Quotidienne en France et en Allemagne (1945-2005)* (Strasbourg, 2008).

pages became 'too difficult' to understand. Organizing news items by importance is no longer 'spontaneously' accessible. Attracting the readers comes down to the 'layout' of daily newspapers. The importance of a news item is determined by the front page and its headline and no longer by the 'number of columns' it is featured in. The clarification of the 'reading contract established with its readers goes through a much more rigorous selection process of editing spaces.'[17] In other words, design reforms change the newsgathering organization in order to 'rationalize' the copy-flow.

This process has also modified the way journalists write their news and bring 'proof' of truth: they write articles on serious issues (politics) in a more audience-oriented way. We would thus expect more soft news on the front page and less political news in this newly market-oriented system. Thus, we have to successively address the issue of the transformation of the front-page as well as the consecutive arrival of a marketing *discourse* before analyzing the resulting organizational transformations.[18]

'This Newspaper Showcase': Optimising the Impacts of Front Pages[19]

The difficult commercial situation leads to the idea that graphic design might be the solution to editorial strategic problems. From 'showcasing', 'stands', 'windows', to 'added value', journalists devote special investment to the front page in order to sell. The relationship existing between journalists and readers is now seen through a seller-buyer relationship. The first rule for every new formula is 'to get out of one's mind the idea that reading *Le Monde* is something that has to be earned. We constantly have to make the reader want to read us and more especially to read us regularly-ideally every day.'[20] Moreover, to earn readers, journalistic reports adopt the reader's psychologizing tone whether it is a matter of positively connoted words with regard to pleasure or desire or pejorative words with regard to merit, hard work or masochistic pathology as shown in the example below.

---

[17] *Le Monde, Le Style du Monde* (Paris, 2002), p. 71.
[18] This paper is based on an analysis drawn from documents collected from *Le Monde*'s and *L'Alsace*'s editorial archives as well as observations and interviews carried out in five French editorial offices between 2000 and 2005. For more details: Hubé, *Décrocher la 'Une'*.
[19] 'L'Alsace, Projet Éditorial 2000', *Internal Document*, September 3, 1999, p. 13.
[20] *Le Monde, Le Nouveau 'Le Monde'*, p. 7. We found the same idea three years earlier in an article entitled: A "*Monde*" plus "*Monde*". *Foreword for the meeting on June 6th*, June 2, 1993, p. 5; Note reproduced, documentation services' archives, "Layout" box.

To be innovative in the way we address events: the picture, the graphic work or the presentation that constitute a newspaper's layout can be surprising, interesting and why not also, *pleasing to the reader*, for whom buying a newspaper is not a *masochistic* act.[21]

Up until the beginning of the 1990s, the concept of *new formula* basically refers to modifications of an editorial line. Layout and press design were out of sight. During the 1980s, the solutions suggested by editors were simple adjustments of what already existed and the attention of actors was mainly focused on content and political leaning.[22] This also applied to the layout elaborated by *Libération* on August 2, 1986, even though it revealed some elements of modernity. This layout corresponded to the daily newspaper's process of a 'general reform' by granting a 'professional charter, and a functional organization' to the editorial office with the aim of putting the 1981 reform to an end (see below).[23] In other words, graphic layouts were constrained by organizational modifications.

However, journalists progressively believe in the idea of using graphic design as a means of winning readers' attention. The editor-in-chief of *Libération*, Serge July, in analyzing the development of magazines in this day and age, summarized this idea. 'Magazines are what is modern in the French press. Daily newspapers still cannot rid themselves of their political conception of news in the broad sense of the term.'[24] On October 16, 1989, *Le Parisien* modified its formula for reasons that were clearly commercial. As its editor-in-chief explained, the new layout was designed following the advice the newspaper was given by the marketing department, which had put in place a research program based on Vu-Lu (Seen-Read), U&A (Use and Attitude) and comparative tests. The idea behind generating this data was to have thorough understanding of the readership and their expectations.[25] In the end, the new formula had more pictures, shorter expressions, and a new typography and its aim was to present the 'newspaper of the future'. 'Make sure that the newspaper appeals to the eye in order to be read.'[26] Interestingly, this layout reform was introduced and conducted by a non-journalist staff member for the first time in French daily journalism.

---

[21] *L'Alsace, projet éditorial 2000,* p. 4. The term is in italics in this original document.

[22] Juhem, 'Alternance Politiques', pp. 185-208.

[23] Berger, F., *Journaux Intimes: Les Aventures Tragi-Comiques de la Presse sous François Mitterrand* (Paris, 1992), p. 317.

[24] July, S., 'Entretien', *Médiaspouvoirs*, 19 (1990), pp. 81-87.

[25] Taslé D'Heliand, G., 'Le Parisien: L'Innovation au Quotidien', *Ibidem*, p. 110.

[26] *Ibidem*, p. 112.

Less than five years later, all journalism professionals expressed this view. 'Design is content', so wrote Le *Monde*'s director for its journalists as a way of justifying the new formula.[27] Ever since then, these arguments remain unchanged, from *Le Monde* in 1995 to *Nord Éclair* in 2009.[28] The headline, the photo, or the caricaturist Plantu's drawings in *Le Monde* for example, are there to bring the page to life and call on to the reader's attention in the same way as any publicity promoting a product would. The lexical field applied by journalists (noted during our interviews with them as well as in published articles) to explain graphic design is always that of movement and modernity: for example notions like 'dynamism', 'punch', 'striking', 'surprise', 'richness' are proposed in opposition to the 'monotony' or 'depressing' nature of certain front pages. In a 'rush for information', the image is conveyed in an impetuous manner. It is up to actors to distinguish themselves in the market through graphic design capable of producing 'label' effects that differentiate one product from another. Therefore, press directors' views become interchangeable and they all take up this idea.

Social and Spatial Identity of Daily Newspapers: Winning Over the Non-readers

Gaining readership encourages journalists to build up an image that is socially and spatially rooted, whilst at the same time reserving a generalist stance. Contrary to magazines, general information media claim to be the bearer of generalist views suitable for all social classes. Asserting the role of the front page does not mean that the choices are 'only' commercial. The synthesis of these two views is a rather significant challenge for newspaper directors. Successive 'new formula' claim to offer an answer to the problem of newspapers' turnover. The ideology used to create a formula that the reader understands is similar to that of advertising. Their profile corresponds to that of a standard individual – a consumer as any other – rather than a subject of complex 'psychology'. Graphic design and new formulas are henceforth thought of as a means to catch them.

The attention paid to a targeted readership is a means of carrying out choices 'by default', i.e. eliminating front page topics in order to keep them for the inside pages. Topics that do not really 'sell' – topics that are less directly concerned with the everyday-life of a socially situated readership – are abandoned in favor of other topics. By making these strategic choices

---

[27] *Le Monde, Le Nouveau* 'Monde', p. 11.
[28] Bail, A., 'Cosmétique Rédactionnelle: Le Marketing en Charge de la Modernisation de Nord Eclair', *Dissertation, Institute of Political Science* (Lille, 2009).

(politically and commercially speaking) for front-page news, editorial decisions acquire their own symbolic capital, allowing newspapers to position themselves daily on the journalistic field.[29] The political content of a 'working class' newspaper is based on the representation of a readership that is not very interested in politics. On the contrary, the readership of quality newspapers is composed of *politicized* and upper-class readers. This is reinforced by scientific studies on the topic and the statistical data with which the journalists work. The content *can* and *should* be mostly political, whilst at the same time promoting the plurality of tastes and cultural practices of the readers.[30]

The lay-out reforms aim to win over new readers by respecting the *tradition* of the newspaper, a tradition which is strongly promoted. *L'Alsace*, for example, publicly defines itself as the newspaper of 'four proximities': chronological, geographical, thematic and emotional. 'We have a monopoly which is that of local news ... not even regional news.'[31] In the same way, *Le Parisien* declares itself a 'working-class newspaper' before being a regional newspaper. As a testimony to its quality, it clearly shows that 'it is one of the leading newspapers' on the French daily newspaper market and that it's 'readership structure [is] very similar to the population of Ile-de-France.'[32] For *Le Parisien*, it is based on the three-folded concept, 'reveal, shock and tell.'[33] Based on figures and graphs, the daily newspaper proudly defends its success. It has a 'readership that is transforming', into a young and popular readership, a near perfect carbon copy of the French population.[34] As for social indicators in contrast to spatial indicators, national daily newspapers are situated in a domain, which they claim is national, one that remains much centered on Paris, the place of major diffusion.[35] To sum up, the similarity shown with the readership is at stake when choosing the issues and their general handling (choice of sequences, writing). Winning over a socially defined reader is achieved by attracting them with the news *and* advertising.

---

[29] Bourdieu, P., *On Television* (New York, 1998), pp. 39-43.

[30] Bourdieu, P., *Distinction: A Social Critique of the Judgement of Taste* (Cambridge, 1984), pp. 440-451; Charpentier, I., 'Une Pratique Rare et Sélective: La Lecture de la Presse d'information Générale et Politique', in: Legavre, J.-B., ed, *La Presse Écrite: Objets Délaissés* (Paris, 2004), pp. 315-335.

[31] Interview with artistic director, *L'Alsace*, January 31, 2000.

[32] 'Le Parisien, En un Clin D'œil', *Publicity Brochure*, 2001, pp. 8-9.

[33] In French, the acronym RER is used for this sentence "Révéler, Etonner, Raconter", which is also the name of one major public transport in Paris.

[34] 'Le Parisien, En un Clin D'œil', *Publicity Brochure*, 1997, p. 7.

[35] *Figaro's* readership (excluding sales abroad) is 59% in Ile-de-France, *Libération* and *Le Monde* is 58%. Sources: Diffusion contrôle, paid diffusion 2001-2002.

Corporate Branding and Corporate Management

This conceptual shift is grounded on and helped by the development of new management methods, based on corporate branding and corporate management. Readers as well as journalists are conceived as stakeholders in this process.

An example of this is using the newspaper's logo to identify their 'brand'. There was a progressive change from a semiotic identity – the name of a paper being a signifier for its reader – to a 'brand identity'. The reformer of *Libération*'s logo in May 1981, Claude Maggiori, a newspaper graphic designer, affirms that 'the problem is not with design and/or content, but rather with the newspaper's image, as in brand images.'[36] He also states 'a newspaper is an object that should satisfy us.'[37] This was how he explained the reforms that he put in place in various newspapers such as *L'Echos des Savanes, Libération, Sud-Ouest, La Marseillaise* and the *Nouvel Observateur* in the early 1980s.[38] The headline that is considered as a 'brand', matches with different graphic elements and thus, differs even more from the rest of the pages. For editors, producing 'labels' that identify 'newspaper brands', involves the modification of a set of styles, character fonts and 'easily identifiable' graphic signs in order to differentiate each newspaper and make it 'one of a kind', what they call in professional terms (and in English): *editing*. Along the same line, *Le Monde* invented a new typographic character with its new design in 1995: A *Le Monde* character. This reform continued in 2002. *Libération* adopted this reform in 2003 and, *Le Figaro* adopted a new dropped initial in 1999. Thus, the success of news magazines has become a major competitive horizon. Their success is due to their cover price policy. They create an example of a front page in which they rely on 'editorial marketing' and in which the layout plays a major role.

During those years, this arousal of the reader's loyalty by brands was achieved through advertising campaigns. *Le Monde* for instance opened its marketing department in 1985 and conducted its first campaign in 1986. This was a reaction to its loss of readers as well as *Libération*'s success.[39] Later on in 1994, 1995, 1998, 1999 and 2000, it increased the number of its campaigns to 'remind readers of the key attributes, the core values of *Le*

---

[36] De Maulde, F., 'La Presse: Maggiori de me Voir si Belle: Un Entretien Avec le Zorro du Look', *Le Matin*, June 12, 1985.

[37] *Ibidem*

[38] *Ibidem*

[39] Erignac, H., 'Quand Le Monde Fait sa Publicité', *Dissertation, Université Paris II-Assas* (Paris, 2000).

Monde.[40] The campaign conducted in October 1998, 'we know nothing if we do not know everything' was one example of journalistic brand advertising done with the aim of 'making their position clear, using graphic design: there is us and then there are others. There are those who are meaningful and those who are not.'[41] This necessity to distinguish oneself from others leads to an overflow of news in daily newspapers but at the same time shows their specificity or added-value marketing. However, advertising only accounts for a very small part of the marketing procedure,[42] and does not play a big part in the everyday planning of the newspaper's content.

As soon as it is admitted that graphic design favors content, journalists as well as readers could reject the different meanings of this *marketing* revolution. Editorials all emphasize the congruence of readers' and editors' expectations that is promoted to justify the reforms. They are described as the result of months of observations of readers by non-editorial or editorial staff and of consultation of the journalists. The idea is to prevent criticism. If it happens, journalists were constantly reminded by their hierarchy that 'our reform is not dedicated to layout, but to content. Be careful not to favor just the cosmetic aspect.'[43]

These reforms also include readers' management. Some editors have hired someone to act as a mediator (at *Le Monde* and for TV France 2). This person's job is to explain these transformations amply.[44] *Le Figaro* and *Le Monde* publish publicity supplements in which they emphasize that a newspaper's aim is to 'inform on its own' and that 'in a world that is more complex, *Le Monde* becomes even more clear' or 'more complete'. *Le Monde's* document – *Le Livre de Style* – is not for external use only but also for internal use: it was published for the first time in 2002, updated in 2004 and was to be used as a brief 'deontology summary [that would allow it to present] the rules and regulations that govern the creation of a newspaper, ... *vade mecum* for editors, a foundation of the contract that *Le Monde* signed with its readers.'[45] As well as the supplement on its new formula in 2003, *Libération* produced a document boasting its linguistic modernity two

---

[40] B. Billiard, marketing director of *Le Monde*, quoted in: *Ibidem*, p. 102.

[41] G. Morax, communication manager of *Le Monde*, quoted in: *Ibidem,* p. 78.

[42] For example, at *Le Monde*, the marketing department in 1999 was in possession of 20 million francs, representing 1.5% to 2% of their total turnover.

[43] 'Libération, Principes D'Editing', *Internal Document*, October 1998, p. 9.

[44] Champagne, P., 'Le Médiateur Entre Deux Monde, Actes de la Recherche en Sciences Sociales', *Actes de la Recherche en Sciences Sociales* 131-132 (2000), pp. 8-29.; Goulet, V., 'Le Médiateur de la Rédaction de France 2: L'institutionnalisation d'un Public Idéal', *Question de Communication* 5 (2004), pp. 281-299.

[45] *Le Monde, Le tour du monde en 80 journaux, Le Monde's* supplement, December 5, 2003, p. XXVII.

months later.[46] The failure of *Libé III* in 1994 was associated with an information overflow and too many columns, which made it an inaccessible
newspaper for the public. *Libé III* claimed to be 'an important newspaper
playing a decisive role in the diversity of what daily newspapers were offering, pulling out all the stops and using the whole spectrum of the written
press.'[47] The commercial failure was presented as the result of the reader's
'incapacity' to understand the challenges presented by these reforms: 'the
traditional readers of *Libération* ... have been disorientated.'[48] It is not a
hazard, that throughout this period, newspapers were publishing collections
of front-pages in order to show their evolution. As Serge July claims in his
preface of *Libération's* collection: 'the future of the daily press lies in its
ability to bring more value to its readers and the front-pages are the physical
and symbolic traces of this added value.'[49]

When Managers Rule the Newsrooms

As in the US press, these changes in professional representations are the
product of the arrival of a new management staff in the editorial board. [50]
But, they are not the only promoter of this new marketing discourse. This
view is expressed by actors who are in favor of marketing (editors, managers), and is endorsed by others who are also in its favor in other social activity domains (designers, art directors). More generally, the gradual adoption
of a market-oriented discourse in public policies by the French society has
facilitated its adoption by French journalists.[51] The most striking example of
this conversion to this discourse is *Libération*. The conjunction of these elements promotes the idea of a *necessity* to invite newspaper managers to
'contain the fire or to save ships in distress.'[52] These managers introduce a
new idea of the newspapers' management as 'products' just the same way

---

[46] *Libération*, Dictionnaire Le Robert, Libé. *30 ans de mots*, *Libération*'s
supplement, December 16, 2003.
[47] Internal document quoted *in*: Guisnel, *Libération. La Biographie,* pp. 310-333.
[48] July (S.), 'Letter to readers', *Libération*, January 30, 1995, p. 40.
[49] July (S.), 'Preface', *La Une*, Libération, *1973-1997* (Paris, 1997); included by the
same editor is a collection of front-pages from the following newspapers:
L'Humanité (1904-1998), *Figaro* (1866-1998), Le *Monde* (1944-1999). *Ouest-
France* produces its own collection in 2001 for the period 1899-2000.
[50] Benson, R., 'Tearing Down the 'Wall' in American Journalism', *International
Journal of the Humanities* 1 (2001), pp. 102-113; Underwood, D., *When MBAs Rule
the Newsroom* (New-York, 1995).
[51] Jobert, B., ed, *Le Tournant Néo-Libéral en Europe: Idées et Recettes dans les
Pratiques Gouvernementales* (Paris, 1994), pp. 21-86.
[52] Charon J.-M., 'Managers au quotidien', *Médiaspouvoirs* 16 (1989), pp. 112-123.

the press magazine did during the past two decades.[53] They introduce marketing, management, finances, planning and strategy by setting up research units, by the development and the management of human resources.[54]

These managers have special profiles. This process is concerning the whole French journalistic field: more commercialization, concentration by industrial groups, more profit-oriented.[55] It took also place at the same time in audiovisual and magazine media (particularly in the Prisma press group). They are member of what Bourdieu called the *State Nobility*.[56] They have studied at French prestigious schools – the so-called *Grandes Ecoles* – or are graduates of business schools; they are business lawyers or coming from big – former state – industry companies (Saint-Gobain, Sema, Manurhin, etc.), or from supermarket companies.[57] Some of them have been shortly involved in TV and radio projects before arriving in newspapers.

The story of *Libération* is certainly the most typical of this structural change. Created by Serge July and Jean-Paul Sartre (among others) in 1973, *Libération* was at the time of its founding the revolutionary avant-garde of (left and/or Maoist) alternative journalism. Serge July, before being an engaged journalist, was one of the leaders of the French Student Trade-Union (UNEF), an activist in May 1968 in Paris, and then co-founder of the Maoist party, La Gauche Prolétarienne in 1969. In 1980, after years of conflicts and revenue loss, the paper folded. *Libération* was born again in 1981 with the project of becoming more 'professional' but still leftist, although this shifted to center-leftist. This professionalization of *Libération* has been a progressive adaptation to the rule of the journalistic field and a reorientation of the political leanings. In 1996, investment into *Libération's* was invited for left-leaning entrepreneurs. In 2006, Edouard de Rotschild bought the newspaper and fired Serge July.

---

[53] Charon, J.-M., 'Le Lecteur à Satisfaire: Le Marketing en Presse Magazine', in: Dreyer E. and Le Floch P., eds, *Le lecteur. Approche Sociologique, Économique et Juridique* (Paris, 2004), pp. 19-45.

[54] Charon, 'Managers au Quotidien', pp. 112-123; Toussaint-Desmoulins, N., 'Comment le Management Vint aux Médias?', *Médiaspouvoirs* 16 (1989), pp. 100-105.

[55] Bourdieu, *On Television*, pp. 39-68; Chupin, et al, *Histoire Politique*, pp. 90-110.

[56] Bourdieu, P., *State Nobility: Elite Schools in the Field of Power* (Cambridge, 1996).

[57] For example: The ex-Polytechnic student, Jacques Lesourne and his Deputy, former student of the École centrale, Jacques Guiu who were managers of *Le Monde* during the years 1991-1994; For example: Martin Desprez at Amaury Editions, Puy Martin at *Dernières nouvelles d'Alsace*, Bernard Roux at *Courier Picard* or that of Jacques Lesourne, Jacques Guiu and Bernard Wouts at *Le* Monde; For example: Yves de Chaisemartin at *Figaro* and *France-Soir*.

The first arrival of managers at *Libération* between 1996-2006 is ideal-typical of the changes in the field. The profiles outlined are not specific to this daily newspaper, but typical to this new staff in French journalism.[58] They show a profile that has become rather common in the actual media. Evence-Charles Coppée was appointed Executive Director in 1996 and left Serge July in charge of editorial management. Coppée is a member of the Seydoux family, a rich liberal and leftist family engaged in cultural industries with a background in industry. When appointed, he brought on board three other people, who had all studied marketing and economics and had experience running marketing divisions for large companies.

The presence of these staff members does not automatically influence editorial methods, but rather introduces concentration on sales development research, which is not indifferent to another new category of staff (art directors) that is more directly in charge of content.[59] The idea of the need to adopt graphic design became widespread after *Libération*'s success during the 1980s. Again, *Libération* is typical of this process, in that design was the leader of these changes. The true actors of these projects gradually started to become press graphic design 'experts'.

The art director position only started to be really common in editorial offices with the new designs of the 1990s. At *Le Monde*, this position was created in 1995; for *L'Alsace* this position was created with the new reorientation in January 2000. These hirings and the introduction of new types of staff demonstrate the increasing prevalence of design in the strategic emphasis of many publishers.

When Design Rationalisation Goes Hand in Hand with Organisational Rationalisation

Trying to attract readers in the climate of an economic crisis does not only mean new management. It also means adapting work techniques to marketing. This adaptation is based on a new organizational plan that requires the participation of editorial staff, and thus changes the previous set-up. Providing a product that is immediately accessible *involves* reducing possible divisions. The readers should be given fewer, well-ordered, typified divisions of 'reality' so that they no longer see the newspaper as a succession of columns, but 'chapters'. 'Marquetry should be henceforth avoided, i.e. the overlapping of articles without any apparent rationality.'[60] The layout was

---

[58] Sources: *Who's who in France*, 2008-2009.
[59] Nerone, J. and Barnhurst, K.G., 'Visual Mapping and Cultural Authority', pp. 9-43.
[60] *Le Monde*, 'Un "*Monde*" plus "*Monde*". Foreword for the meeting on 6 June', June

modified to merge content into 'story sequences' producing a horizontal construction of pages which are divided into a series of editing sections. For the reader, this means a few thematic sequences (international, politics, society, etc.), rather than a multitude of overlapping columns and sections (defense, diplomacy, socialist party, justice, education, etc.). For journalists, it means less autonomy and a more integrated copy-flow and services. It also implies adapting the editorial staff to a more Anglo-Saxon model, with more bureaucratized and hierarchical organizational structures, clearly divided between newsgatherers and news processors.[61] In other words, similar to Frank Esser's findings, French editorial structures have been going from a social order similar to German one to a more British one.[62]

Every section, and by this, every service, sees itself progressively in charge of producing 'pages', and not complete papers. The order of the importance of news items is no longer done from the top-down (once the columns are in the editing process) but from the bottom-up, within the services which each produces opening pages. The column is no longer valid as a unity of measuring the power of a service but a unity of horizontal importance accorded to an article. The opening page thus becomes a necessary correlative to this conception of journalism. From the 'first article at the top left' to a page deprived of any other function besides that of being informative in 1979, the 'opener' [in French: l'ouverture] becomes 'the headlines for the first page of each of the sections of the newspaper' in 1991.[63] In 2000, it corresponds 'to the most important story of the day for this section': a full-page.[64] As a result, this editing space has four functions. This 'opener' first-ly ensures a symbolic function of reassurance for the daily newspapers on their capacity to react to news by showing 'a more dynamic and transversal organization in relation to important topics.'[65] The opening page decreases the need to deal with organizational uncertainties of meeting deadlines. By giving a particular salience to a specific topic, each section reduces the space of possible subjects of the front-page. Choosing the front-page headline is done in light of the topics already ordered within the sections. The opening pages (deemed good enough to be front-pages), give meaning to the front-page, whose role is to seduce the reader with the best story. Final-

---

2, 1993, note reproduced, documentation services' archives of *Le Monde*, p. 5.

[61] Tunstall, J., *Journalists at Work (London, 1971)*.

[62] Esser, 'Editorial structures'. For a France-US comparison before these changes: Padioleau, *Le Monde et le Washington Post*.

[63] Respectively: Agnès (Y.), Croissandeau (J.-M.), *Lire le journal* (Saint-Julien-du-Sault, 1979), pp. 135-136; *Le Monde, Lexique de la presse*, public relation services, February 1991, documentation services' archives of the *Monde*.

[64] *Le Monde, Portrait d'un quotidien*, supplement, February 2000.

[65] *Ibidem*, p. 2.

ly, resulting from that is a greater cooperation within the sections. Several systems are also therefore used to accompany the process of 'rationalization' such as an increase in the number of editing and sections conferences, the use of a 'flat plan', and the opening pages. The opening page therefore guarantees a graphic rationalization function. The visual line breaks are clearly highlighted and can be easily seen in the horizontal organization of the *flat plan*. Just like a locomotive, the opening page of each section is clearly defined and can be easily spotted visually.

The opening page thus acts as a technical tool of pacification between sections and a technical tool of centralization of the process around a more structured 'leadership'.[66] The injunction of a stronger ranking of topics within the sections modifies the organizational function by reinforcing the editorial structure of sections-services and, hence, their hierarchical leaders. The place occupied by the opening pages, the role of the selection process throughout editing conferences and the increase in the number of these meetings, give those in charge of the different sections a considerable amount of power, and thus the task of dealing with the journalist's uncertainty of whether their articles will be published or not.[67] The allotment of a more or less permanent volume of pages reduces tensions between different sections for new columns. However, putting the opening pages together requires cooperation between the columnists of the same section. The journalist now needs his section director's intermediary to gain access to the front-page. He is now the one who centralizes the demands of the journalists. The process of coordination is thus the director's responsibility, who will then negotiate with his or her colleagues and the editor-in-chief during the numerous central editorial conferences.

Parallel to these editorial transformations, the period is marked by technical transformations affecting non-journalist groups. With the computerization and the appearance of new manufacturing techniques, the limits between different jobs have become unstable. Some jobs such as lino typists have disappeared while others have been transformed by PAO (production assisted by computer). They have similar functions. Editorial staffs were forced to negotiate from 1985 onwards with the strong *Syndicat du Livre-CGT* (trade union for workers in book and press companies) in relation to the evolution of these jobs. When *Le Monde* and *L'Alsace* created their new

---

[66] Hubé, N, 'Face aux Pairs. Centralisation des Rédactions, Contraintes de Rôle et Publicité des Discussions', in: Dauvin, P. and Legavre J.-B., eds, *Les Publics des Journalistes* (Paris, 2007), pp. 85-106.

[67] Clayman, S.E. and Reisner, A., 'Gatekeeping in Action: Editorial Conferences and Assessments of Newsworthiness', *American Sociological Review* 63 (1998), pp. 178-199; Esser, 'Editorial Structures and Work Principles', pp. 375-405; Hubé, *Décrocher la 'Une'*; Tunstall, *Journalists at Work*.

formulas they also created new editing and graphic design jobs. Other daily newspapers (*Le Figaro* or *L'Humanité* for example) also now have an 'editorial core. The organizational order pursued by these enterprises aims at reorganising the services and at the same time reinforcing an 'editing' core within the editorial staff, following in the footsteps of the initial model of *Libération*.[68] Again, it implies adapting the editorial structure to a more Anglo-Saxon model with the creation of copy-editor job, whose name have changed from 'redaction secretary' to 'editor' directly taken from the Anglophone world.[69]

A Weak Impact of Tabloizidation on Front-page Content?

If it is supposedly efficient to attract new readers thanks to the diversity of the news and illustrations offered, and a new kind of more 'sexy' headlines, we could hypothesize that the issues raised on headlines were more 'soft' news that 'hard'. But, when we look at them over this period (1971-2002), it appears that headlines aren't so much *tabloidized* (see tables 1 and 2). In fact, newspapers still continue to provide articles about political topics. The *tabloidization* process in France means nonetheless more articles about national politics (instead of international), politics treated as society problems (immigration, educations, etc.) and a little bit more economy. Headlines are in no way focused upon soft news (see fig. 2 and 3).

Journalists change the way they tell stories in the headlines: they write paper on hard issues (politics) in a more audience-oriented and softer way, concentrate on the political game instead of the policy discussions (but to a lesser extent than expected) with the help of polls results.[70] French quality newspapers are at the middle of the British and the German process of tabloidization, changing their presentation but keeping politically oriented newspapers.[71] Their news selection process is a 'negative' one: editors do not speak about what will not interest their readers, but still assume any national *political news* could interest them.

The front-page thus has a double function. It is in charge of bringing the important news of the day to the reader and at the same time, it has a commercial function of attracting the reader. In France the permanent crisis of national and regional daily newspapers ended with the permanent layout transformation as the method *par excellence*. An internal note in *Le Monde*

---

[68] Blin, F., 'Les Secrétaires de Rédaction et les éditeurs de Libération: Des Journalistes Spécialisés dans le Journal', *Réseaux* 111 (2002), pp. 163-190.

[69] Tunstall, *Journalists at Work*.

[70] For more results : Hubé, *Décrocher la 'Une'*, pp. 83-153.

[71] Esser, F., 'Tabloidization of News, pp. 291-324.

in 2005 was a reminder that in 1995, 'it was important to modernize *Le Monde*. This success should not be undermined because since 1995 we have gained several thousand readers.'[72] The process of *tabloidization* described here is due to the dramatic economic situation of the daily press in the 1990s. But this tabloidization follows the 'American rhetoric and business approach, while maintaining the French professional practice and style.'[73] Journalists write paper on serious issues (politics) in a more audience-oriented way. The marketing discourse and the journalistic practices have considerably changed. I close this chapter with two final remarks. The first is methodological. It is important not to leave out organizational transformations concomitant with the evolution of the front-page layout in analysis, because, as a social practice, in order to be effective, the layout comes from the actors before they put it in place. The second is contextual. If in the digital age French journalism faces increasing competition on the information market and entertainment is becoming even more prominent, this new process only reinforces the structural tabloidization that has begun over the past 15 years. News outlets now have to face up to the economic demands placed upon them by ownership that is increasingly concentrated and corporatist. Design reforms, in this market, have become routines.

---

[72] 'A Propos de la Nouvelle Formule', *Le Monde*, Internal Note, September 16, 2005.
[73] Benson, 'La Fin du Monde', p. 120.

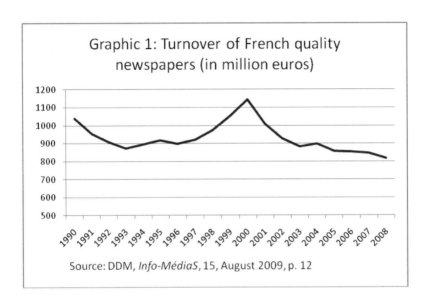

Graphic 1: Turnover of French quality newspapers (in million euros)

Source: DDM, *Info-MédiaS*, 15, August 2009, p. 12

N=907	1971 Le Monde		1971 Le Figaro		1981 Le Monde		1981 Le Figaro		1991 Le Monde		1991 Le Figaro	
	n =	%	n =	%	n =	%	n =	%	n =	%	n =	%
Politics	21	13,3	32	20,8	53	36,3	48	32,9	24	15,9	32	21,1
International	110	69,6	80	51,9	78	53,4	53	36,3	88	58,3	65	42,8
EU	5	3,2	7	4,5	4	2,7	1	0,7	12	7,9	9	5,9
Society	9	5,7	27	17,5	3	2,1	26	17,8	19	12,6	14	9,2
Sub-total political news :	145	91,8	146	94,8	138	94,5	128	87,7	143	94,7	120	78,9
Economy	2	1,3	1	0,6	8	5,5	13	8,9	8	5,3	5	3,3
Sport	0	0,0	1	0,6	0	0,0	1	0,7	0	0,0	14	9,2
Culture	1	0,6	2	1,3	0	0,0	3	2,1	0	0,0	9	5,9
Sciences	1	0,6	4	2,6	0	0,0	1	0,7	0	0,0	4	2,6
Total	158	100	154	100	146	100	146	100	151	100	152	100

2. First and Second Headlines in French Newspapers (October 1st – December 31st)

N = 668	Le Monde		Libération		Le Figaro		L'Alsace		Parisien	
	n =	%	n =	%	n =	%	n =	%	n =	%
Politics	65	43,3	45	31,3	34	27,6	27	21,6	30	22,1
International	28	18,7	33	22,9	26	21,1	10	8	4	2,9
EU	5	3,3	2	1,4	6	4,9	3	2,4	1	0,7
Society	23	15,3	22	15,3	20	16,3	15	12	24	17,6
Sub-total political news :	**121**	**80,7**	**92**	**63,9**	**86**	**69,9**	**55**	**44**	**59**	**43,4**
Economy	23	15,3	11	7,6	14	11,4	9	7,2	8	5,9
Region/local	0	0	1	0,7	0	0	32	25,6	4	2,9
Sport	3	2	13	9	15	12,2	21	16,8	46	33,8
Culture	2	1,3	11	7,6	5	4,1	4	3,2	13	9,6
Sciences	1	0,7	6	4,2	3	2,4	4	3,2	6	4,4
TOTAL	**150**	**100**	**144**	**100**	**123**	**100**	**125**	**100**	**136**	**100**

3. First and Second Headlines in French Newspapers (May-July 2002)

Part III

———

STORYTELLING PRACTICE

THAT'S THE WAY IT WAS

TRANSITIONS IN *CBS EVENING NEWS* FROM CRONKITE TO COURIC

Chris Peters

The words stuck in my throat. A sob wanted to replace them. A gulp or two quashed the sob, which metamorphosed into tears forming in the corners of my eyes. I fought back the emotion and regained my professionalism, but it was touch and go there for a few seconds before I could continue…
Walter Cronkite, A Reporter's Life (1996) – reflecting upon announcing the Kennedy assassination, an iconic moment that throws into relief 20th century professional journalism standards through their threatened momentary breach.

When journalists are considered in popular culture, the names that most often spring to mind are from broadcast, especially over the past few decades. From early stalwarts of the medium, like Edward R. Murrow, to reporters such as Barbara Walters or Diane Sawyer, whose exclusive interviews are among some of the most watched pieces of journalism, it seems that broadcast is more likely than print to generate celebrity status. And at the head of this journalism hierarchy is arguably the network news anchor, a role that began in earnest with Walter Cronkite in the 1960s and reached its zenith with the 'big three' anchors of Tom Brokaw, Dan Rather and Peter Jennings who were the faces of network news for most of the 1980s and 90s. The anchor, it has been argued, occupies, 'a strange position in the American scheme of status. Not quite movie stars, not quite officialdom, they are more famous than most movie stars and more powerful than most politicians'.[1]

However, in the 21st century, more-and-more genres of broadcast journalism seem to be 'trusted' sources of news and a diverse range of voices and formats are influential.[2] Accordingly, this chapter examines to what ex-

---

[1] Rich, F., 'The Weight of an Anchor', *New York Times*, available from: http://query.nytimes.com/gst/fullpage.html?res=9C06E5DC1439F93AA25756C0A9 649C8B63# (May 19, 2002).

[2] Peters, C., 'No-Spin Zones: The Rise of the American Cable News Magazine and Bill O'Reilly', *Journalism Studies* 11 (2010), no. 6, pp. 832-51; Peters, C., 'Emotion Aside or Emotional Side?: Crafting an 'Experience of Involvement' in the News', *Journalism* 12 (2011), no. 3, pp. 297-316; Peters, C., 'Even Better than being Informed: Media Literacy and The Daily Show', in: Peters, C. and Broersma,

tent network evening newscasts are changing as they adapt to this tumultuous journalism landscape. Specifically, it compares one of the bastions of broadcast journalism, the *CBS Evening News*, under what appears to be two vastly different stewardships – that of Walter Cronkite and that of Katie Couric. By counterpoising *CBS Evening News* under Cronkite with the same broadcast under Couric a few decades later, one gets a better sense whether this journalism mainstay has indeed begun to incorporate elements associated with its 'softer' counterparts, and if so, to what extent.

The apparent changes in broadcast news over the past few decades have met with much discussion and, at times, derision. For instance, the rise of cable, breakfast, and satirical news are just a few examples which correspond to what some commentators assert is a more generalized infotaining, personalizing, or conversationalizing tendency across the journalism industry.[3] Michael Delli Carpini and Bruce Williams and Norman Fairclough note that this trend towards informalization is widespread, being increasingly evident in politics and other civic walks of life as well.[4] Franklin speaks of tabloidization, derisively referring to what he terms the appearance of 'newzak' in broadcast journalism, while Bourdieu's *On Television* offers a fairly scathing assessment of the ongoing trivialization of television news.[5] While these assertions are persuasive, they oftentimes lack empirical depth in terms of outlining what, precisely, these changes entail. This chapter attempts to rectify this.

Drawing upon two weeks' worth of episodes, from May 7th to 11th and May 14th to 18th, 2007, I provide a detailed textual analysis of the *CBS Evening News* under Katie Couric.[6] This data set is part of a larger research project, which endeavored to understand the changes in form and style of American broadcast journalism in conjunction with the technological, economic and tonal shifts impacting the news industry over the past few dec-

---

M., eds, *Rethinking Journalism: Trust and Participation in a Transformed News Landscape* (London, 2012), pp. 171-188.

[3] Kovach, B. and Rosenstiel, T., *Warp Speed: America in the Age of Mixed Media* (New York, 1999); MacDonald, M., 'Rethinking Personalization in Current Affairs Journalism', in: Sparks, C. and Tulloch, J., eds, *Tabloid Tales: Global Debates over Media Standards* (Oxford, 2000), pp. 251-266; Cameron, D., 'Language. Truth or Dare?', *Critical Quarterly* 46 (2004), no. 2, 124-127.

[4] Delli Carpini, M. and B. Williams., 'Let Us Infotain You: Politics in the New Media Environment', in: Bennett, W. L. and Entman. R. M., eds, *Mediated Politics: Communication in the Future of Democracy* (Cambridge, 2001), pp. 160-181; Fairclough, N., *Media Discourse* (London 1985).

[5] Franklin, B., *Newzak and the News Media* (London, 1997).

[6] This falls during the Nielsen ratings' May sweeps, one of four periods each year used to set advertising rates, which are thus associated with 'branding' in the television industry. In 2007, this period ran from April 26, 2007 to May 23, 2007.

ades. This reading is then contrasted with a similar textual analysis of a more limited number of *CBS Evening News* broadcasts in 1979. Through the Vanderbilt television news archive, four episodes were selected from this year: March 28th, May 14th, November 5th and November 21st, 1979. These choices were not random but were arrived at after consulting the detailed list of program descriptions for the years 1979-1980 (which note not only each topic covered in the nightly broadcast, but also the anchor, progression, length, and opening paragraphs for each segment's transcript). The rationale was not to analyze multiple weeks of broadcast but to select a diversity of story types that fit closely in terms of content to the 2007 period under study for comparative purpose. The November programs came during the height of the Iran hostage crisis and offered a potentially interesting parallel to the U.S. presence in Iraq in 2007. The May program considered the early days of Presidential primaries, something in common with the 2007 period examined, while the March broadcast contained a variety of international and economic stories.

The Significance of Network Evening News

Studying what, if any, changes have occurred over the past few decades in network news is important if for no other reason than when one considers the state of the media as a whole, the network evening newscasts are still, far-and-away, the most consumed individual news products within American journalism.[7] While a greater total number of Americans subscribe to a daily newspaper or watch local news, when it comes to a single news program these three newscasts still bring in, by far, the largest audience, from 52 million in 1980, to 26 million when Couric was appointed in 2006, to 22.1 million in 2013.[8] By association, one can identify an interpretive dis-

---

[7] Project for Excellence in Journalism (PEJ), *State of the News Media: An Annual Report on American Journalism*, 2006; 2007; 2008; 2013.

[8] This despite the fact that the cumulative viewership for the evening news has dropped some 50 per cent over the past 25 years, from an average of 52 million viewers per evening in 1980, to 26 million in 2006 when Couric was appointed – a consistent decline of about 1 million viewers per year that has since held relatively steady since this study was initially conducted. The most recent numbers for 2013 are an average of 22.1 million. A more telling statistic comes when we consider ratings – the number of televisions tuned into a given program at a given time – and share – the percentage of televisions in use tuned into a specific program – for the past 5, 25, and nearly 40 years. As the 2007 PEJ report notes: 'In 1969, the three network newscasts had a combined 50 rating and an 85 share. In 1980, the year that CNN was launched, they had a 37 rating and a 75 share. As of November 2006, ratings had fallen 64% since 1969, 51% since 1980, and 23% since 2000 [to 18.2].

course within the journalism industry and within the academic study of it, which places expectations on network news to act as a sort of litmus test for the state of the news media.[9] Accordingly, the anchor is often looked to as more than simply an archetype; it is assumed that they will bear close affinity to the ideal type of the professional journalist and what we traditionally refer to as hard news.[10]

Walter Cronkite is often held up as a prototypical example of what we have come to expect from a professional news anchor, an approach still frequently imitated in terms of presentation, tone, emotive posture and so forth. His style of presentation emphasized information over involvement with the audience or subject matter at hand, and lent itself to a cool, detached persona; a manner that dovetails with what we might consider a very 'masculine' form of storytelling.[11] The complement – as opposed to counter – to this style of news is evidenced in many of the emerging broadcast news options to appear over the past few decades, such as cable magazine shows or breakfast television.[12] Such programs depart from the traditional objectivity regime by presenting journalism in an involved manner. The journalist does not merely read and recount information, they attempt to help the audience engage with the material by pre-digesting and 'feeling' stories. In this sense, opinions and belief – things that are shunned in traditional newscasts – come to the fore of presentation and are considered alongside facts and expertise to represent 'reality' and get at the 'truth'.

When Couric was signed by CBS, this ability to 'connect' with audiences was often held up as one of the definitive rationales for her selection. As the host of NBC's popular *Today Show*, a breakfast newscast, Couric was noted for her friendly demeanor and ability to connect with interviewees. Her ascension to the anchor desk was widely considered a crucial moment in the transition of female journalists, for it was taken as a sign by many that a female could be taken 'seriously' enough to hold down one of the most prestigious positions in an industry which still values 'masculine' traits such as gravitas and authority.[13]   However, a change in gender was

---

Share, meanwhile, had fallen 60% since 1969, 55% since 1980, and 23% since 2000 [to 34].'

[9] Cf. Zelizer, B., 'Journalists as Interpretive Communities', *Critical Studies in Mass Communication* 10 (1993), pp. 219-237.

[10] Weber, M., *The Methodology of the Social Sciences* (New York, 1949).

[11] Peters, 'Emotion Aside'; Van Zoonen, L., 'One of the Girls?: The Changing Gender of Journalism', in Carter, C., Branston, G. and Allan, S., eds, *News, Gender and Power* (London, 1998), pp. 33-46.

[12] Peters, 'No-Spin Zones'.

[13] See Hagan, J., 'Alas, Poor Couric: But Pity Her Not', *New York Magazine*, available from: http://nymag.com/news/features/34452/ (2007); cf. Carter, C. et al., "Set-

only one of many developments in how this mainstay of American broadcast went about rebranding its broadcast.

While it is one thing to say that the past few decades have seen the rise
of emerging forms of journalism that redefine the style and tone of broadcast journalism – a rather trivial observation in light of the rapidity of cable
and satellite expansion during this period – it is quite another to investigate
what, if any, pressures this has placed on the networks to adapt. By getting a
specific sense of exactly how the *CBS Evening News* has changed in the period spanning Cronkite to Couric, one can get a more substantive idea about
how 'traditional' broadcast journalism goes about making the news in the
increasingly mediated, technological, fragmented and commercialized landscape that helps define the state of the media in the 21st century. To sum, if
a confluence of factors, including the decline or questioning of the notion of
objectivity in media work, the rapid proliferation of news outlets, the increasing sophistication of news presentation, and the fragmentation of audiences has provided a fertile climate for many broadcast alternatives to flourish, one wonders to what extent these same transformations beget a shift in
the style and form of the network evening newscasts.

CBS News Under Cronkite

The irony of the quote that leads this paper is that a defining moment of one
of the pillars of American journalism is so notable not for personifying his
career but for its incongruity to it. When Walter Cronkite announced the
death of John F. Kennedy in 1963, the anchor was visibly shaken, removing
the glasses he was wearing to read the incoming copy as tears formed at the
edges of his eyes, briefly clearing his throat as he regained his poise before
continuing with the bulletin.[14] As CBS news remembers it: 'On that most
frantic of days, the voice delivering the horrifying news was calm, measured. CBS newsman Walter Cronkite's composure wavered only once: at
the moment when the unthinkable was confirmed'.[15] This moment became
etched in American journalistic lore not just for the magnitude of the event,
but because it so evidently transcended the naturalized image Cronkite had
crafted for the American public. Put otherwise, Cronkite's 'emotion' mo-
mentarily shattered the myth of the professional journalist.[16] His degree of
involvement in reading the news was fleetingly 'hot', a deviation from the

---

ting New(s) Agendas: An Introduction', in: Carter, C., Branston, C. and Allan, S.,
eds, *News, Gender and Power* (London, 1998), pp. 1-12.
[14] The video is available online as part of the CBS news archives.
[15] *CBS Early Show.*, *'Cronkite Remembers JFK: Newsman Walter Cronkite's Impressions on the Fallen President', Early Show (2003).*
[16] Cf. Barthes, R., *Mythologies* (Paris, 1957).

traditional 'cool' posture one expected from the news.[17] But just how did Cronkite go about crafting this persona, and what role did this persona play in the overall success of *CBS Evening News* during his reign? To answer this, one needs to consider not only his performance but also the role of the anchor in the broader journalism field of his day.

In 1963, Cronkite's *CBS Evening News* was the first nightly newscast to move from 15 to 30 minutes. It took four years for him to pass the top-rated *Huntley-Brinkley Report* on NBC as the nation's most-watched newscast, and although there are various theories as to why this happened, it is generally agreed that during his tenure, Cronkite established the level of celebrity and status since afforded to the television news anchor.[18] As Rich notes, 'It was in 1963 that the network anchors as we define them today were born: a man (and still almost always a man) who is at once an authoritative reporter, a cool news reader and the nation's emotional proxy at history's events.'[19] Cronkite is credited with being the first newsreader to don the title of 'anchor', a moniker given to him by CBS news executives when he hosted the 1952 political conventions.[20] This term, interestingly, bears close affinity to the semiotic sense of anchorage coined by Barthes in that the news anchor serves to stabilize the floating meanings, which swirl around news stories.[21] Cronkite stands as the first of his kind, a sort of trusted 'father figure' Americans tuned into, especially during crises, to understand how events would impact the nation.[22] Reflecting this, retrospectives invariably refer to him by his enduring legacy as 'the most trusted man in

---

[17] Peters, 'Emotion Aside'; cf. Stearns, P., *American Cool: Constructing a 20th Century Emotional Style* (New York, 1994); cf. Barbalet, J., *Emotion, Social Theory, and Social Structure: A Macrosociological Approach* (Cambridge, 1998).

[18] Some of the more noted include: the aftermath of a union strike which damaged Huntley and Brinkley's relationship, CBS's position at the forefront of satellite and visual technology, consistency arising from Cronkite's appointment as the first anchor/managing editor, and his demeanour, which some have said was well-suited to calm the 'average' American during turbulent times. Socolow, 'Anchors Away'; *Ibidem.*.

[19] Rich, F., 'The Weight of an Anchor', *New York Times*, available from: http://query.nytimes.com/gst/fullpage.html?res=9C06E5DC1439F93AA25756C0A9 649C8B63# (May 19, 2002).

[20] Ashton, B., 'The Anchorman', *The Quill* 92 (2004), no. 7.

[21] Barthes, R., 'The Rhetoric of the Image', in: Heath, S., ed, *Image, Music, Text* (New York, 1977), pp. 32-51.

[22] As Rich ('Weight of An Anchor') notes, further evidence that this was the case was offered up again on September 11th. In the face of ongoing prognostications of the death of the network anchor, Americans tuned overwhelming into coverage being hosted by the 'big three', who were widely credited as taking a more calm and reasoned approach to the day's events than their cable counterparts.

America,' a title which came to prominence during his tenure as anchor of the *CBS Evening News*. It is instructive to see how Cronkite forged this valued reputation; for if there is one constant in journalism, it is that trust is arguably the currency of the industry.

What is immediately evident from watching a Cronkite broadcast is the near unwavering constancy of his pace, delivery and tone.[23] This is why rare instances like his announcement of the Kennedy assassination, his awe in watching the moon landing in 1969, and an atypical moment of editorializing – an anti-Vietnam war piece appearing at the end of the broadcast which prompted President Johnson to declare, 'If I've lost Cronkite, I've lost middle America,' – are frequently held up when discussing his legacy.[24] These occasions are so notable in a career that spans the last half-century precisely because, especially during the 19 years Cronkite anchored the *CBS Evening News*, he so rarely broke from his measured and detached delivery. When he did, it became a newsworthy event in and of itself. As viewers, these moments stand out because they are clear instances of a violation of the journalistic 'rules of truth' embodied within Cronkite's persona – by contravening the communicative regularities of the profession, these moments demand greater involvement on behalf of the audience as we can recognize that something 'unnatural' is occurring.[25] And the fact that only a few circumstances witnessed this shift in performance illustrates that such moments could only be brought about by the truly exceptional.

However, it can generally be said that from night-to-night, segment-to-segment, Cronkite and the *CBS Evening News* during his tenure was remarkably consistent. Each episode examined for this chapter begins with a male voice simply intoning: 'This is the *CBS Evening News* with Walter Cronkite,' as a shot of the newsroom from the side comes into view, showing Cronkite at his desk and other reporters in the background. A simple graphical overlay of the show title with the CBS logo merged with a globe appears, gradually shrinking until it borders the image of Cronkite at the anchor desk (see fig. 1). At this point, Cronkite simply declares, 'Good Evening,' and delves straight into the top news story of the day with no fanfare. Whether the story and words are sensational, Cronkite's delivery could

---

[23] A claim with some prevalence is that Cronkite trained himself to speak at 124 words per minute, below the average speed of most Americans, to facilitate understanding. While this is difficult to verify, there is little doubt that Cronkite's delivery is constant, measured, and slower than typical conversation.

[24] Ashton, 'The Anchorman'.

[25] Cf. Kress, G. and Van Leeuwen, T., *Reading Images: The Grammar of Visual Design* (London, 1996).

best be described as a sort of matter-of-fact gravitas.[26] For instance, a fairly dull story which led the news on March 28, 1979, about a non-confidence vote dissolving the James Callaghan government in the United Kingdom, is introduced with the exact same pitch, tone, and intonation as a 'horror story' in the Central African Republic where, 'several hundred students were rounded up by the Emperor's imperial guard, and as many as a hundred of the young people, aged 8 to 16 years old, were killed with bayonets, clubs, and stones'.[27] As Dahlgren notes, Cronkite in this sense acts as the 'Prime Knower,' who is 'different from most other people – he appears as a wise, urbane, and stoic father figure;' a persona which encapsulates the fact that he is able to marshal the vast resources of the news division and cover the world for us, shedding light on seemingly any event in a calm and collected manner.[28]

While Cronkite's trademark delivery and steady persona is arguably the constant that led to his status as the 'most trusted man in America', and accordingly the *CBS Evening News'* supremacy over his competitors during his tenure, the rest of the show's format augments this sense of calmness, gravitas, and predictability. Every time we return in studio after a piece filed by a correspondent, there is a brief pause before Cronkite returns his gaze to us, from what we naturally assume is a monitor to his right that we do not see on-screen. This visual cue gives the appearance that Cronkite is engaged with all facets of the newscast.[29] Consistency of performance is mirrored in the consistency of timing. Each episode of his *CBS Evening News* is interspersed with five 1-minute commercial breaks, each composed of two 30-second spots. The first break occurs at different points in the broadcast but generally follows a lead set of stories that are arranged thematically.[30] The second commercial break follows the next round of stories, which are generally field reports introduced by Cronkite. The third follows

---

[26] Dahlgren, P., 'TV News as a Social Relation', *Media, Culture and Society* 3 (1981), pp. 291-302.
[27] CBS Evening News, Newscast Aired on March 28th, 1979; CBS Evening News., Newscast Aired on May 14th, 1979.
[28] Dahlgren, 'TV News as a Social Relation', p. 294, p. 293.
[29] Cf. Helmers, M. and Hill, C., 'Introduction', in: Hall, C. and Helmers, M., eds, *Defining Visual Rhetorics* (Mahwah NJ, 2004), pp. 1-24.
[30] For the 'fast' news days involving the Iranian hostage crisis in November, the break occurred later in the broadcast after all stories relating to the developments were aired (CBS, November 5, 1979; November 21, 1979). On the two 'slower' news days examined, the break came much earlier in the broadcast, after the story about Margaret Thatcher's successful non-confidence vote in the United Kingdom (CBS, March 28, 1979), and after a summary of the weekend activities of the assumed frontrunners for the Democratic ticket in the 1980 Presidential race (CBS, May 14, 1979).

a sequence of shorter stories, often 10-30 second updates simply read by the anchor, while the fourth break often precedes a longer human interest or special report segment. The fifth break separates Cronkite's sign off from the credits. Consistency of format is a primary technique that helps establish the grammar of journalistic communication and the process through which we consume news.[31]

There is no verbal segue into any of these interruptions, simply a side shot of Cronkite and the studio which replicates the opening to the show. The only time this format shifts is for the third or fourth break, a graphic of the stock market activity, with the trends succinctly summarized by Cronkite: 'the stock market today: down in heavy trading'.[32] The implication behind these transitions to commercial interruption is likely not lost on the audience. First, the absence of segueing, teasing, or 'happy talk', either going into the commercial break or returning from it, implies that airtime is a limited resource not to be wasted. It also suggests a direct contradiction to the banality of the advertisements; re-establishing the newscast's sense of substance. The shot of the studio invariably shows the journalists 'hard at work', from Cronkite examining or altering copy, to people typing away and moving hurriedly in the background. One of Cronkite's first directives as managing editor of the nightly newscast was to turn the newsroom into the studio.[33] The desired effect, he said, was to show that that CBS team was collecting and updating the news directly until the end of the broadcast.

When one considers this sense of ongoing work against what became Cronkite's trademark sign off, the transition is quite remarkable. Despite appearing to update the news until the last instance of the broadcast, Cronkite's nightly signoff – 'And that's the way it is,' followed by the date and 'This is Walter Cronkite, CBS News. Good night.' – provides a sense of closure to the newscast. The effect of this closing is twofold. Most evidently, it implies that the viewer is caught up on the events of the day. There is no sense of incompleteness or need to go beyond the purview of the broadcast; this sort of definitive statement leaves little ambiguity or doubt. His final words are another subtle reinforcement of this stance. 'Good night,' is decisive, being tied to a cultural understanding of finality that is associated with going to bed.[34] While it is obvious that few people go to bed at 7:00 pm, this closing salutation implies that, at least when it comes to the news of the day, Cronkite's audience can rest easy. The combination of these two sign-offs is even more intriguing when one compares it to the

---

[31] Cf. Kress and van Leeuwen, *Reading Images*.
[32] CBS, March 28, 1979.
[33] Ashton, 'The Anchorman'.
[34] Cf. Barthes, *Mythologies*.

opening; for the first words Cronkite greats us with, a mere half hour earlier, are "Good evening," a salutation associated with transition – a return from work, arriving at a restaurant for dinner, and so forth – a culture referent that is not connected to conclusiveness and satiation but to beginnings and anticipation.

For the duration of his role of host of the *CBS Evening News*, Cronkite crafted a style of journalism that was the embodiment of what the ideal type of objectivity would demand from a broadcast anchor. He was engaged but neutral, detached but not indifferent, delivering the facts of the day in a style that was unflappable, steady and predictable.[35] Such was the success of his delivery that his style was replicated quite closely by the anchors who followed him in the 1980s and 90s. While Brokaw, Jennings, and Rather allowed 'personality' to come through with slightly greater regularity, the effect of their nightly broadcast was similarly 'cool'.[36] Although Cronkite's term at CBS has been called the halcyon age of broadcast news, and the end of the reign of big three has been heralded by many media analysts as the death of the evening news, some argue there is still a place in journalism for a product that is relies on its 'Authority. Gravitas. Solemnity. A reliable, calm anchorperson on whom you can depend. Every weeknight.'[37] Many of the conventions forged by Cronkite live on today. However, a balancing act is simultaneously evident, as the *CBS Evening News* endeavors to remodel its style, not just in terms of technology, but also in terms of its tone.

CBS News Under Couric

When the big three network anchors stepped down from their broadcasts in 2005, there was talk in the industry that this presented a moment to potentially re-brand the evening news, to shore up ratings which had been steadily deteriorating since the 1980s. While the death of the network news division and star anchors had been predicted by various media critics for much of the 1990s, the replacement of all three stalwarts was seen by many media critics as the final nail in the coffin of the evening news:

> Talking heads are dead. Forget the Internet sucking away younger viewers – they don't watch network news in any great number and haven't for years. Network news watchers are older. Much older ... There's no real allure to the

---

[35] Peters, 'Emotion Aside'; cf. Ward, S., *The Invention of Journalism Ethics: The Path to Objectivity and Beyond* (Montreal, 2005).
[36] Rich, 'The Weight of an Anchor'.
[37] O'Brien, M., 'Lost Cause? Network Executives Say Evening News Shows Remain Viable', *The Quill* 94 (2006), no. 1, pp. 24-31.

nightly network news without the comforting attraction of the iconic anchors (Brokaw, Jennings, Rather). Without them, you've got 22 minutes of storytelling that the bulk of the available demographic has already either read online or will check out later in the night on cable. Let's recap: Outdated delivery system. Airs too early. Appeals to declining, elderly audience.[38]

This sort of doomsday prognostication was perhaps not echoed by network news executives, who pointed to the superior ratings still experienced by the evening news in comparison to other broadcast alternatives. However, there was a general acknowledgement that the networks needed to do something to update the evening news for the new millennium, to halt the downward progression that had plagued them for the past 25 years.[39]

When CBS announced the hiring of Couric to become the new permanent anchor of their evening newscast, a sense of revitalization was evident in its press release. The executive producer noted: 'In the past year, the *CBS Evening News* has begun to build a broadcast with a fresh, accessible approach, and viewers have responded. ... Katie is the perfect person to complete that process'.[40] This use of terminology such as 'fresh' and 'accessible' has echoes of the gendered descriptions of 'skills' often ascribed to female reporters.[41] Further press releases heralded shifts that were to complement Couric's inaugural broadcast, among them a simulcast of the program on the internet, for those unable to be in front of their television; a 'Couric and Company' blog where, 'Couric and the Evening News team will create a transparent, two-way, continuing dialogue with viewers and readers that encourages online comments and questions'; 'Katie Couric's Notebook', where Couric would offer a vlog on stories that caught her attention; and a 'First Look' segment where a video preview of potential news stories for the evening newscast would be available mid-afternoon on the CBS news website.[42] But for all these shifts and changes, the 'fresh' new *CBS Evening News* remains faithful to many of the traditions and techniques that stretch back to Cronkite's tenure as anchor.

---

[38] Tim Goodman, *San Francisco Chronicle*, 2005, quoted in O'Brien, 2006.

[39] *Ibidem*; Project for Excellence in Journalism (PEJ)., *State of the News Media 2007: An Annual Report on American Journalism*, available from: http://www.stateofthemedia.org/2007/ (2007).

[40] CBS Evening News., 'Katie Couric is Joining CBS News: Couric Will Become Anchor and Managing Editor of The CBS Evening News', *CBS News*, available from: http://www.cbscorporation.com/news/ (2006).

[41] See Carter *et al.*, 'Setting New(s) Agendas'.

[42] CBS Evening News., 'Katie Couric is Joining CBS News: Couric Will Become Anchor and Managing Editor of The CBS Evening News', *CBS News*, available from: http://www.cbscorporation.com/news/ (2006).

Similarities with Cronkite

When we consider a product like the *CBS Evening News*, it is important to remember what parts of the objectivity regime still thrive in journalism. Accuracy, balance, factuality and a desire to generate trustworthy accounts are some of the hallmarks of 20th-century American journalism that are still widely witnessed in the rhetoric emanating from newsrooms, industry publications and academic investigations of the industry.[43] It would be reasonable to expect that remnants from the 'rules of truth' manifested in journalistic practice during Cronkite's heyday are more likely to be witnessed in today's evening newscasts as opposed to the emerging broadcast alternatives appearing over the past decade. And one only needs a quick glance at an episode of the *CBS Evening News* under Couric to confirm this supposition. Many of the standardized frames and techniques deployed under Cronkite are still widely employed.[44]

Standard storytelling archetypes from the *CBS Evening News* in 1979 have seen little change over the past 25 years in terms of a basic format. Additionally, such stories are still subject to a host of techniques, from relying on official sources, attribution, statistics, and other positivist indicators that do work in creating what Tuchman calls a 'web of facticity'.[45] Simply put, the approach employed on many stories to make 'objective' reportage apparent to the journalist and visible to the audience often remains unchanged. A comparison of two similar instances covered by the *CBS Evening News*, despite occurring some 28 years apart, quickly illustrates this. Consider the telling of the Iranian hostage crisis in 1979. After the basic facts concerning the takeover of the U.S. embassy in Tehran and resultant hostages is briefly set up by Cronkite, he introduces the reporter for the story, the State Department correspondent for CBS, Marvin Kalb. Kalb offers background, before interviewing the U.S. Secretary of State, counterpoising these comments against the Iranian Chargé d'affaires, then stating the captors' demands and the U.S. State Department's plan of action. These narratives are woven together before ending the story with a stand-up in front of

---

[43] Ericson et al., *Visualizing Deviance: A Study of News Organization* (Toronto, 1987); Schudson, M., 'The Objectivity Norm in American Journalism', *Journalism* 2 (2001), no. 2, pp. 149-170; Ward, *The Invention of Journalism Ethics*.
[44] Cf. Pan, Z. and Kosicki, G., 'Framing Analysis: An Approach to News Discourse', *Political Communication* 10 (1993), pp. 55-75.
[45] Tuchman, G., *Making News: A Study in the Construction of Reality* (New York, 1978).

the State Department pressroom, noting what to expect from the days ahead.[46]

The 2007 Iraqi equivalent, a hostage taking of U.S. soldiers, is told in near-identical fashion. Couric gives the basic facts of the case before handing over to Mark Strassmann, a Baghdad correspondent. Strassman gives the background and details of the hostage taking before interviewing a high-ranking U.S. army spokesman. An Arabic language newspaper editor is called upon to offer a prediction about what might happen, which is counterpoised against the U.S. army commander's summary of the actions the army is taking to recover the hostages. The piece ends with Strassmann detailing the hostage-takers' demands while performing a stand-up from Baghdad, looking forward to what might happen next.[47] This is just one of many examples which illustrates how the basic frames, journalistic credentials, progression, sources, and formats relied upon to convey common narratives has remained relatively unchanged over the years (see fig. 2).

A few more similarities outside of format are worth noting. From 1979 to 2007, we see the same type of expert sources in the crafting of this story, something that is common across the ongoing stories and beat reports that provide the glut of day-to-day coverage. This is a fact not lost on critical theorists in the tradition of Herman and Chomsky who note that elite-engineered accounts are still overwhelmingly relied upon, which potentially co-opts journalism.[48] Additionally, graphics such as maps and charts, which aid in summarizing the factual elements of a story, are utilized frequently by both broadcasts. Similarly, the types of shots one sees are often unchanged: the flyover of the Three Mile Island nuclear plant when it suffered a near-meltdown in 1979 is emblematic of the sweeping panoramas used to set the scene for 'disaster' stories.[49] The 2007 equivalent, a segment on 'Nature's Fury', a series of damaging wildfires, floods, and tornadoes, is nearly identical.[50] The difference in modern broadcast news is thus not a desire for eye-catching graphics and highly visualized material (see fig. 3). Rather what has shifted is the ease of generating such graphics and the sophistication not just of them, but of their integration into the broader newscast. There is a

---

[46] CBS Evening News., Newscast Aired on November 5th, 1979.

[47] CBS Evening News., Newscast Aired on May 14th, 2007.

[48] Herman, E. and Chomsky, N., Manufacturing Consent: The Political Economy of the Mass Media (New York, 1988); Altheide, D., Creating Fear: News and the Construction of Crisis (New York, 2002); McChesney, R., 'September 11 and the Structural Limitations of U.S. Journalism', Zelizer, B. and Allan, S., eds, Journalism After September 11: When Trauma Shapes the News (London, 2002), pp. 91-100.

[49] CBS, March 28, 1979; Cf. Lule, J., Daily News, Eternal Stories: The Mythological Role of Journalism (London, 2001).

[50] CBS Evening News., Newscast Aired on May 9th, 2007.

'smoothness' in their assimilation, not evident in earlier footage, which allows current graphics packages to do a better job 'setting the tone' for an individual story or entire broadcast.[51] Other conventions that aid a sense of verisimilitude and immediacy, such as the reporter stand-up in front of a location directly referenced in the story, are prominent in both newscasts. The association with the 'global' – both Cronkite and Couric's introduction feature an overlaid graphic of the world – and the over-the-shoulder visual cues that introduces each story, are further constants that span the decades separating these newscasts.

Divergences from Cronkite

Each evening of Couric's broadcast begins with a fast three-note 'sounder', 'notes that function as a subliminal come-to-attention signal to viewers'.[52] From a wide-angel shot of Couric in studio at the anchor desk, the camera quickly zooms in while she announces, 'I'm Katie Couric, tonight,' before delving into a series of teasers for the stories to follow, similar in style and presentation to many of the introductions seen leading into the top-rated programs on cable news. Brief, often emotive-laden descriptions of the main stories of the evening are quickly described by Couric as related images flash across the screen. Each teaser has a title, often a play-on-words – as in a report on Barack Obama's potential Irish roots, 'Barack O'Bama'– but without the same degree of tongue-in-cheek as satirical news.[53]   As Couric reads these short previews, the music is lowered in the background, being brought up again as the title sequence is launched upon the completion of the trailers. This graphical compilation relies on a stately dark blue and gold color palette to intersperse the name of the broadcast with the sort of global graphic that has come to be a leitmotif of broadcast news (see fig. 4). As we return to a wide-angled shot of Couric in studio, the history of the *CBS Evening News*, and all associations this brings forth, are harnessed as Walter Cronkite intones, 'This is the *CBS Evening News*, with Katie Couric'.[54]

   This altered opening is telling for number of reasons. First is that the existence of teasers, as the industry term suggests, implies that an increasingly fickle audience needs to be wooed into staying tuned for an entire broadcast. This change, and many which I will subsequently describe, are

---

[51] Cf. Helmers and Hill, *Defining Visual Rhetorics*.
[52] Barnes, B., 'CBS, Katie Couric Have Already Made Sweet Music Together,' *Wall Street Journal*, September 5, 2006, A1.
[53] CBS, May 16, 2007.
[54] CBS, May 7, 2007 – May 18, 2007.

fairly telling indicators of the impact of the triumvirate of fragmentation, declining trust in mainstream news, and commercialization of the industry on traditional newscasts. The fact that teasers for upcoming segments of the newscast are usually offered by Couric before each commercial break is further evidence that the modern viewer is assumed to need encouragement to 'stay tuned'.[55] The second implication, as evidenced in the language employed in these openings, is that news content, in-and-of-itself, is insufficient incentive to watch – the content needs to be dressed up in language that oftentimes implies some personal relevance for the viewer or, alternatively, amuses or begets suspense. So an upcoming story on global warming, is previewed to us as 'Forecast: HOT!' noting, 'If you think summers are hot now, you ain't seen nothing yet. A report that will really make you sweat'.[56] A report on the declining bee population, 'Mystery Killer' is introduced by noting, 'Something is bringing the bees to their knees. Why that is a threat to our food supply'.[57] This trend is also mirrored in the headlines – such as 'Toxic trailers' or 'Terror plot' – which now adorn the over-the-shoulder graphics that announce each story.[58]

These teasers, both at the start and throughout the show, can be seen as part of a broader effort to 'involve' the audience from the outset and throughout each broadcast using a variety of techniques rather than chancing this to content. Music was considered by network executives one of the most important elements in remodeling the tone of the show news consultants noting that many people often listen rather than watch the news.[59] When CBS commissioned James Horner, a Hollywood composer best known for creating the score for *Titanic*, to create a new theme song to accompany Couric's debut as anchor, the executive producer noted the theme 'must be urgent and serious, yet light. Flexible, yet memorable. Regal and encompassing the grand history of CBS News, yet moving forward'.[60] Horner noted that he did not want to replicate the Romanesque fanfares of NBC and ABC and wanted to respect Couric's desire to have music that invoked 'wheat fields blowing rather than Manhattan skyline.' Furthermore, Horner created slight variations on the theme which could reflect the type of news day it was – more drums to reflect anxiety-producing stories leading the news cycle or a more notable trumpet solo to set the tone for introspective news days. Another consideration with an eye to inclusion was altering

---

[55] Kovach and Rosenstiel, *Warp Speed.*
[56] CBS, May 10, 2007.
[57] CBS, May 7, 2007.
[58] CBS, May 16, 2007; CBS, May 8, 2007.
[59] See also Bull, M., 'The World According to Sound', *New Media and Society* 3 (2001), no. 2, pp. 179-197.
[60] Barnes, 'CBS, Katie Couric'.

the colors in the studio to be 'warmer' on camera.[61] These aesthetic considerations point to a re-branding designed to comfort the viewer by harnessing
traits associated with the 'feminine'; gaining trust not through the paternalistic style personified by Cronkite but in a maternal style associated with
protecting the viewer.[62]

There are a few other clues that the *CBS Evening News* is seeking to
address a hold over an audience that is far more tenuous today than it was
during Cronkite's era. One of the more evident examples of this is the timing of commercials. Under Cronkite, the first break occurred at variable
points in the broadcast, whenever the first set of thematic stories had been
completed, sometimes as early as two-and-a-half minutes into the broadcast.
In the 2007 broadcast, the first commercial is consistently aired eleven-and-
a-half minutes into the program, with the frequency of commercial breaks
increasing as the news nears its conclusion. This timing mirrors entertain-
ment-based programming, the purpose of which, one imagines, is to 'hook'
the viewer into the program. Teasing the audience before each commercial
break reinforces this loyalty, giving further incentive to return. This parallels the blurring of entertainment and information-based programming.

Further trends such as personalization, conversationalization, and informalization can also be witnessed in the *CBS Evening News*, for instance,
in how the telling of stories appears to have seen a subtle shift that sees an
effort to contextualize broader themes in a manner that relates them to the
individual viewer. For example in 2007, when Daimler sold off Chrysler
corporation, 'the divorce of the year in the corporate world,' the two-way
conversation that followed spoke of what impact it would have on consumers who owned Chrysler vehicles or had vehicles under lease.[63] A four-day
special, 'Gotta Have It! The Hard Sell To Kids', offered advice and websites to help families resolve issues such as credit card debt and cell-phone
misuse among young people.[64] Couric notes that when she joined CBS the
goal was to make the show, 'more personable, more accessible, a little less
formal, a little more approachable'.[65] Her decision to switch the opening
greeting, initially to 'Hi everybody' from 'Good evening', appears a conscious effort on the part of CBS news to give the viewer a greater sense of
involvement and more 'welcoming' news watching experience.

---

[61] *Ibidem.*
[62] Cf. Van Zoonen, 'One of the Girls?'; Dahlgren, 'TV News as a Social Relation';
Rich, 'The Weight of an Anchor'.
[63] CBS, May 14, 2007.
[64] CBS, May 14, 2007 – May 17, 2007.
[65] Hagan, J., 'Alas, Poor Couric: But Pity Her Not'.

COLBERT: You added a real touch of, a little casual touch at the top of the news; you say 'Hi everybody.'
COURIC: Well now it's a little formal; it's 'Hello everyone.'
COLBERT: But it's inviting right?
COURIC: 'Well I thought about it and you know the only people who say 'good evening' are doormen and maître d's … But I found it to be, just to be, a little pretentious and portentous so I thought something a little more relaxed and casual would be more accessible.[66]

This move seems to be an evident informalization of the news, making the discourse more in line with 'everyday' speech, a recent logic in vogue among political and media consultants who believe that bureaucratic and official discourse comes across as more-stilted, less-empathetic, and accordingly more-distancing.[67] This trend is infused throughout each broadcast and creeps into individual segments. Questions like Couric asking a congressman if he was 'mad as heck right now' over proposed immigration reform is just part of a more extensive shift in language that attempts a familiar form of address.[68] In this regard, there appears to be an effort in the national newscasts to engage more directly with audiences, a style pioneered by local and cable news. However, as the *CBS Evening News'* continued difficulty with ratings indicates, there are significant challenges a traditional newscast faces when it tries to update its look.

Incorporating Interactivity into Network News

Some media commentators assert that the day of the 'trusted father figure' is coming to be replaced by the knowledgeable older brother (or perhaps in Couric's case, sister) – a less paternal connection that is nonetheless 'looked-up-to' for advice and knowledge. This is only one of many personae that we now witness on news-related programming, from the intelligent witty friend, Jon Stewart, to the righteous beat-cop, Bill O'Reilly, the full-throated populist, Glenn Beck, and the jovial conversationalists who are most morning news anchors. Even the supposedly disappearing fatherly types, such as Jim Lehrer, still hold a place on various programs. The field of journalism increasingly comprises a diverse range of emotional spaces, accepted styles of journalistic involvement that mark a departure from the

---

[66] The Colbert Report., 'Interview with Katie Couric', *Comedy Central*, Episode Aired on March 22nd, 2007.
[67] Fairclough, *Media Discourse*; Delli Carpini and Williams, 'Let us Infotain You'.
[68] CBS, May 17, 2007.

cool style that defined most broadcast newscasts in the time of Cronkite.[69] When one looks at the *CBS Evening News* under Couric, it seems that while much of the reportage has stayed true to form in terms of the authoritative 'distance' demanded under the objectivity regime, there is evidence that one of the crucial elements seen under emerging newscasts – the need to generate a more accessible form of involvement – has crept into the evening news. From making a conscientious effort to personalize stories, to informalizing elements of discourse, and increasing the avenues for interaction, the current version of the *CBS Evening News* conveys a sense that it is not only covering the news, but covering the news *for you*.

Technology has certainly played a role in facilitating this sense of involvement and CBS is quite candid in its desire to shift its broadcast in this direction. Part of the somewhat ingratiating explanation for 'Couric & Co.', the online blog of *CBS Evening News*, states:

> In fact, we'll try to make ourselves of some mild use by steering you to material on CBS shows, on CBSNews.com, in the newspapers or around the Web that we find intriguing, unexpected, important and funny. Especially funny. We like funny. And we consider you — the people on the other side of the computer screen, our viewers and readers — a big part of the 'Co.' of 'Couric & Co.,' too. This is important — it's not a gimmick, it's not marketing. The 'Evening News' has never really been able to talk back to you; and you really haven't been able to talk back to us. We really want to change that, and this blog is a big start. We hope you'll drop us a line, leave a comment and offer your feedback. Get into arguments with us. Send story ideas. Tell us what we're ignoring.[70]

As Hallin notes, by the early 1990s, the network newscasts began, to a much lesser extent, adopting a practice more often associated with local news, of 'dropping neutrality and presenting the journalist as a "regular person" who shares and champions the emotions of the audience.'[71] This is not to say that Couric has strayed too far from the cool demeanor, which demands a sort of detachment from the story matter being conveyed. She does not bemoan, yell, or pontificate in the manner that we have come to expect from cable anchors, nor does she act in a manner that could be defined as anything other than 'serious' throughout the bulk of her broadcast. Yet in

---

[69] Peters, 'Emotion Aside'.
[70] CBS Evening News., 'Couric & Co', *CBS News*, available from: http://www.cbsnews.com/sections/couricandco/main500803.shtml (2008).
[71] Hallin, D., 'The Passing of the "High Modernism" of American Journalism', *Journal of Communication* 42 (1992), no. 3, p. 22.

certain segments, those which can have an immediate impact on the audience, she adopts a conversational tone that stands in marked contrast to the professorial-like imparting of information seen under Cronkite. When possible, Couric interacts with or on behalf of her audience, rather than just talking at it.

Two formats where this is often evident are the two-way conversations with correspondents and in-studio discussions that follow specific segments. As Cameron notes, these moments are 'less formal in tone and style than the preceding parts of the item. It is essentially an informalizing or conversationalizing device for presenting news stories: instead of being on the receiving end of an impersonal, mass public announcement, viewers or listeners are repositioned as eavesdroppers on an apparently "natural" exchange between two specific individuals.'[72] The effect is, again, a somewhat contrived sense of involvement. It is not that Couric adopts a different persona for these moments – she is still the concerned anchor – however with this format she is able to display the less formal approach she popularized as host of the *Today Show*, NBC's morning news.

Another place where we witness a change is in the greetings and sign-offs used by Cronkite versus those employed by Couric. As noted above, Couric went through two greetings, 'Hi Everybody' and 'Hello Everyone', which are informal compared to Cronkite's 'Good evening'. The sign-off is similarly toned down. No longer are we told, 'And that's the way it is,' instead Couric refers to us directly, noting, 'And that's the *CBS Evening News* for tonight. I'm Katie Couric. Thanks for watching. I'll see you tomorrow. Good night.'[73] Again, this appears more attentive toward forging a connection with an audience and building a relationship as opposed to just promoting ritual viewership.

Working to encourage involvement, of course, can be generated not only by shifts in tone but in shifts in the types of stories being told. While the beginning of the newscast still covers the similar sort of serious fare – wars, disasters, political developments and the like – that was seen during Cronkite, the latter segments of the *CBS Evening News* now appear to be a place where stories with a more human interest or 'feel good' narrative come to the fore, and to a greater extent than its NBC or ABC equivalents.[74] An attention to narrative is nothing new; as Graber notes, in 1963, the executive producer for NBC's *Huntley-Brinkley Report* instructed his staff that,

---

[72] Cameron, D., 'Language. Truth or Dare?', *Critical Quarterly* 46 (2004), no. 2, p. 125.

[73] On Friday evenings this is altered slightly, with Couric noting, "Thank you for watching again this week. I'll see you again Monday, until then, have a great weekend" (CBS, May 11, 2007; May 18, 2007.).

[74] Project for Excellence in Journalism (PEJ)., 2007.

Every news story should, without any sacrifice of probity or responsibility, display the attributes of fiction, of drama. It should have a structure and conflict, problem and denouement, rising action and falling action, a beginning, a middle and an end. These are not only the essentials of drama; they are the essentials of narrative.[75]

The *CBS Evening News* seems to increasingly echo this thinking. A shift which is no doubt apparent to critics who argue that television news is becoming trivialized is an overall reduction in time devoted to the newscast magnified by the parallel introduction of a near nightly 'kicker'.[76] While the final segment under Cronkite was often an in-depth consideration of a specific story, the typical final segment in 2007 is primarily human-interest stories or features on prominent Americans, such as excerpts from Ronald Reagan's posthumous diary.[77] Financial imperatives should not be ignored as part of this shift. Whereas in 1991 the budget for the *CBS Evening News* was about $65 million a year, by 2000 this number had fallen to $35 million.[78]

---

[75] Graber, D., 'The Infotainment Quotient in Routine Television News: A Director's Perspective', *Discourse & Society* 5 (1994), no. 4, p. 483.

[76] In terms of the total time each broadcast devotes to news, *CBS Evening News* now airs approximately three minutes less coverage in a single broadcast than it did during Cronkite's time. Accounting for the five 1-mintue commercial breaks that occurred each broadcast, and discounting the credits which roll at the end of each newscast, the time devoted to news under Cronkite was approximately 23.5 minutes. Under Couric, this same calculation drops to 21 minutes – commercial time has risen by 2.5 minutes. If we subtract the teasers before each commercial break, much longer introduction, and cross-promotion (largely irrelevant in terms of the duration of the 'news'), this figure drops to approximately 20 minutes. When critics factor in the vacuous nature of many of the nightly 'kickers', which often last two to three minutes, it gives some legitimacy to the contention that nightly newscasts are diminishing their content.

[77] In the four episodes examined of the *CBS Evening News* under Cronkite, only one of the final segments could be termed a conventional kicker (the death of Emmett Kelly – CBS, March 28, 1979); whereas the others were similarly serious fare as the stories which preceded it (early parole release of kidnapper; Kentucky gubernatorial race, Islam in turmoil – CBS, May 14, 1979; November 5, 1979; November 21, 1979). A look over one year of Vanderbilt television archives, which details every story filed on the nightly newscasts, seems to confirm this. The bulk of the final segments under Cronkite in 1979 are longer pieces (often 3 or 4 minutes) similar to stories from news magazines like *60 Minutes*: investigative journalism, international affairs, broad social issues, and so forth; CBS, May 17, 2007.

[78] Hagan, J., 'Alas, Poor Couric: But Pity Her Not'.

The *CBS Evening News* even instituted a set Friday-evening kicker. In 2006 CBS launched 'American Stories', a recurring segment with viewers encouraged to send in story ideas to CBS for a report that would occur at end of the newscast, every Friday. After the report, usually about a 'unique' individual living up to some element of the American dream, correspondent Steve Hartman sits down with Couric in studio, in an atmosphere reminiscent of the morning news shows, to update previous stories and to offer a preview on three potential story ideas for the upcoming week. Based upon audience response on the *CBS Evening News* website, Hartman files whichever story garners the most votes. The news-value of these reports is unclear, and certainly brings one in mind of Stephen Colbert's truthiness quip about trying to 'feel the news, at you.' By asking the audience to vote, this segment takes the one-way exchange of news and changes it to a (minimal) mutually constituted dialogue.

Yet while such stories are heavily laced with pathos, adversity and triumph, themes with a fictionalized quality, when it comes to the first portion of the *CBS Evening News*, the tone is relatively unchanged. Some of the dialogue, such as referring to the Sunni triangle in Iraq as the 'triangle of death' may seem like emotively infused language creeping into the newscast, but as we saw, such discourse was also present during Cronkite's tenure.[79] Similarly, the pitch and cadence for stories such as troubles in the Middle East, manufacturing job losses and the like may be slightly more varied under Couric, but generally speaking, it could be said that her overall tone and delivery is akin to Cronkite. For television news to credibly claim to serve the broader public, stories of suffering and emotion must be contemplated at a distance. These types of 'objective' accounts, which we have come to expect from network news, still dominate the majority of each broadcast of the *CBS Evening News*.

That's The Way it Will Be?

On the whole, the 2007 *CBS Evening News* simply appears like a more technologically advanced, and slightly more welcoming and interactive version of its 1979 counterpart. In this respect, CBS still remains one of the places viewers who want a 'serious' summary of the day's events are likely to turn. However, the overall uniformity of the program has been altered in terms of incorporating 'on-your-side' investigative pieces; faithfully airing a nightly kicker that acts to soften the more depressing fare that overwhelms the early part of each newscast; adopting a more conversational and person-

---

[79] CBS, May 14, 2007.

al tone, when possible; and adding teasers that juxtapose the somber tone of many of the stories, either by attempting to amuse, entice or concern.

Demographics are an element of the drop-off in the audience levels for network news, as the median age of viewers was roughly 60 when Couric took over at CBS.[80] The problems with having such an elderly demographic were twofold. First, as audience members age and die off, younger viewers need to replace them to maintain ratings. Although exact numbers are imprecise, at the time of Couric's hiring it was accepted wisdom among network executives that this was not occurring.[81] The second issue, which dovetails with the first, is that advertising revenue is primarily centered on the 25-54 age range, which means that network newscasts face pressure not only in terms of population dynamics but in terms of commercial imperatives to appeal younger. The balance, as *CBS Evening News* found in the initial months after Katie Couric started, is a tenuous one, as trying to appeal to a younger audience can simultaneously antagonize core viewers.[82]

While the current manifestation of the *CBS Evening News* is still very much a recounting of the day's events to an 'average' audience, there is a notable effort towards making the broadcast more interactive and more accessible. Unlike Cronkite's tenure, it is seemingly no longer enough just to inform – the contemporary version of the *CBS Evening News* also appears to try to appeal and involve. Whether it is using technology to facilitate interaction, making a greater effort to bring the personal relevance of broader themes evident, speaking from time-to-time in a more colloquial style, or adopting a stance of being 'on the side' of the audience, this chapter demonstrates how the *CBS Evening News* incorporated a number of shifts to craft a form of news that aims to generate a greater sense of involvement on behalf of its viewers.[83] However, as CBS adjusted to its new anchor and style, both Couric and CBS executives noted that, at first, they swung the pendulum too far in this direction. As one correspondent notes, '[CBS CEO] Moonves said people don't want to listen to the 'voice of God' anymore. And it's exactly what they want'.[84]

When one considers this in relation to the über-consistent tone that defined Cronkite's *Evening News*, it seems the newscast no longer represents itself as a homogeneous, stand-alone broadcast but as part of a news division that adopts a variety of tones. It is still the sober flagship of the divi-

---

[80] Project for Excellence in Journalism (PEJ), 2006.

[81] While audience demographics have not been consistently collected, MagnaGlobal USA, a television research firm, has noted no significant change in the median age of network news viewers since 2002 (PEJ, 2007).

[82] Hagan, J., 'Alas, Poor Couric: But Pity Her Not'.

[83] Peters, 'Even Better than Being Informed'.

[84] *Ibidem.*

sion, but it now has hints of the light-hearted fare that its early morning relative, *The Early Show*, specializes in producing, while incorporating investigative segments and one-on-one interviews more the purview of *60 Minutes*. One such parallel led to what is arguably Couric's most successful moment since beginning at CBS, her interview with Republican Vice-Presidential candidate Sarah Palin in 2008. In the midst of a media environment where press access to the relatively unknown Alaskan Governor was tightly controlled, Couric's serious yet involved interview appeared to be viewed as the most instructive into Palin's relative experience, or lack thereof, for the office. By being decisive yet conversational in her questioning, Couric's seemed to generate a bond with Palin, whose relaxed demeanor helped illustrate the scripted nature of many of her responses and lack of familiarity with matters of serious national policy. The resonance of this interview was indicative of the potential strength of Couric's contemporary interpretation of the role of the news anchor. Remediation of the interview, discussion in other news outlets and in popular culture, and apparent impact on polling figures made it perhaps the most widely discussed and analyzed moment of the 2008 election campaign.

The foundation of how the *CBS Evening News* is produced under Couric's tenure marks it as obviously descended from Cronkite. At a sort of genetic level, the two are closely related, having the same fundamental building blocks in terms of how they go about making news. However, while the genetics of the *CBS Evening News* under Couric are relatively unchanged, the style has certainly altered. In terms of how the news is presented, the *CBS Evening News* now shares stylistic similarities to many of the emerging broadcast news alternatives that have come to prominence over the past few decades in an effort to replicate their success. In this period of increased competition, media fragmentation, dwindling audiences and shrinking revenues, that – to borrow the old signoff – is the way it is.[85]

---

[85] See Peters and Broersma, *Rethinking Journalism*, especially Broersma and Peters 'Introduction: Rethinking Journalism'.

1. Opening Moments of the CBS Evening News in 1979.[86]

---

[86] My appreciation to CBS for granting permission to use the screen captures which appear in this paper.

2. A Report on Hostage Taking in Iran, 1979, and its 2007 Iraqi Equivalent.

3. Common Stories, Common Images: Discussion on Fuel Prices and Auto Layoffs from 1979 and 2007.

4. New, Longer Opening of CBS Evening News in 2007.

TIME TO GET SERIOUS?

PROCESS NEWS AND BRITISH POLITICS

Daniel Jackson

The proposition that the news media increasingly report about the 'process' of politics over the 'issues' has gathered general acceptance amongst the political class and academic observers. Thomas Patterson documented 'a quiet revolution' in American political journalism in the past 40 years, whereby there was a fundamental shift from issue-based stories to process-based ones.[1] Frank Esser et al. outline three stages of this development, which have also been witnessed in other Western democracies such as the UK.[2] In the period of *issue* orientation that prevailed until the early 1970s, the news was primarily concerned with the key issues each candidate/party stood for and what their victory would mean for the average voter. Since then, in the *strategic* stage, focus shifted towards how parties/candidates ran their campaigns and how this might affect their electoral prospects. Since the early 1990s, political journalism has added a *meta* level to its coverage, whereby it examines how politicians and their handlers are utilising the media for their own ends, as well as reflecting on its own involvement in the political process.

For the past four UK general elections, the Electoral Commission has commissioned a comprehensive content analysis of election news coverage wherein the main themes of news are classified, with process news being one such theme. These studies define process news as: 'campaigning strategies, opinion polls/horse race news, passing references to the chosen daily topic agendas of political parties, political tensions and infighting within parties, party spin/PR/news management, and other themes'.[3] Most observers of campaign news and its critiques will be familiar with these terms, though various other concepts are included in this definition. For example, process news captures the tendency for the news media to focus on *political*

---

[1] Patterson, T.E., *Out of Order* (New York, 1993).

[2] Esser, F., Reinemann, C. and Fan, D., 'Spin Doctors in the United States, Great Britain, and Germany: Metacommunication about Media Manipulation', *Harvard International Journal of Press/ Politics* 6 (2001), no. 1, pp.16-45.

[3] Deacon, D. et al., *Reporting the 2005 UK General Election* (London, 2005).

strategy and its emphasis on winning and losing, campaign tactics and personal battles in the political arena.[4] Process news also encapsulates aspects of *metacoverage*, where journalists turn the spotlight inward and report on themselves, and the communication–related publicity efforts aimed at them, as integral parts of their stories.[5] Whilst its roots lie in analyses of election news, elements of process news also apply to everyday politics outside of election periods.[6]

Evidence from the Electoral Commission studies shows how the amount of process news during UK elections now regularly accounts for around half of overall coverage, with a peak of 70 percent recorded at the 2010 election, leading Ivor Gaber to describe it as a 'policy-free environment'.[7] Longitudinal studies from UK elections are scarce, but content analyses of general elections dating back to the early 1970s suggest that process news used to be far less prominent, typically accounting for around 20-30 percent of election campaign news.[8]

The rise of process news therefore represents one of the most profound shifts in journalistic style in recent decades. With the intense scrutiny supplied by the concerns over the decline in political engagement in recent

---

[4] Cappella, J.N. and Jamieson, K.H., *Spiral of Cynicism: The Press and the Public Good* (New York, 1997).

[5] See Esser, F. and Spanier, B., 'News Management as News: How Media Politics Leads to Metacoverage', *Journal of Political Marketing* 4 (2005), no.4, pp. 27-58.

[6] Esser, F. 'Metacoverage of Mediated Wars: How the Press Framed the Role of the News Media and of Military News Management in the Iraq Wars of 1991 and 2003', *American Behavioral Scientist* 52 (2009), no. 5, pp. 709-734; Jackson, D., 'Strategic News Frames and Public Policy Debates: Press and Television News Coverage of the Euro in the UK', *Communications* 36 (2011), no. 2, pp. 169-194; Skorkjaer Binderkrantz, A. and Green-Pedersen, C., 'Policy or Processes in Focus?', *The Harvard International Journal of Press/ Politics* 14 (2009), pp. 166-185.

[7] See Deacon, D., Golding, P. and Billig, M., 'Press and Broadcasting: "Real Issues" and Real Coverage', in: Norris, P., ed, *Britain Votes 2001* (Oxford, 2001), pp. 103-114; Deacon et al., *Reporting the 2005 UK General Election*; Wring, D. and Deacon, D., 'Patterns of Press Partisanship in the 2010 General Election', *British Politics* 5 (2010), no. 4, pp. 436–454; Wring, D., 'The Media and the Election', in: Geddes, A. and Tonge, J., eds, *Labour's Landslide: The British General Election 1997* (Manchester, 1997), pp. 70-83; Gaber, I., 'Election 2010: a Policy-Free Environment', *Presented at the IPSA/ MPG Joint International Conference on Political Communication, Loughborough University* (November, 2010).

[8] See Harrop, M., 'Press', in: Butler, D. and Kavanagh, D., eds., *The British General Election of 1983* (London, 1984), pp.; Semetko, H.A. et al., *The Formation of Campaign Agendas* (Hillsdale, NJ, 1991); Seymour-Ure, C., 'The Press', in: Butler, D. and Kavanagh, D., eds, *The British General of February 1974* (London, 1974); Seymour-Ure, C., 'Fleet Street', in: Butler, D. and Pinto-Duschinsky, M., eds, *The British General Election of 1970* (London, 1971).

years, many have offered these changes in journalistic style as a causal explanation. In this chapter I will take up some of these normative questions. I will firstly document the driving forces behind process news, and then examine the democratic implications of its rise. Whilst there is no shortage of debate on aspects of process news, it is often polarized and not evidence-based. I argue that there are many dimensions to debates on process news: while many critiques of process news underestimate its value in demystifying aspects of political reality that were once invisible, we should also be concerned about the amount of process news and the tendency for it to be framed cynically. In the final section I explore what practical steps could be made to rectify some of the problems associated with process news, in order to create an environment in which citizenship might thrive.

The Changing Environment of Political Newsmaking and its Consequences

There are many reasons for the striking rise in process news. Firstly, there are a number of well-documented cultural developments that have impacted on political journalism in particular.[9] In the United States, some scholars have identified the fall-out from Vietnam and Watergate as important milestones in the transformation of the culture of political journalism.[10] In Britain, even without the seismic moment of Watergate, the same changes in the 'media-politics nexus' took place.[11] These events had the effect of redefining the deference that journalists had towards politicians, as they came to realize that they had, for too long, been complicit in the government information agenda. Whilst the daily news agenda remained largely determined by the actions of politicians, the congeniality and fraternity between journalists and politicians was supplemented by greater hostility and distrust. Journalists felt emboldened to draw attention to the rivalries and backstage elements of politics, often with a cynical slant. In fact, Patterson believes that for many reporters, conflict and controversy are now actually seen as the real issues of politics, and so this explains their obsession with it:

---

[9] See Swanson, D., 'Political Communication Research and the Mutations of Democracy', in: Gudykunst, W.B., ed, *Communications Yearbook 24* (Thousand Oaks, 2001).

[10] Patterson, *Out of Order*; Sabato, L.J., *Feeding Frenzy: How Attack Journalism has Transformed American Politics* (New York, 1993).

[11] Schlesinger, P., 'Is There a Crisis in British Journalism?', *Media, Culture & Society* 28 (2006), no. 2, pp. 343-351.

The press deals with charge and countercharge, rarely digging into the details of political positions or social conditions underlying policy problems. It is not simply that the press neglects issues in favor of the strategic game: issues, even when covered, are subordinated to the drama of conflict generated by the opposing sides.[12]

In the past 30 years we have witnessed the ongoing 'mediatization' of politics, whereby politics is increasingly carried out through the media, as that is where it is 'located'.[13] For politicians, mediatization is a thorny matter, as it gives them opportunities to communicate with voters, but not always on their own terms, creating a tension with their own 'political logic'.[14] As a large body of literature has documented, party communications across the world have undergone a process of professionalization in order to control or at least manage the demands of the media.[15] This in turn has had major implications for the relationship between politicians and journalists. The relentless and at times aggressive promotion of political messages by party and government spin doctors places great strains on the autonomy of journalists.[16] Process news is one of the strategies they have developed to counter this, as it draws specific attention to attempts to influence the presentation of politics through news management. John Zaller draws upon the concept of professionalism to explain this process. He concludes that journalists would cease to be professionals if they were forced into the role of newsreaders or mere conduits for politicians.[17] So whilst politicians are still very successful at setting the news agenda, in order to retain a sense of professional self-esteem, reporters therefore want to add something to the news, by being a professional that not only reports but also selects, frames, comments upon, investigates, interprets and regulates the flow of political communication. In their view, 'what journalists add should be, in their ideal, as arresting and manifestly important as possible – if possible, the most

---

[12] Patterson, T.E., 'The News Media: An Effective Political Actor?', *Political Communication* 14 (1997), p. 450.

[13] Mazzoleni, G. and Schultz, W., '"Mediatization" of Politics: A Challenge for Democracy?', *Political Communication* 16 (1999), no. 3, pp. 247-261.

[14] Brants, K. and Van Praag, P., 'Signs of Media Logic: Half a Century of Political Communication in the Netherlands', *Javnost—the Public* 13 (2006), pp. 25–40; Strömbäck, J., 'Four Phases of Mediatization: An Analysis of the Mediatization of Politics', *The International Journal of Press/Politics* 13 (2008), no. 3, pp. 228-246.

[15] See Lilleker, D. G., Negrine, R. and Stanyer, J., 'A Vicious Circle: Politicians and Journalists in Britain's Media Democracy', *Political Studies Review* (2002).

[16] Blumler. J.G., 'Origins of the Crisis of Communication for Citizenship', *Political Communication* 14 (1997), pp. 395-404.

[17] Zaller, J., *A Theory of Media Politics: How the Interests of Politicians, Journalists, and Citizens Shape the News*, unpublished manuscript (1999).

important aspect of each news report, so as to call attention to journalists and the importance of their work'.[18]

Mediatization also – quite legitimately – gives the news media license to report on itself, as it no longer solely looks upon politics from the outside, but is a political institution of considerable power.[19] Process news, or more specifically metacoverage, is a logical outgrowth of this, and describes the inclination of reporters to turn the spotlight inward and treat themselves as actors, even autonomous sources, in their own stories. Other times it might include 'self reverential' discussions of the media's own impact on an election campaign, or a politician's appearance on one medium (e.g. television) being the subject of a story on another (e.g. press).[20] Such reporting has been facilitated by the growth of specialist media pages in the press, themselves a reflection of the media's central role in contemporary culture and politics. Similarly, the internet has facilitated metacoverage, as the mainstream news media pick up on trending topics on Twitter, for example, or commission navel-gazing features on the impact of new media on politics.

Structural Changes

In the last 20-30 years, the news media environment has changed dramatically. This has been driven by technological developments: satellite, cable and latterly digital signals have opened the door for new television channels to be launched without great costs, including 24-hour news channels; likewise in the newspaper sector, falling printing costs have been one reason for greater pagination and the launch of freesheets; technology also provided an entirely new platform for media expansion with the internet. Alongside technology, governments have allowed a liberalization of media markets, thus ending the days of spectrum scarcity and enabling a more commercially based media system. These developments transformed the information environment, seeing an explosion in the number of news outlets, and subsequent fragmentation of news audiences.[21]

---

[18] *Ibidem.*, p. 24.
[19] Esser, F., Reinemann, C. and Fan, D., 'Spin Doctors in the United States'.
[20] Johnson, T. J. and Boudreau, T., 'Turning the Spotlight Inward: How Leading News Organizations Covered the Media in the 1992 Presidential Election', *Journalism and Mass Communication Quarterly* 73 (1996), no. 3, pp. 657-671.
[21] Norris, P., *A Virtuous Circle: Political Communication in Post- Industrial Democracies* (Oxford, 2000); Swanson, D., 'Political Communication Research and the Mutations of Democracy', in: Gudykunst, W.B., ed, *Communications Yearbook 24* (Thousand Oaks, 2001).

The dramatic changes in the media environment have been mirrored by important cultural changes in their audience. In particular, we have seen the rise of a consumer culture, which is based around consumption and individuality.[22] News media audiences are thus increasingly behaving like consumers in the media market; given greater choice, they have responded by relinquishing their former loyalties, and increasingly obtain their news from a wider variety of sources.[23] Traditional news outlets such as evening television news broadcasts and newspapers have seen a decline in their audience figures, as more people migrate to alternative news sources offered by new media technologies.

One of the most important consequences of these forces has been the intensification of competition for audiences among news organizations. Journalism has traditionally been a competitive industry, typified by the kudos bequeathed to those who break an 'exclusive' story ahead of their rivals. What has accelerated in the last 20-30 years is the greater exposure of news *organizations* to commercial pressures. As news media output burgeons, so the finite advertising spend is spread more thinly, thus impacting upon overall profitability and as a consequence the budgets that can be allocated to newsgathering.[24] Within the newsroom, a major study by Justin Lewis et al. revealed a number of significant patterns underpinned by the political economy of contemporary news.[25] Firstly, as news organizations diversify into multimedia operations more news space is required to fill, but on the whole more journalists are *not* being hired to fill it. Instead, staff journalists are asked to be more productive, with their sample of journalists producing an average of 4.5 stories per day, and more than two-thirds of those surveyed (30 out of 42) believing that journalists were filing more stories each shift than they were a decade ago.[26]

These pressures place even greater emphasis on news values, and hence for owners and editors concerned with the bottom-line, process news is cheap, quick, and in their view attracts larger audiences than news focused on the substance of policies and politics. For time-pressed journalists, it is

---

[22] Bauman, Z., *The Individualized Society* (Oxford, 2001); Firat, A. and Dholakia, N., *Consuming People: From Political Economy to Theatres of Consumption* (London, 1998).

[23] See Dahlgren, P., 'Media, Citizenship and Civic Culture', in: Curran, J. and Gurevitch, M., eds, *Mass Media and Society* (London, 2000).

[24] Gavin, N.T., *Press and Television in British Politics* (Basingstoke, 2007).

[25] Lewis, J., Williams, A. and Franklin, B., 'Four Rumours and an Explanation', *Journalism Practice* 2 (2008), no. 1, pp. 27–45.

[26] Although it should be noted that the press agency journalists contacted appeared to be producing approximately twice as many stories as their counterparts working on national newspapers.

easier to put a new twist on the day's news by focusing on the game of politics than by researching issues of policy.[27] Process news fits many news values that are important to the selection and presentation of the news, such as 'human interest', 'conflict' and 'controversy'.[28] It is also perpetually new: there will always be another twist, maneuver, or stumble in the game of politics.[29]

Timothy Cook has argued that many 'daily news stories are episodes of larger continuing sagas … Simply put, for news to be produced routinely, journalists must be able to visualize events as part of a larger, broader storyline and must move the plot along from one episode to the next'.[30] These sagas are often said to have a certain 'phase structure', and so the newsworthiness of events is determined by whether or not they move the saga to the 'next' step.[31] When it comes to elections, reporters often treat them as if they fit into a 'master narrative', whereby the election day is the finishing line, and everything that happens during an election campaign is significant only for its relevance towards a candidate's or party's chances of crossing that line.[32] Process news provides the perfect framework for journalists to interpret the election 'master narrative' of the 'race' for the line whereas policy coverage fits much less comfortably. The same can be said of non-election periods.[33] UN resolution votes, public inquiries, or even the saga of the splits in the UK coalition government all share a 'phase structure', whereby journalists can relate the day's news to its likely implications for the ongoing saga through process news.[34]

---

[27] Patterson, 'The News Media'; Fallows, J., *Breaking the News: How the Media Undermine American Democracy* (New York, 1996); Kuhn, R., 'The Media and Politics', in: Dunleavy, P. et al., eds, *Developments in British Politics* 7 (Hampshire: 2003).

[28] McManus, M., *Market Driven Journalism: Let the Citizen Beware?* (London, 1994); Price, V. and Tewksbury, D., 'News Values and Public Opinion: A Theoretical Account of Media Priming and Framing', in: Barnett, G. and Boster, F.J., eds, *Progress in Communication Science* (Greenwich, CT, 1997), pp.173-212.

[29] Patterson, *Out of Order.*

[30] Lawrence, R., 'Game Framing the Issues: Tracking the Strategy Frame in Public Policy News', *Political Communication* 17 (2000), p. 96.

[31] Fishman, M., *Manufacturing the News* (Austin, 1980); Cook, T.E., *Making Laws and Making News* (Washington, 1989), p. 47.

[32] Fallows, *Breaking the News*, pp. 170-173.

[33] See Jackson, 'Strategic News Frames and Public Policy Debates'.

[34] Fishman, *Manufacturing the News.*

The 'Problem' of Process News

This takes us to some of the democratic implications of process news. The list of charges held up against process news (including its close relatives, self-coverage, metacoverage and strategic frames) is serious. Firstly, there is a complaint that process news is largely trivial. Its replacement of substantial and weighty news has stifled learning about political issues, and the ability of audiences to engage with political life has been compromised. For Lance Bennett the result of a media concerned with the spectacle of news is that it can disconnect its audience from the power to participate actively in political life.[35] They are 'passive receivers, no longer active participants, in the dialogue of democracy' and the ability to understand policy issues, generate opinions, and hold politicians to account is thus lost.[36]

This can then result in or aggravate a second problem: disenchantment and cynicism towards the political process. Many aspects of what constitutes process news are 'inherently cynical' according to Kerbel, Apee and Ross: politics is presented as a game played by ruthless, Machiavellian, power-hungry politicians.[37] As Fallows explains: 'By choosing to present public life as a contest between scheming political leaders, all of whom the public should view with suspicion, the mass media helps bring about that very result'.[38]

Such a sweeping critique is tempting to subscribe to, and regularly is by both media critics and politicians keen to move the focus towards 'real issues'. But it is underpinned by a number of assumptions, some of which are sustainable and others that are flawed. These will be explored in the following sections.

It is Becoming Harder to Sustain the Normative Distinction between 'Issues' and 'Process'.

Dichotomies can be appealing and convenient, but sometimes mask a more complex truth. Whilst the rise in process news is quite clear and unambiguous, its status as a 'non-issue' is less so. Firstly, the UK represents a postmodern political culture where the distinction between the 'political' and

---

[35] Bennett, W.L., *The Governing Crisis* (New York, 1992).
[36] Franklin, B., *Packaging Politics: Political Communications in Britain's Media Democracy* (London, 2004), p. 14.
[37] Kerbel, M.R., Apee, S. and Ross, M.H., 'PBS ain't so Different: Public Broadcasting, Election Frames, and Democratic Empowerment', *The Harvard International Journal of Press/Politics* 5 (2000), no. 8, pp. 8-32.
[38] Fallows, *Breaking the* News, p. 7.

entertainment is increasingly blurred.[39] The private lives of politicians, their personality traits, looks, dress sense, personal rivalries and presentational performance have all become more important in our increasingly emotionalized public sphere.[40] In the context of the 2010 UK General election, Ipsos Mori found that voters ranked the image of the leaders as important as their policies in deciding how to vote.[41] This was the first time leaders were ranked as high as policies since they first asked this question in 1987. Of course, this cultural shift towards image and personality may be partly a *result* of media coverage, but it would seem unfair to dismiss all process news as trivial in this context.

Secondly, the extensive use of sophisticated communications methods by governments and political parties is an issue of democratic concern, and so worthy of reportage. Ten years ago, a UK government special advisor's internal announcement that 9/11 was 'a good day to bury bad news' seemed to encapsulate a government obsessed by 'spin', and accompanied a wider critique of a 'symbolic state' in which the *perception* of policy delivery was more important than actual delivery.[42] The subsequent 'demystification' of spin offered by journalists was both a rational response to a changing environment, and the raising of an issue of public interest which represents a progressive evolution in our political culture towards one of greater transparency and scrutiny.[43] Whilst coverage of news management and political PR is process news, it is not necessarily a 'non-issue'.

Who Says you Cannot Learn from Process News?

Alternative forms of journalism such as blogs, breakfast news, panel and debate shows, and even satirical news shows such as *The Daily Show* or *10 O'clock Live* are gaining increasing acceptance as a legitimate part of the informational diet of citizens.[44] Whilst process news does not represent an

---

[39] Street, J., *Mass Media, Politics and Democracy* (London, 2001).

[40] Richards, B., *Emotional Governance: Politics, Media and Terror* (Basingstoke, 2007).

[41] Ipsos-MORI., 'The Political Triangle 1987-2010', *Ipsos*, available from: http://www.ipsos-mori.com/researchpublications (2010).

[42] O'Shaughnessy, N., 'The Symbolic State: a British Experience', *Journal of Public Affairs* 3 (2003), no. 4, pp. 297-312.

[43] McNair, B., *Cultural Chaos: Journalism, News and Power in a Globalised World* (London, 2006).

[44] See Atton, C. and Hamilton, J., *Alternative Journalism* (London, 2008); Jones J., *Entertaining Politics* (New York, 2005); Peters, C., 'Emotion Aside or Emotional Side?: Crafting an 'Experience of Involvement in the News', *Journalism: Theory, Practice and Criticism* 12 (2011), no. 3, pp. 297-316.

alternative form of journalism, it can give citizens a more rounded picture of political reality than information on policies alone. Brian McNair cautiously welcomes process news as 'the emergence of a demystificatory, potentially empowering commentary on the nature of the political process; an ongoing deconstruction of the relationship between journalism and the powerful which adds to, rather than detracts from, the stock of useful information available to the average citizen'.[45] Of course, this rests on the assumptions that: a) citizens are likely to be able to easily access coverage of policies as well as process and b) most process news is presented in an empowering way. These two issues will be taken up later.

The Problematic Role of Politicians in Process News

As mentioned earlier, as both campaigning and governing have become increasingly media-centered, so politicians must accommodate the 'media logic' and standards of newsworthiness, which privilege the visual; dramatic, conflict or scandal-based; human interest; and episodic (as opposed to thematic).[46] Thus whilst politicians may complain of the media obsession with process over issues (for e.g. see Tony Blair's final speech as Prime Minister, 2007), they have often been complicit in its rise to prominence. However, it is interesting to note that academic studies of process news invariably take a media-centric perspective, thus placing the blame for its deleterious consequences on the news media. There are serious limitations to this.

Conflict – including attack and counter attack – is a deeply embedded part of the UK's political culture and is theatrically performed weekly during Prime Minister's Questions. Politicians regularly accuse each other of spin and deception; and will emphasize the divisions in their opponents' ranks for their own political gain. The 'soap opera' of Tony Blair and Gordon Brown's relationship during the last Labour government was an obsession of the media, but news was littered with quotes from opposition politi-

---

[45] McNair, B., *Cultural Chaos: Journalism, News and Power in a Globalised World* (London, 2006), pp. 171-172.

[46] Esser and Spanier, 'News Management as News'; Strömbäck, J., 'Four Phases of Mediatization'; Bucy, E. P. and Grabe, M. E., 'Taking Television Seriously: A Sound and Image Bite Analysis of Presidential Campaign Coverage, 1992-2004', *Journal of Communication* 57 (2007), pp. 652-675; De Vreese, C.H., *Framing Europe: Television News and European Integration* (Amsterdam, 2005); Sabato, L.J., *Feeding Frenzy: How Attack Journalism has Transformed American Politics* (New York, 1993); Strömbäck, J. and Kaid, L.L., eds., *The Handbook of Election News Coverage around the World* (New York, 2008); Iyengar, S., *Is Anyone Responsible? How Television Frames Political Issues* (Chicago, 1991).

cians who were keen to stoke the fire of a story that undermined their rivals.[47] Similarly, the news media are often castigated for employing the language of the 'horse race', war and games in their election coverage but this is also the language that politicians use to both internal and external audiences.[48] For example, in his 'State of the race – memo 4' to Labour party members during the 2010 General Election, Peter Mandelson said:

> We are the underdogs in this fight – always have been. But, with as much as a third of the electorate still undecided, this election remains wide open. The polls are so volatile because people remain in a state of genuine flux. So it is time to up the tempo and fight every inch of the way.[49]

Studies that have examined the agendas of political parties in elections reveal a sharp rise in the focus on political process. For the 1983 election, Holli Semetko et al. found that parties placed a great deal of emphasis on 'substantive issues' (measured through press releases), with a minimum of 60 percent and a maximum of 80 percent of their press releases primarily focused on policies.[50] In 1997, an analysis of party PEBs and press releases found this figure to be 75 percent.[51] By 2005, Gaber reported that in their press releases the parties had made election strategy and tactics their single biggest issue, with Labour and the Conservatives devoting around 47 percent of their announcements to either attacking their opponents, or urging voters to get out and vote or not vote for their opponents, a trend that accelerated in the 2010 election.[52] By feeding the media stories of conflict, splits and spin, politicians can be seen as active agents in the rise of process news.

The 'Negative' Effects of Process News can be Questioned

Part of the critique of process news is rooted in the media malaise thesis that places the media at the center of the process of voter disengagement and cynicism. This is hotly disputed in the political communication literature. Often based on large-scale survey evidence, a major finding of the 'media mobilization' literature is the more a citizen consumes news media, the more likely they are to be politically knowledgeable and engaged, which in turn motivates them to seek out more political information, akin to a 'vir-

---

[47] Jackson, 'Strategic News Frames and Public Policy Debates'.
[48] See Jamieson, K.H., *Dirty Politics* (Oxford, 1992).
[49] Internal memo sent to Labour Party members, 25 April 2010.
[50] Semetko, *The Formation of Campaign Agendas*.
[51] Norris, P. et al., *On Message: Communicating the Campaign* (London, 1999).
[52] Gaber, I., '"Dislocated and Distracted": Media, Parties and the Voters in the 2005 General Election Campaign', *British Politics* 1 (2006), no. 3, pp. 344–366.

tuous circle'.[53] Critics of process news would not dispute this, but instead contend that it still does not discount the possibility of a 'spiral of cynicism' for those who consume the least news, or certain types of news. Indeed, Norris' own data showed that those who consumed the least news on the European elections were less likely to believe they could trust Brussels bureaucrats and MEPs, and this pattern was likely to be self-reinforcing – so people who know least about the EU and have minimal trust, will probably pay little attention to news about EU, on rational grounds.[54] The virtuous circle and spiral of cynicism theories are therefore arguably more compatible than many would believe. For those who are interested in politics, there is a mutually reinforcing cycle of news consumption and political engagement. But this can work the opposite way for the disengaged: because people lack interest and feel detached from politics, they are less likely to consume political news, which again reinforces their detachment from politics.

The spiral of cynicism thesis posits that strategically framed news (emphasizing the tactics employed by politicians in pursuing policy/electoral goals, as well as their performance, styles of campaigning, and personal battles in the political arena) can activate cynicism towards the politicians involved, as well as the wider political process.[55] Meanwhile, issue-based news has been found to potentially reverse the spiral of cynicism for young voters.[56] Empirical support for the thesis has been found in a number of contexts, though levels of political engagement and sophistication have been often found to moderate the effects of such frames.[57] When metacoverage (news about the press' own role in political affairs, and attempts by politicians to gain publicity) is framed strategically, similar results have been found.[58] The effects of this news should be cause for concern, but

---

[53] Norris, *A Virtuous Circle*; Newton, K., 'Politics and the News Media: Mobilisation or Videomalaise?', in: Jowell, R., et al., eds, *British Social Attitudes: The 14th Report* (Aldershot, 1997), pp. 151-163.
[54] Norris, *A Virtuous Circle*, p. 250.
[55] See Cappella and Jamieson, *Spiral of Cynicism*.
[56] Adriaansen, M. L., van Praag, P. and De Vreese, C. H., 'Substance Matters: How News Content can Reduce Political Cynicism', *International Journal of Public Opinion Research* 22 (2010), no. 4, pp. 433-457.
[57] De Vreese, C.H., *Framing Europe: Television News and European Integration* (Amsterdam, 2005); Jackson, D., 'Strategic Media, Cynical Public?'; Valentino, N.A., Beckmann, M.N. and Buhr, T.A., 'A Spiral of Cynicism for Some: The Contingent Effects of Campaign News Frames on Participation and Confidence in Government', *Political Communication* 18 (2001), pp. 347-367.
[58] D'Angelo, P. and Lombard, M., 'The Power of the Press: The Effects of Press Frames in Political Campaign News on Media Perceptions', *Atlantic Journal of Communication* 16 (2008), no. 1, pp. 1-32; De Vreese, C.H. and Elenbaas, M., 'Media in the Game of Politics: Effects of Strategic Metacoverage on Political Cyni-

whilst the link between strategic frames and voter cynicism is well established, the relationship between cynicism and political engagement is less
so, meaning it is possible that under some circumstances, voters can be both
'cynical and engaged'.[59] Nevertheless, it would be misguided to dismiss the
concerns raised by the effects of strategically framed process news given
the balance of evidence garnered to date.

Perhaps Citizens Prefer Process News to Policy

It might be fair to assume that because strategically framed process news
activates cynicism in some individuals, they will be less favorable to this
type of news presentation. This is based on Joseph Cappella and Kathleen
Jamieson's evidence that the spiral of cynicism can spread from cynicism
about those politicians portrayed as Machiavellian in news reports, to cynicism towards the media as the messenger.[60] On the other hand, process
news is partly a result of market pressures, which demand that news be presented in a format that has significant entertainment and interest value, even
at the expense of civic or educational value.[61] The assumption here being
that the uncertainty and suspense associated with the depiction of politicians
as strategic players, plus the focus on personality-related stories, are more
likely to catch and hold the audience's attention than more substantive aspects of the election or issue.

    It seems previous research has provided evidence for both propositions.
In the US, public opinion surveys have shown that citizens are not happy
about campaign formats that inject cynical views of the political process.[62]
Calls for more 'substantive' reporting of politics by Thomas Patterson and
Bob Franklin contain the implicit assumption that the public would be hap-
pier if campaigns provided more and 'better' information (with a greater

---

cism', *Harvard International Journal of Press/ Politics* 13 (2008), no. 3, pp.285-
309.
[59] De Vreese, C.H. and Semetko, H.A., 'Cynical and Engaged: Strategic Campaign
Coverage, Public Opinion and Mobilisation in a Referendum', *Communication Research* 29 (2006), no. 6, pp. 615-641.
[60] Cappella and Jamieson, *Spiral of Cynicism*.
[61] Hahn, K., Iyengar, S. and Norpoth, H., 'Consumer Demand for Election News:
The Horserace Sells', *Presented at the Annual Meeting of the American Political
Science Association* (Boston, 2002).
[62] Just, M., 'Talk is Cheap: Thoughts on Improving Voter Information in Light of
the 1992 Campaign', *Harvard International Journal of Press/Politics* 1 (1996), pp.
152-160; Lichter, R., 'Was TV Election News Better This Time: A Content Analysis
of 1988 and 1992 Campaign Coverage', *Journal of Political Science* 21 (1993), pp.
3-25.

commitment to explaining issues as opposed to dramatizing them).[63] This
view was challenged by John Hibbing and Elizabeth Theiss-Morse, who
found that while citizens indeed dislike campaigns, they do not necessarily
desire more deliberation around the issues.[64] Instead, they want simple cues
so they can size up candidates with minimal effort. If anything, election
coverage should therefore be less demanding (i.e. substantive and issue-
focused). Barry Lipsitz et al. place themselves somewhere in between the
'deliberative' and 'undemanding' perspectives. They found attitudes to
campaigns vary considerably based on various attitudinal and demographic
factors. Most importantly, politically involved citizens desire more 'substantive' campaigns, whereas the less involved are more open to process
news.[65]

As with the US studies, most evidence of audience evaluations of the
news in the UK is based on a campaign context. Recent election opinion
surveys asking the public to rate the media's performance have found them
to be generally happy with the amount of news, but more critical of its content. In 2001 and 2005 for example, the majority thought coverage should
be less leader focused and more policy and local candidate focused.[66] Other
evidence suggests that a substantial part of the population feel short of information during elections, though it does not explicitly say this is a result
of a media focus on process over issues.[67] Qualitative reports about young
people and politics offer some more useful evidence towards this debate.
Clarissa White et al., for example, found them to view media coverage of
politics as too often framed around party squabbles in Parliament, which
reinforced their view of it as 'boring'.[68] The young also appear to have
picked up on media cynicism. Their message to the media was 'Make politics interesting and exciting for us – relate it to our lives but don't trivialize
it with stories about politicians' private lives or political in-fighting – we're
not interested'.[69] The handful of studies that have examined audience evalu-

---

[63] Franklin, *Packaging Politics*; Patterson, *Out of Order*.

[64] Hibbing, J. and Theiss-Morse, E., *Stealth Democracy: Americans' Beliefs about
how Government Should Work* (Cambridge, 2002).

[65] Lipsitz, K. et al., 'What Voters Want from Political Campaign Communication',
Political Communication 20 (2005), pp. 337-354.

[66] Ofcom., '*Viewers and Voters: Attitudes to Television Coverage of the 2005 General* Election', available from:
http://www.ofcom.org.uk/research/tv/reports/election/ (2005); Worcester, R. and
Mortimore. R., *Explaining Labour's Second Landslide* (London, 2002).

[67] E.g. Worcester and Mortimore, *Explaining Labour's Second Landslide*.

[68] White, C., Bruce, S. and Ritchie, J., Young People's Politics: Political Interest and
Engagement Amongst 14 to 24-year –olds (London, 2000).

[69] Children and Young People's Unit., *Young People and Politics: A Report on the
Yvote?/ Ynot? Project* (London, 2002).

ations of strategically-framed process news versus issue-based news have found (perhaps unsurprisingly) that citizens have both a greater sense of learning from issue-based news, as well as placing a higher value on its informational content.[70]

Despite some of the contradictions, all of this research supports the idea of an electorate who are critical of the media's current coverage of political affairs. This is set against a backdrop of declining levels of trust in news organizations, particularly newspapers.[71] Importantly, what the evidence does tell us is that we should challenge part of the logic behind why process news is so commonly used in everyday political journalism: the belief that it holds more news value and therefore appeals to audiences. Whilst there is unquestionably some audience demand for process news, including 'political junkies' (like your author) who want to know about both the substance of political issues and the 'politics' of them, the evidence does not support a demand for the amount of process news that we regularly see in UK news, especially in recent elections.

Coming to Terms with Process News

Whilst defending the importance of process news in a diet of news consumption, alongside its empowering and demystifying potential; and recognizing the active role politicians play in the cycle of political gossip, speculation and tactical maneuverings; there are two main conditions this defense rests upon. The first is the balance of issue-based versus process news that the average citizen is likely to encounter. The second condition is the framing of process news in cynical or edifying terms. There is reason for concern about both of these.

It is the Sheer Amount of Process News

John Zaller rightly argues that many media critics expect an unrealistic standard of journalism, and questions whether most citizens would be willing or capable enough to fully process what he calls the 'full news stand-

---

[70] D'Angelo and Lombard, 'The Power of the Press'; Jackson, D., 'Framing Democratic Politics: An Investigation into the Presence and Effects of 'Strategy' News Frames in the UK', *PhD thesis, Bournemouth University* (2009); Pinkleton, B.E. and Austin, E.W., 'Exploring Relationships among Media Use Frequency, Perceived Media Importance, and Media Satisfaction in Political Disaffection and Efficacy', *Mass Communication and Society*, 5 (2002), pp. 113-140.

[71] See Hargreaves, I. and Thomas, J., 'New News, Old News', *ITC/BSC Report*, available from: http://www.itc.org.uk/itc_publications/audience_research/index.asp (2002); Schlesinger, P., 'Is There a Crisis in British Journalism?', pp. 343-351.

ard'.[72] But whilst accepting the case for 'multidimensional public spheres' to suit the needs of different sections of the public, the weight of evidence from existing content analyses suggests that most citizens are likely to find it increasingly hard to learn about policy issues.[73] During elections, when the focus on process news intensifies, typically between 50-80 percent of stories focus primarily on political process.[74] Whilst there are not the same number of campaign set-piece events or opinion polls to write about in-between elections – and therefore less process news – it is clear that it penetrates into the governing process as well.

But beyond the sheer amount of process news lie deeper concerns for the average citizen. In the context of EU news, Jackson found that process news is disproportionately prominent: a) in the news media that is consumed by the most people, namely TV news and tabloid newspapers; and b) at the top of the news agenda, so that readers/viewers would normally have to get beyond the main news stories before encountering issue-based news.[75] Studies have also found how the ebb and flow of news during non-election policy debates privileges process news over policy issues at key times. In the context of various debates in the US and UK, when the policy decision was being discussed and decided both behind closed doors and in the public sphere, the news more commonly offered strategic angles. Once the decision had been announced, the news placed greater emphasis on the policy issues.[76] It is arguably very reasonable for journalists to focus more on the political game when policy is being debated, and that when decided, attention might then turn to its implementation and possible consequences for ordinary citizens. But this phase structure can crowd-out or delay substantive coverage of those issues. For citizens, it means that at precisely the time when public opinion is most likely to be formulated, mobilized, and listened to by politicians, they are given news that encourages them to think about political strategies, party prospects and media management (often

---

[72] Zaller, J., 'A New Standard of News Quality: Burglar Alarms for the Monitorial Citizen', *Political Communication* 20 (2003), no. 1, pp. 109-130.
[73] Temple, M., 'Dumbing Down is Good for you', *British Politics* 1 (2006), pp. 257-273.
[74] See Benoit, W. L., Stein, K. A. and Hansen, G. J., 'New York Times Coverage of Presidential Campaigns', *Journalism and Mass Communication Quarterly* 82 (2005), pp. 356-376; Project for Excellence in Journalism, 'The Last Lap: How the Press Covered the Final Stages of the Campaign', available from: http://www.journalism.org/node/309 (2002); Project for Excellence in Journalism, 'The Debate Effect: How the Press Covered the Pivotal Period of the 2004 Presidential Campaign', available from: http://www.journalism.org/node/163 (2004); Patterson, *Out of Order*.
[75] Jackson, 'Strategic News Frames and Public Policy Debates'.
[76] *Ibidem*; Lawrence, R., 'Game Framing the Issues', pp. 93-114.

framed with a cynical slant); rather than empowering them to be part of the policy debate by explaining what impact the policy may have on their own life.

So whilst process news *can* give citizens a more rounded picture of political reality, there is evidence that it has cut so deeply into issue-based coverage that many citizens are unlikely to receive a sufficient basis for making informed choices of their own.

The Question of Cynicism

Process news is not inherently cynical, and its focus on political motivations, political PR and presentation can be presented in an educational or empowering way. However, too often it is depicted in adversarial and cynical terms. Studies examining metacoverage (during elections) have found that such stories were mainly narrated with (cynical) strategy frames rather than (edifying) accountability frames.[77] Frank Esser et al. highlight the term 'spin doctor' as an example of this.[78] Journalists could not serve their public task without the information provided by PR officials, and as long as this information is presented in a reliable and ethical way then there is nothing inherently undemocratic about the PR function itself. But many news outlets use the term 'spin doctor' to indiscriminately demonize any kind of professional PR.

> The journalistic use of the term spin doctor occurs in a one-sided and problematic sense whenever it serves to discredit the legitimate interest of politicians, parties, and governments in asserting themselves against the autonomous and powerful journalism that pursues an agenda of its own and whose mechanisms and motives are not always exclusively oriented toward the public welfare.[79]

Findings from content analyses to date have therefore found that rather than presenting process news in a way that could empower 'a political public sphere in crisis', more often than not it takes the form of an adversarial battleground that does more to encourage public cynicism and distrust.

---

[77] Esser, Reinemann and Fan , 'Spin doctors in the United States, Great Britain, and Germany'; Esser and D'Angelo, 'Framing the Press and the Publicity Process'; Esser and D'Angelo, 'Framing the Press and Publicity Process in German, British, and U.S. General Elections: A Comparative Study of Metacoverage', *Harvard International Journal of Press/Politics* 11 (2006), no. 3, pp. 44-66.
[78] Esser, Reinemann and Fan, 'Spin doctors in the United States, Great Britain, and Germany'.
[79] *Ibidem*, pp. 39-40.

Retelling Journalism. Retelling Politics

In this chapter I have documented the rise of process news, explaining its appeal to journalists who find themselves in an increasingly fragmented and commercially exposed industry; and faced with a political class who put media strategy at the heart of their campaigning and governing activities. I have defended process news as a necessary element of political journalism due its empowering potential for citizens, and explored how politicians are complicit in its manifestation. However, as it stands, the sheer amount of process news and its cynical presentation means that it often represents an obstacle to democratic empowerment and engagement. The challenges facing political journalism are many: the commercial climate, the pressure to produce more copy for multiple news outlets, the decreasing willingness for politicians to go 'off message', the obstacles to 'truth' in the shape of political spin doctors, plus the difficulty of explaining complex issues to an audience with limited knowledge and interest – all potentially stand in the way of redirecting journalism towards political news that feels less need to present politics as a game played by power-hungry schemers.

Why worry about these challenges? The news media plays a central role in the health of a democracy, and have a duty to exercise this power responsibly. The choices made by journalists when covering politics can have significant implications for how audiences perceive politics, politicians, and indeed the news itself. Given the wider concerns about falling trust in the political class, public disengagement from mainstream politics, not to mention falling trust in and readership of newspapers, the media must bear some of the responsibility, and this may mean considering different ways of covering politics.

What practical steps might be made to meet these challenges and improve the quality of news that citizens receive? Or, to take the theme of the book, how can political journalism be retold? Firstly, they are not straightforward to meet, and in some cases require reciprocal movements from politicians. Secondly, the suggestions offered do not claim to offer anything especially original, given the amount of attention the media and politics nexus has received in recent years. Still, they are worth elucidating as they can help raise the pressure for change, as well as elaborate the positive consequences that change may achieve.

Process news is a product of the culture of journalism, and supported by its adherence to news values. Matthew Kerbel et al. have documented how political reporters are unaware that they are covering politics as a game and are unable to imagine how an election could be covered if not as a horse race. It is therefore important to recognize that *covering politics as a game is a choice, and there are other ways to characterize it, even during elec-*

tions. As they explain, the strategy frame may be particularly appealing for TV journalists during an election campaign because it can be partly driven by an adherence to a norm of objectivity, or 'principled detachment'.[80] For TV journalists, objectivity is a thorny matter, and with a wide range of information available, reporters must make decisions about what subjects and perspectives constitute dispassionate coverage. Having mutually accepted standards for what comprises appropriate election news reduces the risk of appearing biased, and therefore covering elections from the strategic perspective serves this end.[81] Journalists will often therefore try to maintain a healthy distance from accusations of bias by highlighting the daily conflicts in Westminster, addressing how parties are doing in the horse race of opinion polls, and discussing the strategies employed to outmaneuver opponents. This is safer than engaging in substantive issues like the implications of a proposed policy, because there may not be equal amounts of evidence to support both sides.

A senior BBC political correspondent explains this mindset well:

> Here we have our 'Punch and Judy rows'. They are easy to cover because they fall into that 'British-wish-to-have-two-sides'. They are neat because they are told briefly, only need two bits of actuality, and require very little explanation, because people are familiar with the ideas, and you don't need to explain too much.[82]

In this sense, the focus on strategy is probably as well explained by journalistic professional norms as much as an in-built cynical perspective of political affairs. But this is still not without its problems, because if the aim is to increase public understanding of a complex issue, then simply offering conflicting perspectives can be counterproductive, because complex debates are simplified into polarized positions, potentially creating more heat than light.[83] Furthermore, the way these 'Punch and Judy' rows are framed is often not as principled stands, but as cynical maneuvers in order to appeal to a voter segment or outflank opponents. The easiest decision for broadcasters is to continue to avoid engaging in the issues because of the potential accusations of bias associated with it. But reconnecting with their audience does not mean scrapping impartiality, but allowing more voices in.

---

[80] Kerbel, Apee and Ross, 'PBS Ain't So Different'.
[81] *Ibidem.*
[82] De Vreese, *Framing Europe.*
[83] See Bond, M., 'Insular by Default? How the BBC Presents Europe to the British Public', *European Movement Policy Paper 3*, available from: www.euromove.org.uk (2005).

This first suggestion is underpinned by a second, broader one for jour-nalists, which is *to place citizens rather than politicians at the center of their coverage*. This point has been elaborated by Lewis, whose argument is that the majority of news coverage tends to address audiences as passive spectators rather than empowered citizens.[84] Even if the economics of news production are driving process news, through news values, then he argues these should be challenged. After all, once interrogated, many news values serve neither a commercial nor public interest purpose:

> Their operational presence is justified by a tautology: it is news simply because it meets our definition of what news is – what Peter Dahlgren (1992) calls "the aura of the self-evident". Or as David Althiede bluntly puts it: "news is what-ever news people say it is" (1986, p. 17). Thus defined, it need serve no other purpose.[85]

Indeed, we may need to challenge part of the commercial news value basis on which process news is built. The idea that it is more appealing than is-sue-based news is only partially supported by the evidence to date, suggest-ing news organizations may be misunderstanding their audience somewhat. Instead, we might argue for a set of news values in which citizenship is foregrounded. In the case of elections for example, rather than conceiving the 'public interest' as no more than which candidate we find most likeable, and thus focusing on aspects of their media performance and electoral pro-spects, it might mean starting with the question of what difference it actual-ly makes to people's lives if one candidate wins rather than another. Then, according to Justin Lewis, a different type of contest might be encouraged in which what is at stake is less about the fortunes of one politician or an-other, and more about the way that we and others live.[86]

These suggestions do not mean journalists only engaging in worthy, dispassionate policy debates, but making the issues more relevant to peo-ple's lives. It also does not mean neglecting process news altogether, as its exposure of media management, personal rivalries, and the inside story of politics can have a public interest function. And it does not aim to create two kinds of news – one for the well informed, and one for the rest – but instead aims to re-conceive news by focusing on what it is useful for people to know.

---

[84] Lewis, J., 'News and the Empowerment of Citizens', *European Journal of Cul-tural Studies* (2006), no. 3, pp. 303-319.
[85] *Ibidem*, p. 311.
[86] *Ibidem*.

If some of the suggestions for journalists are to be successful, then they must be at least mirrored by a reassessment of relations with the media adopted by politicians. If this is achieved, then it may go some way to *mending the relationship between journalists and politicians*, which is widely regarded as in need of repair, and one of the root causes of cynically framed process news. Indeed, Kees Brants et al. recently characterized this as the 'real spiral of cynicism'.[87] Some progress has been made as a result of the 2004 Phillis Report on UK government communications, such as making more press briefings open and on the record, and introducing new rules governing the conduct of special advisers within the civil service. But the problems run deeper than that.

> Many politicians believe that the national media "are only out to shaft us", that they use MPs to add colour to stories irrespective of the effect on the MP and that they will twist words to suit the story. Consequently, politicians become more defensive and adhere strictly to the party line, refusing to be drawn into debates (…) The result is that the audience are left as bystanders, spectators to an often ugly struggle.[88]

This has been described as a 'vicious' circle evolving at the heart of British politics, where the mutual distrust between politicians, their media handlers and the news media have created an environment where it is difficult for politicians of any side to make meaningful contributions to public debates.[89]

If we take the issue of Britain and the EU as an example, the media and politicians have consistently called for a proper debate on the subject in this country, but it is not likely to happen in the current climate of relations between the two. The media criticize politicians for not speaking their mind, and for stifling debate about the future of the EU. But when they do speak their mind, there are immediate stories of splits, conflicts and crises. The current stand-off between the two means that politicians talk less and less about Europe and simply follow the party line, while the media and political opponents pounce on any opportunity to claim a split. For slightly different reasons, a similar situation existed at the last general election, where the main political parties refused to seriously engage in the two most important issues for the public (public spending cuts and immigration).[90] In both cases, adopting the approach of staying strictly 'on message', whilst focusing

---

[87] Brants, K. et al., 'The Real Spiral of Cynicism? Symbiosis and Mistrust between Politicians and Journalists', *The International Journal of Press/Politics* 15 (2010), no.1, pp. 25-40.
[88] Lilleker, Negrine and Stanyer, 'A Vicious Circle'.
[89] *Ibidem*.
[90] Gaber, 'Election 2010: a Policy-free Environment'.

on superficial points scoring, may save politicians from engaging in complex and difficult discussions. However, it does little to promote wider understanding of the issues facing the country, nor does it appear to inspire the public.

For their part, in order for their complaints about process news to hold weight, *politicians should give more consideration for how their statements may contribute to public understanding of an issue*, rather than their contribution to the political game. Upon becoming leaders of their respective parties, both David Cameron and Ed Milliband promised an end to 'Punch and Judy' style politics, and to pursue a more measured and constructive dialogue. This is a pledge they have failed to keep.[91] If politicians have more confidence that their policy statements will not be interrogated only for their contribution to the political game – such as evidence of splits or an appeal to a voter segment – then they in turn might feel less inclined to stick to the party line and speak in bland sound bites rather than answer straight questions, and rely less on news management techniques, which are some of journalists' main complaints.[92] The result may be the encouragement of a public discourse about politics that is more conducive to open and constructive dialogue, rather than distrust, hostility and cynicism.

Of course, we cannot force people to be interested or active citizens. But we can think about how to facilitate the conditions in which active citizenship may flourish. Reforming some aspects of how politics is conducted and reported national literary models of the recent past.

---

[91] See Kirkup, Kirkup, J., 'Cameron Fails to end 'Punch and Judy' Politics', *The Daily Telegraph*, available from:
http://www.telegraph.co.uk/news/politics/conservative/1908155/David-Cameron-fails-to-end-Punch-and-Judy-politics.html (2008).
[92] See Rusbridger, A., 'Politicians, the Press and Political Language', *The Hetherington Memorial Lecture. The University of Stirling*, available from http://www-fms.stir.ac.uk/ (2001).

'READER, TELL US!'

JOURNALISTIC STRATEGIES TO RE-ESTABLISH A TRUST RELATIONSHIP WITH THE READER

Yael de Haan and Jo Bardoel

The relationship between media and the public is in turmoil. On the one hand, there seems to be a widening gap. The process of secularization and individualization in society and the professionalization of journalism have led to a greater distance between media and their public. At the same time, due to these trends, the citizen has distanced him or herself from traditional values and norms, has become better educated, resulting in a more assertive citizen, making ever greater demands on society and the media.[1] On the other hand, media trends like concentration, fragmentation and commercialization, show that media are focused more on reaching out to the public, trying to amend the gap.[2] To top it all, new technologies have created both opportunities and pitfalls for public trust in journalism.[3] Consultation, hypertextuality, multimediality and interactivity are four unique characteristics of the internet that strengthened the position of the media. However, the growing number of amateur journalists and the problem of regulation on the internet has undermined the credibility of news coverage.[4]

The attention for the role of citizens and consumers is now greater than ever. Using the Netherlands as a case study, the question this chapter addresses is how the media are attempting to come closer to the public and possibly redefine journalism to improve its relationship with the public.

---

[1] Bardoel J., and D'Haenens L., 'Media Meet the Citizen: Beyond Market Mechanisms and Government Regulations', *European Journal of Communication* 2 (2004), pp.165-194; Mitchell, J., and Blumler, J.G., 'In Conclusion: Beyond the State and the Market', in: Mitchell, J. and Blumler, G., eds, *Television and the Viewer Interest: Explorations in the Responsiveness of European Broadcasters* (London, 1994), pp. 227-240; Pritchard, D., Holding the Media Accountable: Citizens, Ethics and the Law (Bloomington, Indiana, 2000).

[2] Van Cuilenburg, J., 'On Competition, Access and Diversity in Media, Old and New', *New Media & Society* 2 (1998), pp. 183–207.

[3] Lowrey, W. and Anderson, W., 'The Journalist Behind the Curtain: Participatory Functions on the Internet and Their Impact on Perceptions of the Work of journalism', *Journal of Computer-Mediated Communication* 10 (2005), no. 3, available from: http://jcmc.indiana.edu/vol10/issue3/lowrey.html

[4] McQuail, D., *Media Accountability and Freedom of Publication* (Oxford, 2003).

This fragile relationship is not only instigated by larger structural trends, but also by the rise in criticism on media performance and a subsequent decreasing trust in the media. This trust in journalism and the media *tout court* constitutes, in our view, a crucial prerequisite for the future social and democratic role of professional journalism in general and journalistic storytelling in particular.

Historically the media have, often after a long fight for independence and press freedom, been entrusted with the responsibility to make sense of and give meaning to what happens in the world around us. Free from political or economic interests, media are to provide the public with information on the issues and different points of view that exist in society and critically control those elected to represent us. Recently, trust in the media has been put into question. Its role as a responsible informer is increasingly being criticized and a greater demand for accountability and responsiveness is being heard. In the public debate, media have been placed under heavy scrutiny, especially after specific incidents become subject to public opinion. In the Netherlands, two cases stand out. First, the Srebrenica massacres during the Balkan war (1995) and the way journalists reported them led to an intense internal media debate. Seven years later, in an official review commissioned by the government, the Dutch Institute for War Documentation (NIOD) concluded that next to political and military mistakes, the performance of the media had to be questioned. Extensive content research showed that Dutch news coverage was biased, portraying the Serbians as the 'bad guys' and siding with the Bosnians, and all of it laden with strong emotions.[5]

Second, Dutch media were again under fire in 2002, accused of demonizing the Dutch populist politician Pim Fortuyn. In his criticism of the political establishment Fortuyn had included the media, which, he claimed, failed to see the ills of contemporary society, particularly the effects of immigration. He was murdered in 2002 by a Dutch environmental activist and his followers blamed the 'left-wing' political and media elite for having created an atmosphere of hate against the populist politician, which ultimately led to his death. This once again triggered a debate about the responsibility of the media.[6] Politicians and government officials nervously ob-

---

[5] Wieten, J., *Srebrenica en de Journalistiek: Achtergronden en Invloed van de Berichtgeving over het Conflict in Voormalig Joegoslavië in de Periode 1991-1995: Een Onderzoek naar Opvattingen en Werkwijze van Nederlandse Journalisten* (Amsterdam, 2002).

[6] Brants, K. and Bardoel, J., 'Death Duties: Kelly, Fortuyn, and Their Challenge to Media Governance', *European Journal of Communication* 4 (2008), pp. 471-489.

served and complained about the apparent increasing power of the media.[7] They were dissatisfied with the kind of attention they got, the cynicism of the press and focus on scandal, sound bites and hypes, and they blamed the media for telling half-truths and whole lies.[8]

It seems as if media institutions, entrusted with a public service to de- mocracy, are losing the trust of both the public and politicians. In this con- text the key question is how media are responding to this alleged loss of trust. Has it attempted new ways to bring stories to the public? Are media responding to the increasing demand for more accountability and respon- siveness? How are media otherwise coming closer to the public? In this contribution we analyse how journalistic practice is currently responding to the criticism on its public role in terms of accountability and responsive- ness. Although the empirical focus of this research is on the Netherlands, the context and findings might well resonate in other Western European countries.

A case study was conducted of the Dutch national newspaper *de Volkskrant*, as this type of research method provides an in-depth look at a phenomenon in its natural setting.[9] We not only wanted to describe the dif- ferent accountability and responsiveness instruments the newspaper adheres to or introduced, but also how these different instruments are adopted with- in the organization structure and culture.[10] This chapter offers an insight into how the press is responding to the criticism on its performance and how this affects journalistic practice and the way journalism is being told. First, however, we will elaborate on four theoretical concepts that are central in the debate on media performance: responsibility, trust, accountability, and responsiveness.

---

[7] Raad voor Maatschappelijke Ontwikkelingen, (RMO)., *Medialogica: Over het Krachtenveld Tussen Burgers, Media en Politiek* (Den Haag, 2003); Jansen, T. and Drok, N., *Op Zoek naar Vertrouwen in de Pers* (Amsterdam, 2005).

[8] Vasterman, P., *Mediahypes* (Amsterdam, 2004); Brants, K. and Van Praag, P., *Pol- itiek en Media in Verwarring: De Verkiezingscampagne in het Lange Jaar 2002* (Amsterdam, 2005); Von Krogh, T., 'Introduction: Media Accountability: A 60- year-old Compromise that Still Holds Promise for the Future', in: Von Krogh,T., ed, *Media Accountability Today... and Tomorrow: Updating the Concept in Theory and Practice* (Göteborg, 2008), pp. 1-12.

[9] Gerring, J., *Case Study Research: Principles and Practices* (Cambridge, 2007); Yin, R.K., *Case Study Research: Design and Methods* (London, 1989).

[10] Methodologically, this was achieved through a comprehensive qualitative analysis of interviews and ethnographic observations.

From Responsibility to Accountability: A Conceptual Shift

Embedded in the tradition of Western liberal thinking, media responsibility consists of three functions. Firstly, the media are responsible for providing citizens with information about political and social life (the information or gatekeeper function). Secondly, they should provide citizens with a platform for dialogue to be able to express their wishes and opinions (the expression or platform function). And finally, the media should serve as a watchdog for the public regarding the conduct of political and other actors and institutions (the critical or watchdog function).[11] Until quite recently, in most European countries trust in the media was not a manifest issue and, it was almost taken for granted that the media performed in a socially responsible way. However, both media scholars and the public indicate that trust in the media and their performance has become a pressing issue as media responsibility is questioned.[12] Entrusted with the power and responsibility of meaning construction and sense making, the media particularly lose trust of the political elite, who blame them not only for a distorted portrayal of their trade but also for the public's mistrust of it. Therefore, media scholars have recently responded and emphasized the importance of trust in a modern democracy as a prerequisite for social cohesion.[13] The assumption is that if media are not trusted, the public might not engage in the use of the media, which can have negative consequences for democratic performance and thus social order in society. Swift and McCandless state that due to the

---

[11] Wildenmann, R. and Kaltefleiter, W., *Funktionen der Massenmedien* (Frankfurt am Main, 1965).

[12] Sociaal Cultureel Planbureau, SCP., *De Sociale Staat van Nederland 2009* (Den Haag, 2009); Directorate General Communication., 'Eurobarometer 66: Public Opinion in the European Union', *European Commission*, available from: http://ec.europa.eu/public_opinion/archives/eb/eb66/eb66_highlights_en.pdf (2006); Directorate General Communication., 'Eurobarometer 72: Public Opinion in the European Union', *European Commission*, available from: http://ec.europa.eu/public_opinion/archives/eb/eb72/eb72_en.htm (2010); Bakir,V. and Barlow, D. M., 'Exploring Relationships Between Trust Studies and Media Studies', in: Bakir, V. and Barlow, D.M., eds, *Communication in the Age of Suspicion: Trust and the Media* (New York, 2007), pp. 9-24; Jansen and Drok., *Op Zoek naar Vertrouwen.*

[13] Bakir and Barlow., *Exploring Relationships*; McQuail, *Media Accountability*; Tsfati,Y., 'Media Skepticism and Climate of Opinion Perception', *International Journal of Public Opinion Research* 1 (2003), pp. 64-82.

perceived lack of trust in public institutions, there is a greater need for explicit accountability relations. [14]

In this context we note a clear shift over the last decade from general and abstract thinking about media responsibility to more practical and concrete mechanisms through which media are held accountable. This more recent notion of accountability is a broad concept though, not only limited to formal regulation, but also embracing the wider obligations media have to their stakeholders and the way in which they account for their performance in a dynamic interaction between parties involved.[15]

McQuail and Bardoel & D'Haenens distinguish four accountability types, each having a different, although not mutually exclusive approach: political, market, professional and public accountability.[16] Political accountability relates first and foremost to formal law and regulation and is therefore enforceable. Market accountability is primarily based on the notion of a free market and the market principle of supply and demand.[17] Here media are held accountable and judged primarily by (the interest of) the consumer. The other two types of accountability, public and professional, are more self-regulatory, which means that these initiatives function on a voluntary and non-enforceable basis. Professional accountability is associated with professionalism primarily and has as its goal to enhance the quality of media performance positively.[18] The more recent type of public accountability is often linked to indirect public pressure and its main objective is that the media are supposed to operate on behalf of the public and voluntarily choose an active participatory role in society.[19] The latter, informal and voluntary, types of professional and public accountability mechanisms are most preferred by media institutions and professionals, since they supposedly do not interfere with the principle of freedom of the press. These self-regulatory accountability types are not only discussed more frequently, but

---

[14] Swift,T., 'Trust, Reputation and Corporate Accountability to Stakeholders', *Business Ethics: A European Review* 1 (2001), pp. 16-26; McCandless, H. E., *A Citizen's Guide to Public Accountability: Changing the Relationship Between Citizens and Authorities* (Victoria, 2001).

[15] Plaisance, P. L., 'The Concept of Media Accountability Reconsidered', *Journal of Mass Media Ethics* 4 (2000), pp. 257-268; Pritchard, *Holding the Media Accountable*; McQuail, D., *McQuail's Mass Communication Theory* (London, 2005).

[16] *Ibidem*; Bardoel, J., and d' Haenens, L., 'Media Responsibility and Accountability: New Conceptualizations and Practices', *Communications* 1 (2004), pp. 5-25.

[17] Crouteau, D., and Hoynes, W., *The Business of Media: Corporate Media and the Public Interest* (Thousand Oaks, 2001).

[18] McQuail, *Media Accountability*, p. 224.

[19] *Ibidem*, p. 224; Bardoel and D' Haenens, 'Media Responsibility and Accountability', pp. 5-25.

also put forward more by the media themselves as an answer to the current crisis of trust in the media.

In this debate on trust in the media Brants and De Haan note that there is not only a greater demand for accountability.[20] Among journalists and within media organizations there is also a growing need for a new professional attitude that is more focused on the public. There is a need to be more responsive to the public in order to regain its trust. Whereas accountability puts the emphasis on responding to the public after publication, being responsive to the public takes place prior to publication by involving the public in order to convey the story in a more accessible and understandable manner. The concept responsiveness indicates that media take the public's concerns and wishes into consideration more (pro)actively, 'whether media listen to and provide a platform for the expression of anxieties, wants and opinions, or whether they focus on needs defined more in market terms'.[21] While responsiveness focuses on taking the issues of the public into account proactively, public accountability means justifying to the public for media performance afterwards. In the Netherlands, the Fortuyn incident in particular opened the eyes of the media to take the concerns of citizens into consideration.

Brants and de Haan distinguish between civic, strategic and empathic responsiveness.[22] The first is based on taking the *public* as citizens into account, listening to and connecting with them and putting their agenda first. The starting point is the public agenda in order to be socially responsible and to bridge the gap with the public. Media are also connecting with the public as a way of binding to one's public as *consumers*, taking the form of more commercial or strategic responsiveness. This relates much to market accountability. Market accountability at most is being accountable by advertisers and shareholders. Lastly, empathic responsiveness means that journalists side with the public *victims*, who have become embroiled in problematic situations with public authorities. Journalists function as the people's advocate and bond with the public or victim and speak on behalf of this person or group to try to solve the problem. In the following sections, these rather theoretical concepts of accountability and responsiveness are translated into concrete instruments that *de Volkskrant* uses.

---

[20] Brants, K. and De Haan, Y., 'Taking the Public Seriously: Three Models of Responsiveness in Media and Journalism', *Media, Culture & Society* 3 (2010), pp. 411-428.

[21] Brants, K. and Bardoel, J., 'Death Duties', p. 475.

[22] Brants. K. and De Haan, Y., 'Taking the Public Seriously', pp. 411-428.

Case Study of de Volkskrant

The Dutch daily *de Volkskrant* was selected as a case because in the past ten years the newspaper's role and coverage has been questioned several times during specific incidents, such as the Balkan war in the nineties and the Iraq war in 2003. At the time of research, its editor-in-chief had also been chair of the Netherlands Association of Editors-in-Chief (until 2006) and had been actively involved with the debate on media performance and accountability. Moreover, the newspaper presented itself as an early-adopter in initiating accountability instruments. Finally, this newspaper has a solid reputation as a quality paper in combination with high circulation figures, which is the authentication of its prominent place in the public debate.

The data for this case study were gathered between April and June 2009. Being almost full-time at the newsroom, the first author started with an observation period to become acquainted with the relevant people and organizational structures, to understand the different journalistic processes, and to detect instruments of accountability and responsiveness. The observations varied from joining a range of daily meetings to having informal talks. During this observation period, we also collected internal documents, including policy papers, internal updates from the editor-in-chief, updates on the intranet and broadcasting and evaluation reports. Based on the document analysis and an analysis of the observation period, we composed a topic list to conduct 33 semi-structured interviews. At management level we spoke with the three deputy editors and the editor-in-chief. At professional level the heads and journalists of the different editorial desks were interviewed. Next to that, the first author spoke to the publisher.

Through a triangulation method of observations, in-depth interviews and document analysis the data were analyzed systematically through an inductive and iterative process of coding the documents, observation notes and transcribed interviews with the support of the qualitative software program MAXQDA.[23]

An Avalanche of Accountability Instruments?

The results of our case study suggest that there were an avalanche of accountability instruments introduced over the last decade in order to come closer to the public and restore the alleged crisis of the trust in the media (see fig. 1). There seems to be a shift from a type of journalism that primari-

---

[23] Miles, M.B. and Huberman, A.M., *Qualitative Data Analysis: An Expanded Sourcebook* (Thousands Oaks, 1994); Patton, M.Q., *Qualitative Evaluation and Research Methods* (Newbury Park, 1990).

ly wants to inform the public top-down to a more bottom-up journalistic approach that includes the critical voice of the public. This increased attention for accountability coincides with trends in other North-western European countries that are increasingly introducing new forms of self-regulatory accountability.[24] In this section we offer an overview of the self-regulatory (public and professional) accountability instruments that have been introduced over time in chronological order.

The oldest and most established mechanism to respond to the readers is the letter to the editor. Since 1948, *de Volkskrant* has a special readers' letters section. A small selection is published in the daily newspaper and, more recently and frequently, also on the website. A separate letters' editor takes account of the letters and is responsible for either publishing them, answering personally or sending them to the appropriate editor to be answered. Over recent decades the readers' letters section has gained prominence in the newspaper, and this also applies to the need felt to take readers' letters seriously and respond, either publicly or privately. Another longstanding and well-established mechanism of public accountability is the *Press Council* (Raad voor de Journalistiek). The press council in the Netherlands was established in 1960 and has the task to evaluate journalistic behavior of both organized and non-organized journalists and if possible, mediate in pending complaints.[25] Its judgments are not enforceable, but the press council highly recommends media to publish a rectification when the complaint is considered well-grounded. Unlike some other media, *de Volkskrant* acknowledges the Press Council, which means that the newspaper goes to hearings when it is summoned, publishes a rectification when the press council decides the complaint is legitimate and pays a financial contribution to this council.

Increasingly, from the end of the 1990s onwards, the newspaper has developed several instruments to be accountable to the reader. The oldest of the plethora of new accountability instruments is the ombudsman. In 1997, the editor-in-chief appointed the first *Volkskrant* ombudsman with the task to 'to give more room for complaints about our coverage. Often journalists do not have time, patience and enough distance to answer the emails and phone calls. The ombudsman should prevent this drawback.'[26] Besides this focus on the reader, the formal tasks of the ombudsman also consist of improving the journalistic quality and stimulating internal self-reflection. The ombudsman writes a weekly column in the Saturday newspaper, based on

---

[24] Eberwein, T. et al., *Mapping Media Accountability: In Europe and Beyond* (Cologne, 2011).

[25] Mentink, H., *Veel Raad, Weinig Baat: Een Onderzoek naar Nut en Noodzaak van de Nederlandse Raad voor de Journalistiek* (Rotterdam, 2006).

[26] De Volkskrant (2002, Jan. 28). Statuut Ombudsman. Internal Document.

an incident that was either pointed out by a reader or that he encountered himself. The columns do not seek to rebuke the involved journalists but rather to raise awareness internally and to provide transparency and explanation externally. An issue that the ombudsman raises internally does not always have implications for his column and is not always visible to the reader, which means he then functions as an internal professional accountability instrument. More recently there have been suggestions to establish a national ombudsman function for the media, but this proposal did acquire insufficient support in both politics and the media. [27]

Another proof of transparency was the new practice to publish the *author's name* together with the article so that journalists can be tracked and addressed personally, with the idea for journalists to respond to readers' questions. In 2004, the newspaper initiated a *correction box* 'Supplements & Improvements' (Aanvullingen & Verbeteringen). This box is published in the newspaper on a regular basis and lists the factual mistakes published in the newspaper.

More recently, public accountability is also offered by including a special section within the article (a *transparency box),* explaining to the reader that the article is based on independent information gathering. A transparency box is particularly provided when commercial organizations – like tour operators - occupy a key role in the story, which might give the impression that such articles are sponsored. Providing transparency gives the reader the possibility to judge the reliability of the story.

Another instrument, which serves both public and professional purposes are self-evaluations. Since 2002, the newspaper has organized self-evaluations on journalistic incidents on a case-by-case basis. The first self-evaluation was meant to respond to the criticism on how *de Volkskrant* had covered the Srebrenica dossier between 1993 and 1995 during the Balkan war. This was done in 2002 after the Netherlands Institute for War Documentation (NIOD) concluded that the performance of the media had to be questioned. [28] *De Volkskrant* decided to initiate research by two people from within the newspaper, the former and current ombudsman at that time. The internal research gave with five recommendations for the editorial department: to emphasize facts instead of opinion in news coverage, to improve the expertise in war reporting, to invest in internal debate on the position of the newspaper in important issues, to set up a special team of journalists

---

[27] RMO, *Medialogica*.
[28] Nederlands Instituut voor Oorlogsdocumentatie, (NIOD)., *Srebrenica, een 'Veilig' Gebied: Reconstructie, Achtergronden, Gevolgen en Analyses van de Val van een Safe Area* (Amsterdam, 2002); Klaassen, J. and Klein, T., *Srebrenica in de Volkskrant: 1991-1995* (Amsterdam, 2002).

during long-term and complicated issues and to invest in independent research to prevent from being almost only dependent of government information.[29]

Five years later, in 2007, the newspaper again initiated a self-evaluation
process, reflecting on its news reporting regarding the supposed maltreat-
ment of Iraqis by the Dutch military. On November 17, 2006 the front page
opened with the title 'Dutch torture Iraqis'. Accusations were heard from
government and military officials stating that it was not torture but mal-
treatment. In June of that same year the official governmental investigation
on the behavior of the Dutch military was finalized, concluding that the
newspaper had failed. The editor-in-chief then decided to set up his own
self-evaluation, conducted by an external journalist and an external lawyer,
to evaluate the so-called torture scoop. This inquiry was primarily meant for
internal self-reflection and 'to have lessons learned for the future.'[30] The
outcomes of the research resulted in a new protocol for scoops, written by a
special formed internal working group.

First and foremost, these two self-evaluations were initiated to reflect
internally on the mistakes the newspaper made and therefore are a form of
professional accountability. However, both cases also illustrate how the
newspaper gave insight in these self-evaluations to the reader and admitted
its mistakes publicly and thus eventually took public accountability.

An external public accountability instrument the newspaper cooperates
with is the media debate organization, Mediadebat. This organization was
founded in 2005 in collaboration with the Dutch Union of Journalists
(NVJ), the Dutch Newspaper Publishers Association (NDP) and the public
broadcaster news organization (NOS) on the recommendation of an independent advisory commission with financial help from the government.[31] Its
goal is to stimulate public and media professional debate on the quality,
trustworthiness and diversity of journalism, which means that the instrument functions both as overt public and overt professional accountability.
De Volkskrant speaks at these debates when invited and representatives of
the newspaper attend the debates regularly. However, in 2010 the organization ceased to organize debates for financial reasons. Since governmental
compensation stopped, it is questionable whether the media sector is willing
to provide the necessary contribution.

A last accountability mechanism to show more transparency to the
public was the publication of the book *Between the Lines* (*Tussen de Re-*

---

[29] *Ibidem.*
[30] De Volkskrant., *Onderzoek Jansen van Galen en Kemper naar Martelprimeur in de Volkskrant* (Amsterdam, 2007).
[31] RMO, *Medialogica.*

gels) in 2006. A number of outsiders, journalists and academics, were asked to reflect on how the newspaper covered specific incidents and issues including the rise and murder of Fortuyn.

To conclude, with the introduction of a range of self-regulatory accountability instruments this newspaper made attempts to respond to the rise of the public's critical voice. Journalists do not solely have the task to inform, but also to respond, to justify journalistic choices and admit mistakes. The newspaper does not only collaborate with external institutions such as the Press Council and a media debate organization, but has also taken on many initiatives itself.

We noticed a distinction between public accountability, where the newspaper communicates with the public about its performance, and professional accountability, where the newspaper stays in touch with the professional community – inside or outside – about quality and standards. However, in practice it seems that professional accountability is affected by a greater focus on amending the alleged gap with the public over the last decade (see fig. 1).

Instruments of Responsiveness

Besides formal and institutionalized instruments of public accountability, the increasing attention to the reader is also visible through a changing attitude and mentality to understand the concerns and desires of the public and to interact with the reader and thus show responsiveness. A first look at the initiatives indicates a primary focus on civic responsiveness to bridge the gap with the public, to understand the issues of concern for the public and to learn through interaction.

In recent years, *de Volkskrant* has started a number of initiatives to (re)connect with their public and to take its agenda into account. However, the idea of putting the readers concerns center stage has already been in place in the *opinion pages* of the newspaper for a long time. As mentioned before, a separate readers' editor handles the *readers' letters*. Besides complaints, the letters also address salient reader concerns, a selection of which is published in the newspaper and online.

The idea of putting the reader more center stage was explicitly brought to attention in the mid-1990s with the appointment of a new editor-in-chief. He declared a shift from institutional news to news that directly affected daily life, approaching the interests of the reader. In response to a changing society and media landscape the editor-in-chief wanted to explore new ways of conveying news stories. There was an emphasis on retelling journalism by coming closer to the public. 'The newspaper should free itself from institutional journalism, in search for the thus far not-reported reality.'[32] This issue again came to the fore during the Fortuyn period, when the media were being criticized for not being aware of the allegedly real problems and popular sentiments within society. The editor-in-chief stimulated a new style of journalistic practice by being more responsive to the public by 'thoroughly listening to and understanding the average citizen.'[33]

More recently, *de Volkskrant* started new styles of journalism to connect with the public and address issues of public concern more directly. In 2005, the newspaper started an *online interactive project*. A so-called 'social agenda' was created, focusing on important issues of society in collaboration with readers allotting priority to specific issues. The focus was not only on describing the problems of society, but noting the possible range and attainability of solutions. The project used several methods to interact with the public. On the website readers were able to rank the best subjects to be discussed and elaborated on, public debates were organized across the country and news articles were generated from these and published in the newspaper and on the website. This year-long project was repeated in following years, focusing on spatial and urban planning, economic and educational issues.

While the internet has made interactivity with the reader easier, more traditional forms of interaction, through *public debates*, are also present within the newspaper. Since 2005, the newspaper has organized ten debates a year on a topical issue under the name 'The Newspaper on Sunday' (De Krant op Zondag). Also, the science desk (wetenschap) regularly organizes public debates, discussing science-related subjects with a panel of invited experts.

Again, prompted by interactive opportunities on the internet, in 2008 the project 'Reader, Tell us' (Lezer, Zeg het maar) was initiated by one of the chief editors. The idea was to anticipate issues of interest or concern to the reader. A call was put in the newspaper asking the readers to send in ideas for news articles. The ten best were supposed to be drawn up and published. However, on the site several critical or cynical visitors took over the discussion and 'captured' it, obliging the newspaper to end the project.

Concluding, historically the newspaper has not only shown its responsibility by informing the public, but increasingly also provides a platform for public expression. In recent years, the newspaper has made several new

---

[32] Ybema, S., *De Koers van de Krant: Vertogen over Identiteit bij Trouw en de Volkskrant* (Amsterdam, 2003), p. 146.
[33] Bruin, W. et al., *Tussen de Regels: Vijf Jaar Verslaggeving in De Volkskrant* (Amsterdam, 2006), p. 35.

attempts to relate to the public and understand its wishes and concerns, whether these are considered as readers, citizens or consumers. A first look at the instruments of responsiveness shows that responsiveness seems to be prompted primarily by civic considerations.

Accountability Versus Professional Responsibility

An initial overview of the introduced instruments of accountability and responsiveness suggests that the newspaper has made serious efforts to invest in the relationship with its reader to improve the quality of its performance, with the ultimate goal to regain or retain public trust. However, initiated and often formally introduced primarily by the editor-in-chief, the question remains to what extent these instruments of a more public-oriented journalism are actually adopted in the organization. Only when these are acknowledged, supported and used on all levels of the organization will they have the aimed effect of taking the public into account and being accountable and transparent to the public and professionals. In the following section we assess, based primarily on interviews, informal talks and observations, to what extent these instruments of accountability and responsiveness are adopted within the organization today.

Based on the interviews we can conclude that there is an overall consensus among journalists on the importance of media accountability by responding to the reader. The vast majority believed the ombudsman fulfills a good role for the reader. The importance of answering readers' letters is also seen as essential in these troubled times, due to a distancing relationship with the public, the decreasing readership and increasing discontent. It is not considered as compulsory to respond to readers, but 'it is just something that is decent and important to do', as stated by a journalist.[34] Journalists said they feel that taking the public into consideration is something that nowadays they cannot turn their back on. In particular, they show their loyalty to the reader who has a subscription. This indicates that responding to readers' complaints is not only prompted by challenges to media performance but is also seen as a way to keep the loyalty of current subscribers and thus also has a strategic or commercial motive.

Besides the importance of responding to readers, the editorial staff demonstrate cooperativeness in using the accountability instruments. For example, even though the journalists and heads of editorial desks dread the ombudsman coming to their editorial department, they take him seriously when he addresses them and they find his function unassailable for the reader. The same goes for answering to readers' letters. Whether they agree

---

[34] Interview, journalist, June 28, 2009.

upon it or not, almost all editors answer the letters of readers. Most of them have experienced that by explaining to the reader how the article came about, much of the reader's initial anger or dissatisfaction is taken away. But again, where the editor-in-chief puts priority in responding to the increasing demand for accountability, the journalists prefer to respond to the public to keep or gain the loyalty of the (potential) reader.

However, there is still quite a defensive attitude. Some do not even want to answer when the complainant is not a subscriber or when the complaints are seen as not relevant, harsh or discriminative. Some plainly stated, 'if you don't like it, just skip to the next page or don't buy the newspaper.'[35] This shows that journalists are still quite reluctant and not always willing to respond or engage with the reader as it touches upon their perceptions of professional responsibility and autonomy. They are still accustomed to and prefer the idea of focusing on their responsibility of informing and do not feel the necessity to engage with the reader. To them accountability is embedded in responsibility and ideally they do not need these formal instruments. This leaves them with an ambivalent feeling, as they believe nowadays one should show his accountability to the public to respond the criticism on their performance and as a way to show loyalty to the reader. However, the majority agreed that this openness should not be exaggerated as this touches upon their professionalism.

Another reason journalists are sometimes hesitant to use the instruments is that it is not always clear when and how instruments of self-evaluation should be deployed, as there are no clear guidelines. Paradoxically, when specific formal guidelines are written, such as the protocol for scoops, many doubt the use and effect of them in daily practice. A head of an editorial desk said, 'Such a protocol is quite stylish to the outside world, but I really have my doubts on the internal effect. A good journalist knows which principles to keep to and won't consult a protocol.'[36] This shows an ambivalent attitude to the formalization of accountability procedures. On the one hand, they need more clarity on how to use the instruments. On the other, they do not believe formal procedures will do their performance any good.

A last reason, which might explain the journalists' hesitance, is that there is no consensus between the editor-in-chief and journalists on the actual purpose of the accountability instruments and the ombudsman. While the management believes the ombudsman and self-evaluations serve the purpose of both public and professional accountability, the journalists believe they merely feed an external purpose. The journalists regard them as a

---

[35] Interview, Head of an Editorial Desk, May 14, 2009.
[36] Interview, Head of an Editorial Desk, June 2, 2009.

tool to explain and be accountable to the reader and many believe they merely serve as a damage-control mechanism, as a way to restore the image of the newspaper, which is felt essential in times of financial insecurity and decreasing circulation figures.

This hesitance to reflect on one's performance or this quite 'closed debate culture' as one journalist called it, has several reasons. One is related to the nature of a newspaper. Once it is published, things cannot be changed and corrections are too late. Therefore, many find it futile to make remarks on about yesterday's newspaper. It might also be related to the conflict between the increasing need of the management for control and professionalization, which conflicts with the traditional journalistic culture of individual freedom and autonomy. Over the years, with newspapers becoming large enterprises, editors-in-chief have taken the position of managing instead of making the newspaper. This shift seems to conflict with a traditional journalistic culture in which journalists are used to working independently. While the journalistic profession is increasingly obliged to adhere to standardized procedures set out by the organization, journalists prefer to keep to their professional autonomy. They believe it is first and foremost the responsibility of the individual journalist to perform well and provide output of high quality, which should not be arranged in formal organizational procedures. A head of an editorial desk said indignantly, 'The result would be a journalism on demand of organizational wishes.'[37]

Responsiveness Versus Professional Autonomy

In relation to the recently introduced concept of responsiveness all editors agree that the idea of taking the reader into account and relating to the issues within society is unavoidable in the current media landscape. One head of an editorial desk said, 'In the past, we would write what we thought was interesting, now we think more in what the reader might find interesting.'[38] While there is a shift visible and being responsive to the public has become more notable, the question remains as to why this shift has taken place and to what extent this idea has been adopted in the organization.

Initiatives to obtain a better understanding of the reader and to increase the dialogue are seen by most interviewees as a positive shift to a less arrogant attitude of journalists and the media towards the reader. Yet, instruments such as the public debates and the online agenda projects seem to be more based on presenting issues important to social elites rather than the actual issues of the ordinary readers. When the average reader was asked to

---

[37] Interview, Head of an Editorial Desk, June 27, 2009.
[38] Interview, Head of an Editorial Desk, May 25, 2009.

contribute in the project 'Reader, tell us', the project was forced to end as a result of a group of people who tried to overrule the discussion.

While formally most instruments of responsiveness seem to have a clear civic motive, the interviews and observation analysis shows that all instruments and initiatives have an underlying strategic motive to try to bind the (potential) reader to the newspaper. Taking the reader into consideration is something the journalists feel they cannot turn their back on since the circulation figures are decreasing, the subscribers are ageing and the younger public is ever harder to attract. A head of an editorial desk stated: 'We, and all newspapers, are desperately seeking for the right recipe to stop the decreasing circulation figures.'[39] Many found it obvious that these initiatives of responsiveness were commercially motivated, trying to retain or attract new readers. A journalist told me they often make jokes about this situation: 'Guys, this is one of our last readers, we have to cherish him.'[40] Besides their democratic task of providing information to citizens, the newspaper is also a commercial venture, which needs to adhere to mechanisms of the market. The recent structural issues such as decreasing circulation figures, a less loyal subscriber market in a fierce competitive media environment has challenged the 'delicate combination between private enterprise and public responsibility'.[41]

Whether based on civic or strategic reasoning, journalists increasingly see the importance of engaging with the public and are familiar and make use of the responsive instruments, which indicates that they are incorporated in the organization. However, there is still quite a lot of resistance to involve the reader in the journalistic process. Readers should preferably only take the role of the end user. If involved, citizens are allowed to contribute in the last stage of the journalistic process: to provide feedback on the news coverage. While in a few projects, such as the reader weblogs, the 'Reader, tell us', and the agenda project, readers were able to contribute to the primary stage of the journalistic process by generating possible ideas, journalists believe it is their primary professional task to select, filter and write the story. There is an overall fear of blurring the borders of professional journalism, believing that listening too much to the public devaluates the profession. One of the heads was very critical and believed the newspaper is making the wrong choices: 'I am not a proponent of the journalist in an ivory tower but at this point the journalist has sunk deep.'[42]

---

[39] Interview, Head of an Editorial Desk, April 29, 2009.
[40] Interview, Journalist, April 9, 2009.
[41] Bardoel and D'Haenens, 'Media Responsibility', p. 15.
[42] Interview, Head of an Editorial Desk, May 14, 2009.

Conclusion

This case study of *de Volkskrant* has shown that this newspaper has developed a deliberate accountability policy to respond to the growing criticism vis-à-vis the media over the last ten to fifteen years, triggered by critical events such as the murder of the populist politician Pim Fortuyn but substantiated by structural trends such as increasing competition and commercialization and a decreasing and more critical readership. Over the last decade an impressive number of instruments of accountability and responsiveness have been introduced to tackle the perceived crisis in trust (see Table 1). These instruments were sometimes stimulated or imposed by third parties but in most cases these were self-initiated and thus self-regulatory. This new accountability policy was introduced by a new editor-in-chief, who wanted to respond (pro)actively to the increasing criticism on the changing social role of the media in general and *de Volkskrant* in particular.

Our study shows that most journalists support this shift towards a more open and responsive type of journalism, but at the same time they seem to prefer a new attitude and mentality of responsiveness above formally implemented accountability measures. Also the reason to make this shift seems to differ considerably; for journalists not the perceived increasing criticism on the performance of the press – as is the case with the editor-in-chief – is the main motive, but rather the rapidly changing and weakening strategic position of the newspaper in relation to the readership, in particular the subscribers.

Behind the new editorial policy of accountability and transparency we notice a clear shift from a paternalistic, top-down journalism, where the selection of news items, news agenda and ways of storytelling are determined by the enlightened professional, to a more open, bottom-up and interactive journalism, in which the public serves more as a partner than a subject. News selection and ways of storytelling seriously take into account the preferences and priorities of the public. At the same time we notice that professional journalists are only at the beginning of a long path of striking a proper balance between old-style paternalism and new-type consumerism and populism. Especially for an elitist quality newspaper with a liberal-progressive identity, it is not easy to find a new equilibrium.

New digital technologies offer new opportunities as well as threats in this respect. The advent of new technologies creates new opportunities for journalistic storytelling with a greater priority for the public. Pavlik notes, 'The once-basic inverted pyramid news-writing style is becoming obsolete in the online news world. It is being supplanted increasingly by immersive and interactive multimedia news reports that can give readers/viewers a feeling of presence at news events like never before.'[43] Research in other media organizations across Europe show that the interactive possibilities of the internet are increasingly used, but also that actual interaction with the public is still limited.[44]

Our study suggests that for many journalists currently responsiveness is more a mechanism to keep the attention and the loyalty of the public rather than the need to engage actively in dialogue with it. Although new interactive technologies have facilitated the dialogue with the public, the problem of trust does not seem to be solved. Actually, it might even have complicated things. Not only is the public skeptical towards the media, it now seems that the other way around is also the case. Among media professionals there are serious worries that the increased interaction between media and the users and the relative power of the latter might weaken the occupation's professional authority.[45]

At the end of the day journalists prefer to invest in their professional performance instead of showing their accountability and responsiveness, as these do not live easily with their autonomy and professional values. Even though the Netherlands might be a frontrunner regarding the implementation of various accountability instruments, the effectiveness of them depends on the acceptance by the journalistic profession. Comparably, in other European countries such as France and Finland, there are doubts about the effect and influence of media accountability instruments on journalistic practice.[46] Where we see a need for a new type of journalism that is more public-oriented and has a more proactive approach, journalistic storytelling in a digital age still faces serious problems related to traditional perceptions of an autonomous journalistic culture.

---

[43] Pavlik, J., 'The Impact of Technology on Journalism', *Journalism studies* 2 (2007), pp. 229-237.
[44] Hermida, A., 'Let's talk: How Blogging is Shaping the BBC' s Relationship with the Public', in: Tunney, S. and Monaghan. G., eds, *Web Journalism: A New Form of Citizenship* (Eastourne, 2010), pp. 306-316; Paulussen, S. et al., 'Doing it Together: Citizen Participation in the Professional News Making Process', *Observatorio Journal* 3(2007), pp.131-154; Neuberger, C. and Nuernbergk, C., 'Competition, Complementarity or Integration?', *Journalism practice* 3(2010), pp. 319-332.
[45] Lowrey and Anderson, 'The Journalist Behind the Curtain'.
[46] Heikki, H. and Kylmala, T., 'Finland: Direction of Change Still Pending', in: Eberwein, T. et al., eds, *Mapping Media Accountability: In Europe and Beyond* (Koln, 2011), pp. 50-62; Baisnée, O. and Balland, L., 'France: Much Ado About (Almost) Nothing', in: Eberwein, T. et al., eds, *Mapping Media Accountability: In Europe and Beyond* (Koln, 2011), pp. 63-76.

Instruments	Level of adoption	Introduction year
Letters to the editor	Incorporated	1948
Press Council	Collaborating	1960
Ombudsman	Incorporated	1997
Publication of author's names	Incorporated	End 90s
Correction box	Incorporated	2004
Media debate organiza-tion	Collaborating	2005
Transparency box	Incorporated	± 2006
Book *Between the Lines*	Incorporated	2006

1. Instruments of Accountability at *de Volkskrant*.

SOURCES, TRANSPARENCY AND NARRATIVE

FOREIGN CORRESPONDENCE IN THE PEOPLE'S REPUBLIC OF CHINA

Bernadette C.M. Kester

Introduction: Context Matters

Foreign correspondents are the main creators of our windows on the world. The way people perceive of other countries and cultures depends largely on how these countries and cultures are portrayed and narrated in news stories. Foreign reporting even affects foreign policy as well. Not surprisingly, and despite the fact that foreign correspondence is often called a profession on the brink of extinction, mainly due to commercialization and the rise of the internet, quality news media still consider their contribution important.[1] Even more, in a world where the interest in international affairs largely depends on geographical and cultural proximity, emphasis on foreign news as such has become a unique selling point.[2] This is not only due to the afore-mentioned reasons, but articles from correspondents are also considered a valuable addition to the flow of foreign news reports coming from the international news agencies.[3] Therefore, particularly in times of austerity measures, nationally located broadsheets such as *The Guardian*, *The New York Times* or *NRC Handelsblad* (a Dutch quality newspaper) and several other news media, maintain this expensive branch of journalism. The stories provided by correspondents add a sense of 'having been there', a phenomenon that could be called the 'dateline-effect'. It strengthens the idea of authenticity through such techniques as eyewitness accounts, which generally still bear the notion of truthfulness. Although every journalist frames his or

---

[1] Schroeder , R., and Stovall, J., ''The Impact of the Internet on Foreign Correspondents' Work Routines', in: Gross, P., and Kopper, G.G., *Understanding Foreign Correspondence: A Euro-American Perspective of Concepts, Methodologies, and Theories* (New York, 2011), p. 188.

[2] Shoemaker, P.J., et al, 'Proximity and Scope as News Values', in: Devereux, E., ed, *Media Studies: Key Issues and Debates* (London, 2007), pp. 231-248.

[3] Hannerz, U., *Foreign News. Exploring the World of Foreign Correspondents* (Chicago, 2004), p. 167; Kopper, G.G. and Bates, B.J., 'Political Economy of Foreign Correspondents', in: Gross, P. and Kopper, G.G., eds, *Understanding Foreign Correspondence*, p. 56.

her news account, correspondents seem to put more effort in framing news events not only by reporting from a more personal angle but also by looking for alternative sources of information. Particularly when the usual, routine sources (such as officials, experts) are propagandistic mouthpieces of a regime, searching for alternatives can even become a necessity. The question is: could this particular constellation have any consequences for the angle of the news narrative and in the long run on the representation of a country in general? Particularly the first part of this question is taken here as the main point of departure.

In order to make a difference and to be able to add an extra dimension to regular news reports, the availability of and the accessibility to a broad range of information sources is crucial for correspondents. Thus a free flow of information, also in the literal sense of freedom of speech, or rather freedom and openness to speak, is paramount for correspondents, particularly when sources are concerned, that is 'the originators of the information that is processed into news'.[4] With the general display of optimism in regard to globalization and particularly to a global flow of information, it is often ignored (also by correspondents themselves) that many foreign correspondents are actually stationed in countries or on continents where information is not flowing freely at all. Indeed ample research has shown that the context of society, or the media system, in which news is produced does matter for the content of news.[5] As we consider news to be a social construction, news content produced in a politically non-free environment is certainly affected by the fact that sources are or might be limited, controlled or frightened to speak.[6] In regimes where (self)censorship reigns, journalists are arrested or even eliminated because of their critical stance towards the power elites and propaganda dominates political communication.[7]

Much has been written about the effects of censorship on journalism, but not from the perspective of foreign correspondence. The position or rather journalistic practice of foreign (western) reporters based in   non-

---

[4] Zelizer, B. and Allan, S., *Keywords in News and Journalism Studies* (New York, 2010), p. 143.

[5] Shoemaker, P. and Reese, S., *Mediating the Message: Theories of Influence on Mass Media Content* (New York, 1996); Sparks, C., 'Media Systems in Transition: Poland, Russia, China', *Chinese Journal of Communication* 1 (2008), p. 7; Hallin, D. C. and Mancini, P., eds, *Comparing Media Systems Beyond the Western World* (Cambridge, 2012).

[6] Tuchman, G., *Making News: A Study in the Construction of Reality* (New York, 1978).

[7] Brady, A.-M., 'Guided Hand: The Role of the CCP Central Propaganda Department in the Current Era', *Westminster Papers in Communication and Culture* 1 (2006), p. 67.

democratic countries – which most countries in the Middle East, Africa and to a lesser degree in Asia are – has hardly ever been problematized in relation to source accessibility, let alone taken as an object of serious investigation. Some observations are indicative, like those of William Hachten and James Scotton who wrote in their *World News Prism*:

> The freedom of access that a foreign reporter enjoys is usually directly related to the amount of independence and access enjoyed by local journalists themselves. If local journalists are harassed or news media controlled by a particular government, so very likely will be the foreign correspondent.[8]

Likewise Joris Luyendijk, a former Dutch correspondent in the Arab world who now calls himself a 'meta-journalist' and wrote a (meta-)critical book on (foreign) journalistic practices in authoritarian states argued:

> The absence of the rule of law has profound impact on the availability and existence of information, on the nature of that information itself and on the possibilities of conveying that information properly to a western audience that has no first-hand experience of a non-democratic system.[9]

Although the internet is considered to be a serious competitor to journalism in providing international news to citizens, it is also assumed that journalists benefit from the abundance of recourses from the internet as well. Moreover the accessibility and boundlessness that is associated with the internet suggests that correspondents could easily circumvent any restrictions on information, which is not completely true. They benefit enormously from the internet as it is a rich source of information, including social media, particularly when one masters the local language. But then at least one condition should be met, the guarantee that information is freely flowing and accessible and not hampered by any restrictions. However, in 'our' western universe the internet is all too often equated with universal accessibility of digital information. This Western-centric view ignores the fact that there are still twelve countries in the world that could be labelled, 'enemies of the in-

---

[8] Hachten, W.A. and Scotton, J.F., *World News Prisms. Global Information in a Satellite Age* (Oxford, 2007), p. 131.
[9] Luyendijk, J., 'Beyond Orientalism', *The International Communication Gazette* 1 (2010), p. 11; Kester, B.C.M., 'Working at the End of the Assembly Line: A Conversation with Joris Luyendijk about the Impossibility of Doing Western-Style Journalism in Arab Countries', *The International Journal of Press/Politics* 4 (2008).

ternet' or in which the internet is 'under surveillance'; China is on this list.[10] To illustrate: in the run up to the Olympics in 2008 China had promised, under international diplomatic pressure, foreign journalists free access to the internet. However, on July 31, 2008, Edward Cody reported on the *Washington Post*-website:

> China, which employs an extensive array of monitoring software to comb through whatever people call up on their screens and block sites that China's security or propaganda officials consider unacceptable. Sites run by Amnesty International, the human rights group; Falun Gong, the spiritual movement; Tibet independence sympathizers; and a host of other human rights groups hostile to aspects of China's Communist Party rule have been targeted by the censorship equipment, which is backed up by an estimated 30,000 monitors employed by the Public Security Bureau.[11]

The main focal point and question of this chapter is whether and how this specific context transpires in the correspondents' news narratives themselves, meaning the selection, nature, presentation and explanation of news sources. In other words, what consequences could the restrictions in a non-free country, in an authoritative state, have on source research and subsequently on the narrative angle of their news articles? And with the future of journalism in mind, what chances are there for the flow of information to be freed from the shackles of state control, or to circumvent control in any way, and again what could this imply for foreign journalists' news narratives? With these questions taken as starting points this chapter addresses the case of foreign correspondence in China during two internal conflicts in 2008 and 2009 respectively.

China: 'One of the Most Challenging Beats in the World'[12]

As the illustrative objects of this study on foreign correspondence in authoritative media systems, I took news narratives surrounding two internal conflicts in China (the Tibetan uprising in 2008; Uighur uprising in 2009), pro-

---

[10] Website *Reporters without Borders* (search string: China, Internet); Deans, P., 'The Internet in the People's Republic of China: Censorship and Participation', in: Abbott, J.P., ed, *The Political Economy of the Internet in Asia and the Pacific: Digital Divides, Economic Competitiveness, and Security Challenges* (Connecticut, 2004), p. 123.

[11] Brady, 'Guided Hand', pp. 67-68; Woo, S., 'China Clings to Control. Press Freedom in 2009', *International Federation of Journalists, Brussels* (2010), p. 2.

[12] MacKinnon, R., 'Blogs and China Correspondence: Lessons about Global Information Flows', *Chinese Journal of Communication* 2 (2008), p. 246.

duced by correspondents from *The New York Times*, *The Guardian* and *NRC Handelsblad*.[13] These three broadsheets were chosen because of their focus on international news reporting and their (still) large number of employed foreign correspondents. China has been chosen as a case for several reasons. Firstly, the country is a clear example of a non-democratic regime, where not all media are state owned, but where ideological restraint and control are nevertheless still very tangible, particularly during times of conflict when the reins are tightened.[14] Secondly, China is not only governing a significant portion of the world population, internationally it has a growing importance not only in economic terms but in terms of international power relations as well. Therefore, trustworthy information about current Chinese affairs is essential. Moreover China is next to the US, Belgium (Brussels) and Israel perhaps the country where most foreign correspondents are based and their numbers are still growing. In 2007 more than 400 correspondents were based in China, according to the Chinese Foreign Ministry.[15]

Claiming that the national, societal context in which news is produced is of importance for the content, how in the case of China does the political or governmental system influence the way news for foreign media comes into being? How do the controlling mechanisms of the political system operate? First, this chapter will draw a general picture of how the Chinese political system works in relation to news media. The issue of press freedom and the accessibility of information will be addressed as well. Subsequently the focus will be turned towards journalistic routines in regard to the use of sources in general and then towards the actual practice of source searching in the Chinese context. Finally the consequences this practice has for the construction of news narratives will be addressed.

Despite the liberal reforms that recently took place in the field of the economy, China first of all represents a case of an authoritarian, non-democratic state, with a one party system. As Colin Sparks notes in his study on media systems in *transition*: China is 'Exceptionally Not Democratic', therefore a transition is not expected to take place soon.[16] Recently (Dec. 2011) the World Democracy Audit showed that China is ranked 121

---

[13] I decided to leave the names of the correspondents out, because this is not about (criticizing or commenting on) individual journalists but about routines and practices mainly.

[14] Brady, 'Guided Hand', p. 67; Brooker, P., *Non-Democratic Regimes* (Hampshire, 2009).

[15] *Ibidem*.

[16] Sparks, C., 'Media Systems in Transition: Poland, Russia, China', *Chinese Journal of Communication* 1 (2008), p. 7.

on a scale of 150.[17] China shared its position with Togo and Kyrgystan. Even less favorable is China's 139th position in the same table, under the heading of Press Freedom Rank. These conclusions are corroborated by academic research as well.[18]

This country of about 1.3 billion people is firmly ruled by the leaders of the Chinese Communist Party (CCP). One of the basic principles of Chinese governance is preventing the country and its people from disorder. Keeping harmony intact on all levels of society is the main goal. This preference for harmony and consensus is deeply ingrained in the Chinese culture at large and accordingly in its journalistic culture. Dissidence, deviancy, protests, criticism (of the political system) is kept within strict limits or not allowed at all.

For Chinese journalists there are two strategies to circumvent or deal with this. On the one hand 'convey criticism between the lines of censored media texts by ways of "double coding,"' and on the other hand in regard to the audience, assume that people will 'skillfully decode these messages by subversive reading' that is, reading between the lines.[19] As all foreign journalists make ample use of indigenous media sources, they too have to be able to read between the lines, which not only implies a good comprehension of the Chinese language(s) but also the possession of a deep cultural knowledge.[20] For instance, nowadays every so often Chinese journalists are allowed to openly indict corrupt local managers or local party members, but this right is merely functioning as a valve or control device to the benefit of the Chinese state. It is assumed that this will channel protests from local people against corruption and industrial accidents and is meant to prevent any real disruption.[21] Despite this strictly monitored and regulated 'freedom' to protest, any other opposition, especially protests coming from cultural and ethnic minorities in China (like for instance by Tibetans or Ui-

---

[17] China: World Democracy Profile, *WorldAudit.org*, available from: http://www.worldaudit.org/countries/china.htm (2001).

[18] Shoemaker, P.J, and Cohen, A.A., *News Around the World: Content, Practitioners and the Public* (New York, 2006), pp. 160-164; Yin, J. and Payne, G., 'Asia and the Pacific', in: De Beer A. S. and Merrill, J. C., eds, *Global Journalism: Topical Issues and Media Systems* (Boston, 2004), pp. 349-386; Ma, E. K.-W., 'Rethinking Media Studies: The Case of China', in: Curran, J., and Park, M.-J., eds, *De-Westernizing Media Studies* (New York, 2000), pp. 17-27.

[19] Hanitzsch, T., 'Deconstructing Journalism Culture: Toward a Universal Theory', *Communication Theory* 17 (2007), p. 373.

[20] Louw, E. P., 'Journalists Reporting from Foreign Places', in: De Beer A. S. and Merrill, J. C., eds, *Global Journalism: Topical Issues and Media Systems* (Boston, 2004), pp. 151-162.

[21] Shirk, S.L., ed, *Changing Media, Changing China* (Oxford, New York, 2011), p. 177; Yin and Payne, 'Asia and the Pacific', p. 349.

ghurs, see below), will be severely repressed and not tolerated by any means.

The 1989 crackdown in Tiananmen Square, where one of the issues at stake was to gain more press freedom, exemplified another case. In its aftermath a new government was formed under the leadership of Jiang Zemin. After a decade of economic liberalization, starting in 1978 when Deng Xiaoping (1978-1994) opened the door ajar to economic reform and free market mechanisms, the reins were tightened again. Nevertheless many media organizations became commercially liberalized (before then they were owned by the state.[22] Although this liberalization meant more freedom for media organizations to compete and gain profits, the ideological content of media was still monitored.[23] This implies that the growing commercialization of media organizations and news products as such coexist with a tight control over media and news content.

Evidently the preference for order and harmony as a part of most people's mental outfit has consequences for the practice of Chinese journalism. Contrary to western forms of journalism it is not as adversarial and cannot be considered a Fourth Estate, with journalists acting as watchdogs.[24] From a western point of view, this striving for harmony could also be considered to be a dominating form of conformism and obedience to and fear of authorities. An extensive network of propaganda and indoctrination mechanisms in the realms of education and media are responsible for this. The tentacles of the Chinese Communist Party (CCP) reach and control the people and the media through various bureaucratic organizations. Indeed, as Anne-Marie Brady, an expert on the Chinese propaganda system writes, the Central Propaganda Department of the CCP has a 'central, guiding role over the whole of Chinese society in the current era. ... the propaganda systems touches on virtually every aspect of life in the PRC.'[25] Ironically, in order to refine its propaganda and control system, the Chinese government has developed and deployed many strategies and tactics in the field of persuasion, PR, mass and political communication that originate in the West.[26]

---

[22] Stockman, D., 'What Kind of Information Does the Public Demand? Getting the News during the 2005 Ant-Japanese Protests', in: Shirk, S., ed, *Changing Media, Changing China*, p. 177.

[23] Brady, 'Guided Hand', p. 59.

[24] Hanitzsch, 'Deconstructing Journalism Culture', p. 373.

[25] Brady, 'Guided Hand', pp. 58-59; Zhao, Y., *Communication in China: Political Economy, Power and Conflict* (New York, 2008), pp. 20-21.

[26] Brady, 'Guided Hand', p. 74.

Internal propaganda is supervised by a 'highly secret organization', the Central Propaganda Department.[27] External propaganda, towards foreigners and the outside world, falls under the responsibility of the Foreign Office of Propaganda. This office, which is partly secret and partly non-secret, 'researches and develops China's foreign publicity activities as well as monitoring, policing and censoring all activities within China which fits within the foreign propaganda ambit, including the *activities of foreign journalists*, monitoring foreign social science research on China, and controlling the internet.'[28] As Karin Deutsch Karlekar and Sarah Cook state: 'China employs a small army of functionaries tasked with monitoring and censoring the content of websites and blogs.'[29] The monitoring and censoring strategies consist of four techniques: technical filtering, pre- and post-publication censorship, and proactive manipulation.[30]

Despite the official strategies and techniques to control the media, the flow of information has been growing substantially. No longer are regulations directed towards monitoring content only, but also towards managing this ever-expanding flow of information. At the same time, because of the decentralization of the economy and the market orientation of many media organizations, Chinese media content shows more diversity than ever before, however, not in its opinion on sensitive political topics. Diversity in Chinese terms means first of all that next to the media owned by the state also commercial and thus more entertainment, sensation, and human interest oriented media content has become available. Recently more Chinese citizens tend to turn their backs on official media (such as the Party paper *People's Daily* or *Reference News* published by the official Xinhua news agency; or the national television station (CCTV) and choose for 'alternative' sources of news, like news provided by commercialized conventional media (after television, newspapers are still the most popular sources for the news!) and the internet.'[31] Particularly, access to the internet makes it hard for the Chinese government to have complete control of and surveillance over the flow of information. However, though the amount of internet users is growing rapidly, in 2009 less than 30 percent of Chinese citizens had ac-

---

[27] *Ibidem.*, p. 60.

[28] *Ibidem.*, p. 63 (quoted from Brady, italics are mine); Zhao, *Communication in China*, p. 21.

[29] Deutsch Karlekar, K. and Cook, S.G., 'Access and Control: A Growing Diversity of Threats to Internet Freedom', in: *Freedom House Report Freedom on the net: A Global Assessment of Internet and Digital Media* 1 (2009), p. 1.

[30] *Ibidem*, p. 37.

[31] Yin and Payne, 'Asia and the Pacific', pp. 348-349, 361; see also Shirk, S.L., 'Changing Media, Changing China', pp. 1-37.

cess to the internet.[32] Clearly it is not the most popular source for the news. Perhaps more surprisingly most citizens also tend to stay within the Great Fire Wall, officially known as the Golden Shield Project (a censoring system) and do not look necessarily for entries that lay outside the reach of the Propaganda Department.[33]

Circumventing the Golden Shield?

The ever expanding flow of information and subsequently the fact that it is technically not feasible for the Chinese government (or any government for that matter) to control every single piece of information and media content that is aired or published, does indicate that the 'wall' has perhaps always been more or less permeable. According to Daniela Stockman, those cracks in the wall are particularly obvious when 'during a crisis, people have a particular keen nose for where to find credible information'.[34] Another fairly recent example of these cracks is the rise in popularity of Chinese microblogging: the so called weibo-posts.[35] Social network sites like Facebook and Twitter are blocked but these Chinese equivalents seem to thrive.

Besides the Chinese equivalent of Twitter, China also knows an extensive blogosphere, which by now probably contains more than the 20 million bloggers it had at the end of 2006 despite the ever-growing surveillance.[36] However, the question is of how much value these weibo-posts and blogs are for foreign correspondents, as most are highly personal and apolitical in content.[37] Interesting though are the writings produced by a relatively small group of several thousand Chinese bloggers 'who engage instead in irony, parody, and innuendo, enabling informed readers to "read between the lines" about the blogger's real point.'[38] Other internet platforms which require the skill of 'reading between the lines' are the online forums, chat rooms or 'bulletin board systems' (BBS) as they are called. According to scholar and former CNN-journalist in China, Rebecca MacKinnon, this is

---

[32] Stockman., 'What Kind of Information Does the Public Demand?'.
[33] *Ibidem.*, p. 188; Woo, S., 'China Clings to Control. Press Freedom in 2009', p. 3.
[34] Shirk, S.L., ed, *Changing Media, Changing China* (Oxford, New York, 2011), p. 23.
[35] Wines, M. and LaFranière, S., 'In Baring Facts of Train Crash, Blogs Erode China Censorship', in: *New York Times* (July 29, 2011).
[36] MacKinnon, R., 'Blogs and China Correspondence: Lessons about Global Information Flows', *Chinese Journal of Communication* 2 (2008), p. 248.
[37] *Ibidem.*
[38] *Ibidem.*

the really popular and 'preferred sphere for public discourse.'[39] In her investigation (a survey) on the internet's value as a resource for foreign correspondents in China, MacKinnon found that correspondents deem blogs particular useful for story ideation: 'story ideas, angles and leads'.[40] Blogs are thus to be considered a different type of journalistic source than sources containing factual information.

Indeed, foreign journalists can find, through these cracks, alternative ways to circumvent the official 'contaminated' sources. This, however, would only be feasible when certain conditions are met like the ones mentioned earlier: proficiency (of the language) and a deep understanding of cultural meanings and the complexities of the country and its political system as well, in order to be able to read between the lines. Speaking the language of the country where one is or will be stationed for a few years is of course highly recommended by the editor but not always considered a prerequisite. Besides it may not seem worth the trouble to learn the language if correspondents tend to spend only three of four years abroad, which is more and more the case nowadays.

In this respect two other phenomena should be mentioned, namely 'bridge blogging' and the 'local foreign reporter'. Among the most popular blogs used by correspondents are a few English-language blogs written by bloggers who literally bridge the language cleavage between China and the international (English-speaking) community.[41] In more than one way do these bloggers 'translate' perspectives on Chinese current affairs and make them accessible to an international audience whether or not mediated by correspondents. Another way to circumvent the language and culture problem is the use of local reporters, working for foreign news organizations. John Maxwell Hamilton and Eric Jenner, predict not so much the end of the foreign correspondent as such, but a process towards more (professional) differentiation.[42] In that respect they expect the 'local foreign correspondent' to become one of the future changes in the professional area of foreign correspondence. However inexpensive and practical the employment of a local reporter could be, one should not overlook the fact that a foreign cor-

---

[39] *Ibidem.*

[40] MacKinnon, 'Blogs and China correspondence', pp. 249-250. Correspondents considered blogs more useful in that sense than 'CCTV (Chinese Central Television), CNN, BBC (radio & TV), oversees forums, domestic forums and BBS, or Chinese radio.' (p. 249).

[41] *Ibidem.* Two most used bridge blogs mentioned by MacKinnon (and which still exist) are: *EastSouthWestNorth* by Roland Soong, and Danwei.com by Jeremy Goldkorn.

[42] Maxwell Hamilton, J. and Jenner, E., 'Redefining Foreign Correspondence', in: *Journalism* 3 (2004), pp. 301-321.

respondent is also expected to stay in touch with the wishes and expectations of her editors as well as readers or viewers at home, in order to be able
to 'domesticate' foreign news.[43] A local reporter could be missing this particular national sensibility.

In short, the picture is perhaps not as black and white as first stated but
nevertheless the conditions in which foreign journalists in China have to
work clearly diverge from a western, democratic environment. Generally
speaking we could argue that the Chinese government by controlling internal news flows (and sources) indirectly controls (or tries to control) foreign
news about China as well.

The 'Official Source Syndrome'[44]

In western countries access to independent information and to a variety of
news sources is considered to be basic for practicing fair and balanced journalism. Nevertheless research on news sources conducted from the seventies onwards found that journalists predominantly use routine channels –
authoritative sources and pseudo-events that is – to back up their stories.[45]
Informal and enterprise sources were generally less popular with journalists.
Nowadays reporters still tend to focus on elite sources as their principal
sources, a tendency some media critics call the 'official source syndrome'.
In free societies news often represents the voices of the so-called 'author-
ized knowers' and 'their authoritative versions of reality' dominate news
discourses and thus acts as 'primary definers' of most people's view on the
world.[46] However limited this may sound, these elite sources do not necessarily represent just one dominant voice but can be diverse or contradictory
as well.[47] This at least is the situation in most free countries. In authoritative
states like China, however, elite sources do usually represent only one dom-

---

[43] Clausen, L., 'Localizing the Global: "Domestication" Processes in International
News Production', *Media, Culture and Society* 1 (2004), p. 28.
[44] Rennen, T., *Journalistiek als Kwestie van Bronnen: Ontwikkeling en Toepassing
van Bron-georiënteerde Benadering van Journalistiek* (Delft, 2000), p. 82.
[45] Sigal, L. V., 'Reporters and Officials: The Organization and Politics of Newsmaking', in: Tumber, H., ed, *News: A Reader* (Oxford, 1999), pp. 224-234; Berkowitz,
M., 'Reporters and Their Sources' in: Wahl-Jorgensen, K., and Hanitzsch, T., eds,
The Handbook of Journalism Studies (New York, 2009), pp. 102-115.
[46] Manning, P., *News and News Sources: A Critical Introduction* (London, 2001), p.
14-17; Ericson, R.V., Baranek, P.M. and Chan, J.B.L., *Negotiating Control: A Study
of News Sources* (London, 1989).
[47] Entman, R.M., *Projections of Power: Framing News, Public Opinion, and U.S.
Foreign Policy* (Chicago, 2004).

inant perspective, which is generally considered to be highly unreliable. The question is, do international reporters, most of them trained in balanced reporting, still tend to select the obvious sources, and if so, do they exercise any source criticism?

Reporting Internal Conflicts: Minorities versus Majority

In my investigation I concentrated on two extreme situations, situations in which we can assume that the government's restrictions on the media were at their strongest. In these circumstances official sources are the untrustworthiest sources journalists could use. This is particularly the case in regard to high risk or taboo issues like conflicts concerning ethnic minorities daring to violently oppose Beijing's rule by attacking Han Chinese on the streets, among other things. Both Tibetans and Uighurs are such (large) minorities, in the southern and western regions of China, who have a history of protest against Beijing's rule. Both regions, which were formerly inhabited mainly by Tibetans and Uighurs respectively, are overrun (and overruled) by Han Chinese who were sent to these regions by the CCP. Since then members of both ethnic minorities feel and are treated like second-rate citizens compared to the Han Chinese. Many local, ethnic and religious (Buddhist and Muslim respectively) customs and beliefs are not allowed to be practiced since the communists took over. Their economic positions lag behind the positions of Han Chinese residents and politically they are principally powerless, politics being the area where Han Chinese occupy all positions.

The leaders or representatives of both Tibetans and Uighurs live in exile. The 14th Dalai Lama Tenzin Gyatso, leader of Tibet and the Tibetan people, escaped in 1959 from Lhasa to India, after Mao Zedong's People Republic of China occupied Tibet, which from then on became known as the Tibetan Autonomous Region. The human rights activist and spokeswoman of the Uighurs, Rebiya Kadeer, originally from China, is living in exile in the United States, since 2005.

The Tibetan uprising took place in March 2008. Unrest first began with demonstrations on the 10th of March, commemorating the uprising in 1959 against Chinese rule and the Dalai Lama's subsequent flight. A few days later, from March 14th onwards, the insurgency worsened and the Chinese army intervened forcefully. Looting, burning and fights were followed by a violent response from the authorities, which led to the deaths of dozens of people.

Although unrest among the Uighur community started around the same time as the Tibetan protests began (albeit without being related), I chose the Uighur uprising that subsequently took place about a year later around July 2009. The reason for this choice is that the Chinese government apparently 'learned' from its oppressive response towards Western media during the Tibetan unrest and decided to change its attitude towards the media during the Uighur riots a year later. For my analysis it is relevant to see if this made any difference in the choice for sources or otherwise.

The Uighur uprising in Ürümqi, the capital of the Xinjiang Uighur Autonomous Region, started on July 5, 2009 after two Uighurs were killed in a fight with Han Chinese, in southern China. Many Uighurs took to the streets demanding a more serious investigation into the case. The protests escalated after the police used excessive force (according to the Uighur) or after it was stirred up by the Uighurs in exile represented by their spokeswoman Rebiya Kadeer, (according to the Chinese government).

Sources

During the first few weeks of both uprisings, 78 articles in all were published by the three newspapers, all of them were taken into account.[48] The results are based on a quantitative content analysis of all news reports from the foreign desks and written by correspondents only, all of them stationed in China. The news source was the primary unit of analysis. As the definition of a source we took the one developed by Toon Rennen, a Dutch scholar in journalism studies, who wrote an extensive and thorough study on journalism and sources. He defined a source as a person, or a collective of persons, from whom the journalist, via a transaction process, retrieved information for his journalistic product.[49] 'Persons' should be understood in a literal sense as well as in the sense of statements made in textual or audio-visual form/sources. With regard to the transaction process the distinction was made between inter-transactional processes (between the journalist and someone else as a source) and intra-transactional processes (when the journalist herself is the source). In the latter case, the source has been typified as 'journalist info'.[50] In my research this source is considered an 'implicit source', a source that is not explicitly mentioned or recognized as a source. Every sentence though that could be attributed to the correspondent's input coming from his own background knowledge was accounted as 'journalist

---

[48] On Tibet 2008: from *The New York Times*, 18 articles were selected, March 14-31; from *The Guardian* 14 articles, March 12-28; from *NRC Handelsblad* 10 articles, 15-29 March. On the Uighurs 2009: from *The NYT* 20 articles, July 6-30; from *The Guardian* 11 articles, July 6-15; from *NRC* 5 articles, July 6-11.

[49] Rennen, *Journalistiek als Kwestie van Bronnen*, p. 50.

[50] *Ibidem*, p. 51.

info'. Often the first paragraph, containing an introduction to or an explanation of the situation at hand, could be accounted for as such.

The aim was to attribute every part of the journalistic text to a source. All sources that an article explicitly referred to were first listed in the same way as how they were mentioned in the journalistic text, be it by their real names, of both persons and organizations, or by generalizations as in 'locals', 'shopkeeper', 'officials', 'Uighurs', etc.. Next, these names and generalizations were labeled in relatable types of sources. In total 14 types of sources and a residual type-category were identified.

When a source was mentioned in the plural, like for instance when reports referred to 'locals', 'officials', 'monks', 'Uighurs', etcetera they were counted as two sources.[51] The source type 'person' may sound like a vague label, but was nevertheless a quite essential designation for those sources, individuals only, that were mentioned in a more general or anonymous way and could not be labeled as one of the other source types.[52] This relatively anonymous source type made it difficult to make a clear distinction between dissidents or opponents to the state and people supportive of state policy. If it would have been possible to make a clear distinction between both sources' positions more could have been concluded on how balanced the reports are in that respect.

The State 'Versus' the People

In the articles that contained the corpus of research materials, a total of 957 sources were identified (including the plural sources counted as two), which equates to an average of 12 sources per article. The overall pattern in the types of sources that dominated the news reporting in general (taking both conflicts and all three newspapers into account) shows a hierarchy in which, according to average percentages, state authorities, local eye witnesses, persons and journalist info occupy the highest ranks (see fig. 1).

That state authorities would take a rather dominant position was more or less to be expected and confirms the 'official source syndrome' once again. As has already been indicated, the easiest sources for journalists to turn to are (often local) official representatives, or spokespersons of the Chinese government, and of course state-owned media as well. Striving to become the primary definers these sources attempt to frame the situation in

---

[51] Perhaps this could be considered a debatable decision but it should be taken into account and we might assume that when a reporter uses the plural she talked at least to not less than two sources.

[52] Organized individuals (e.g. not exiles, but exile *groups*, mostly advocacy groups), individuals representing a people (like the Dalai Lama or Kadeer), politicians from abroad, were typified as 'other civil society actors'.

accordance to state ideology. This 'routine' source is always easily availa-ble, though subsequently to be refuted, contradicted or balanced by other sources like eyewitnesses, the other dominant source. Quite surprisingly, eyewitnesses represent a high percentage of the sources used despite the fact that most people are known or said to be afraid of talking freely or con-tradicting the authorities.

Having to turn to local people and witnesses as sources of infor-mation has important implications for the news stories themselves: they of-ten take on a human-interest frame. This frame 'brings a human face, an in-dividual's story, or an emotional angle to the presentation of an event, issue or problem'.[53] It also offers the reader more insight into the daily life of or-dinary people and of their experiences under extraordinary circumstances. The many quotes from ordinary people that are included in the reports will enhance the 'personal' style many articles from correspondents already have, offering a valuable addition to hard news reports. At the same time it endorses the claim to authenticity, to a 'having-been-there' (-despite-all-the-obstacles, one is inclined to add) and a 'have-been-talking-to-the-people-themselves' which are important and convincing connotations to the date line reporting of foreign correspondents. As a side effect this style of report-ing could result in a more multi-dimensional view on China in general.

The choice for eyewitness sources implies that journalists seem to con-sider these sources trustworthy or at least as a valuable source to counter-balance authoritarian sources. The latter sources are considered untrustwor-thy, although this is never explicitly mentioned. Journalists rather treat the source as any other one, except that sometimes it is mentioned that commu-nication is tightly controlled. A former Dutch correspondent, Garrie van Pinxteren, was quoted on this issue in a guide for foreign (Dutch) journalists in China, in the run up to the 2008 Olympic Games:

> In order to get as many sources as possible for my story, I often interviewed or-dinary people on the streets. I did not always tell them I was a journalist. Of course this is absolutely debatable from an ethical point of view and in the Netherlands this definitely is not common usage, but in China this practice is inevitable as most people are afraid to talk to the media. Apart from state sources not many alternative sources are available. Independent media or opin-

---

[53] Semetko, H. A. and Valkenburg, P. M., 'Framing European Politics: A Content Analysis of Press and Television News', *Journal of Communication* 50 (2000), no. 2, p. 95.

ion polls do not exist. That is why, for a good perspective, you have to include as many Chinese 'voices' (sources) as possible.[54]

For Van Pinxteren the basic dichotomy in the management of sources is the opposition between 'state sources' and 'alternative' sources. In the present research this kind of dichotomy was also taken as a means to distinguish sources from a broader perspective by dividing them in 'state oriented' and 'non-state oriented' sources. Both source categories are predominantly Chinese which is not always the case with sources like 'experts' and 'other', which were therefore put in separate categories.[55]

Arranging sources in *types* gives an indication of the diversity of sources that were used. Dividing sources in broader *categories*, like state and non-state-oriented sources, shows that the second category nevertheless is the largest one, although state-oriented sources still represent a dominant category (see fig. 2).

The results from the present analysis show that correspondents intend to keep quite a clear balance between state and non-state-oriented source categories. Nevertheless we also see that state-oriented sources, despite their relative dominance, are outweighed by the non-state-oriented sources and even more so if we include the 'experts' in the non-state-oriented source category. The question comes up whether it would have made a difference in the relation between state- and non-state-related sources if the sources would have been considered from an ideological or political perspective or opposition. Although the political 'content' of the respective sources was not investigated it still became clear that state-related sources were not by definition counter-balanced only by sources that could be considered enemies of the state. Non-state-oriented sources used in all the reports represent a mixture of Han Chinese and Tibetans or Uighurs, which indicates that the main dichotomy in news reporting is not between state and (all) non-state oriented sources but between state-related sources and a specific type of non-state-related sources, namely ordinary people: locals eye witnesses and persons mainly (no matter what political stance).

Indeed, many reports show a constant changing of perspective displayed by starting almost every paragraph with a different source type. To give a random example:

---

[54] Hulshof, A. and Bronkhorst, D., *De Andere Kant van de Medaille: Een Journalistieke Gids voor China* (Amsterdam, 2007), p. 20.
[55] State oriented sources include: state authorities on all societal levels, local and national media (print, broadcast) and national news agencies; Non-state oriented sources are: eyewitnesses, (other) persons, international NGO's.

Officials said last night ... The EU and the White House urged ... Radio Free Asia ... quoted witnesses ... A tourist in Lhasa told the *Guardian* ... Another eyewitness said he heard an explosion ... A blogger ... describes the violence ... Several witnesses reported ... A Tibetan guide quoted by the Associated Press said ... An eyewitness told the *Guardian* ... About a dozen monks were reportedly detained ... The International Campaign for Tibet said ...[56]

In this respect the situation in an authoritarian country clearly shows a different picture than the source 'management' or strategy in democratic countries where pluralism is not demonstrated by using state versus non-state sources only, but most notably by presenting various, sometimes contradicting sources from within the same political, economic, etc. elite.

In the case presented here it seems to be the other way around. Plurality is sought and found not so much in elite, state-oriented sources, but mostly in non-state related sources and particularly in local people sources. We could say that in this particular context the sources that are usually considered as 'secondary definers' seem to have been granted more credibility and did move up the ladder in the 'hierarchy of credibility'.[57]

The Voice of the Correspondent

From the perspective of space allocated to specific sources, however, the non-elite sources are not the only ones with a dominant voice. If the space that is allocated for each source category is taken into account it becomes clear that the (indirect) 'voice' of the correspondent too is important in framing the story, in both the Uighur and Tibetan case. By definition the journalist, as author, frames the story. Considered from the perspective of space allocated to a source, it seems that space generally is almost equally divided between journalist-as-a-source and the indigenous sources. Chart 3 clearly shows how prominent the voice of the correspondent and subsequently the expert in general has been in defining the situation at hand.[58] The voice of the correspondent – 'journalist info' – represents a beacon for the readers and provides them with the where, when, how and by whom. By its factuality it gives a sense of 'neutrality', which is enhanced by the fact

---

[56] Branigan, T. and Ramesh, R., 'Tibet: Gunfire on the streets of Lhasa as rallies turn violent', *The Guardian*, March 15, 2008, p. 24.
[57] Manning, *News and News Sources*, pp. 14-16.
[58] The space allocated to sources was measured as follows: The mean words per line were counted and then the lines devoted to a source, subsequently we could measure the mean words per source.

the sources where the journalist bases his general information on are seldom mentioned.

Most notably this was the case in *The New York Times* and the Dutch *NRC Handelsblad*. *The Guardian* on the other hand displayed a less frequent use of the voice of the journalist and a minimum use of the expert as source. Many news articles from *The Guardian* addressing the Chinese conflicts formed a concatenation of quotations from various source types (see the example above). This, I found, was also the most conspicuous difference between the three newspapers. *The Guardian* clearly tends to 'hide' the voice of the correspondent the most and seems to want to display a maximum effect of authenticity by stitching quotations together. In both other broadsheets the correspondent's voice is much more prominent, clearly displaying an authoritative and knowledgeable instance.

Obstacles Neglected

I was curious to find out whether the space occupied by the correspondent's 'voice', was by any means also used to explain the difficulties correspondents encountered in reporting under these strict and constraint circumstances. But that was only rarely the case and most of the time not in the articles reporting the news about the conflicts. Although correspondents far from denied the obstructive conditions under which they had to do their job, they told their readers about this in only one or two articles only and separately from their regular reports on the conflicts.[59] Only in a few instances they also mentioned, often in one line only, that China was having a tight grip on the information flow, that certain locations or areas were not accessible for outsiders, or that facts could not be confirmed or checked. It was never openly acknowledged that it would affect their reporting in a more fundamental way. The sources themselves were never really questioned or labeled as unreliable. This means that the news reports or background articles were not very transparent in the sense of indicating the reliability of the sources on which the news about the conflicts was founded (see fig. 3)

---

[59] With regard to Tibet 2008: 'Pressed on Tibet, China berates foreign media', *The New York Times* March 25, 2008, p. 7; 'Tibet violence. Diary: blocked at every turn' *The Guardian* March 22, 2008, p. 7; 'Media, dispatches: Reporting from China: 'Mountain roads are a greater risk than the police' *The Guardian* March 24, 2008, p. 2; 'China geeft nu de 'absoluut correcte' versie van het nieuws; Internationale mediacampagne tegen westerse Tibet-verslaggeving' ('The absolute true version of the news; International media campaign against western Tibet-reporting') *NRC Handelsblad* March 29, p. 4. With regard to the Uighur uprise 2009: 'In latest upheaval, China applies new strategies to control flow of information' *New York Times* (on the Web) July 8.

Another way in which journalists could display a certain degree of transparency – and therewith heighten the trustworthiness of their news – was by addressing or using sources in the most explicit way possible such as by quoting (instead of paraphrasing) and by mentioning the name of the one who is quoted (instead of naming the source in general terms). What the present analysis of the reports show is that about 20 percent is quoted and mentioned by name as well, which is quite surprising considering the dangers the sources are surrounded by. If we include the percentage of sources that was not quoted but nevertheless named (8 percent) we see that almost one in three sources were seemingly not afraid to be named in the reports by foreign reporters. On the other hand no less than an average of 50 percent of the sources is mentioned in general terms only. Despite the percentage of quoted and named sources, this could be an indication of how much ordinary people fear the consequences if their names are displayed in foreign news reports. That in some reports the sources are quoted explicitly anyway (by attributing the quote to a name), indicates that it was probably not the journalist's initiative to make a source anonymous and therewith protect the source from harassment by the authorities (see fig. 4).

Comparing the Uighur and the Tibet-cases

What makes comparing the two incidents interesting is that in both cases the state authorities instigated restrictive conditions for the press, but in the case of Tibet constraints were much stricter than during the Uighur protests a year later (in July 2009). Nevertheless the comparison shows that there is no significant difference in the use of prominent sources like state authorities, local eyewitnesses and journalist info; although reporters used more of all three sources during the Uighur uprising. Significantly more (international) civil society actors were used as a source during the Tibetan uprising and during the Uighur protests many more 'persons' were used as source. This specific difference can be attributed to the fact that the Tibetans have a relatively long history of (national but mostly international by exile groups) protest and their PR, with the Dalai Lama as a much celebrated and in many cases internationally-accepted spokesperson, seems to be more professionalized than that of the Uighurs. Moreover foreign journalists had less opportunity to act as eyewitnesses during the Tibetan protests than during the Uighur protests. The Tibetan Autonomous Region was almost completely isolated from the outside world. Even foreign websites (inside China) were blocked, including *The New York Times*, and foreign broadcasts were censored. According to *The New York Times* 'foreign journalists have been denied access to Tibet and blocked from reaching neighboring regions with large Tibetan populations. Many foreign reporters who managed to get into Tibet after the riots were forced to leave.'[60] Although some journalists were allowed – in one state guided tour – to visit the crisis area (conspicuously enough a correspondent from the *Economist*, not from *The New York Times*!), state authorities took extreme measures to control the flow of information. That the news on Tibet was still based on a sizeable amount of non-state related sources (locals and eyewitnesses, that is) can partly explained by the fact that many foreign journalists mentioned 'reports' (in the plural) as a source, by which was clearly alluded to 'eyewitness reports'. Indeed, the number of references made to 'reports' during the Tibetan crisis outnumbered the mention of this source during the Uighur crisis, which indicates a kind of 'indirectness' and information that resembles rumor.

The situation a year later seemed to be quite different. The Chinese government still 'crippled Internet service, blocked Twitter's micro-blogs, purged search engines of unapproved references to the violence, saturated Chinese media with the state-sanctioned story' as *The New York Times* wrote.[61] During the Uighur protests more special tours for (more) foreign reporters were organized around the area of conflict. This explains the prominence of 'persons' as a source. Apparently reporters were allowed to talk to the people on the streets. Of course this was all meant to encourage a more favorable picture of Chinese state authorities. Nevertheless this PR act could be considered as rather unusual for China but after clamping down on the media during the Tibetan uproar, China received such severe criticism from foreign media representatives, which had flooded the country before and during the Olympic Games a few months later, that state authorities decided to act less restrictive with the next internal conflict.

Concluding Remarks

Analyzing the sources that are used by western foreign reporters in China, gives us an insight in how the news under restrictive circumstances is constructed and what implications this has or could have for news narratives. As indicated, prior research has shown that journalists routinely tend to prefer elite, official or in this case state-related sources and consider those the most reliable and informative. In the case of China though, correspondents are conscious of the fact that this category of sources is far from reliable. Moreover, contrary to official sources in democracies, state related sources

---

[60] Barboza, D., 'Pressed on Tibet, China Berates Foreign Media', *The New York Times*, March 25, 2008.
[61] Wines, M., 'In latest Upheaval, China Applies New Strategies to Control Flow of Information', *The New York Times*, July 8, 2009.

in non-democratic countries do not easily express deviant perspectives, particularly not in regard to controversial matters as minority conflicts. They usually speak with one voice enunciating the same message. However, correspondents do not seem to show any reticence towards this source category, giving this official voice relatively much room.

The most sources that are mentioned though are non-state related sources. This ties in with another routine strategy, which is to seek balanced reporting. As official sources do not particularly meet or fit this routine of balancing, journalists clearly looked for different ways to include alternative perspectives or 'voices' in their reports. In this case they focused predominantly on (non-official) local eyewitnesses and 'persons', alternating between the different parties involved in the conflict, but all on a non-state level. This means pluralism is found between state- and non- state-related sources on the one hand, and between local citizens of both parties (Han Chinese versus Tibetans or Uighurs respectively) on the other hand.

With some caution it could be concluded that news and background narratives from foreign correspondents based in authoritarian states show a tendency to a greater variety of source usage than in democracies, where the official source category dominates the news. Contrary to what was to be expected in an authoritarian regime is the voice of ordinary people heard the most, at least in its variety. This source strategy clearly heightens the authenticity-claim dateline journalism provokes.

Turning to local people and eyewitnesses as sources of information has more implications for the news narrative: it often takes on a human interest frame. On the one hand this could be explained by the news organization's requirement to correspondents to bring context and an alternative ('soft') angle to the hard news. On the other hand, as I have tried to argue in this chapter, it could as well be a result from the context in which the correspondent works.

The intensity of this kind of (crisis) reporting is further enhanced by the space that is devoted to the journalist's own voice, be it not in the news reports about the conflicts themselves though. In most articles this voice takes on a purely informative position. It is the voice that presents the reader any necessary facts and context information but which does not really contribute to an intensive reporting style. What does enhance the intensity though, is the almost inevitable moment at which the reporter has to address the consequences the restrictive measures and circumstances have for his or her own reporting. At that moment, the performative style of journalistic narrative, presented as being a truthful reflection of reality, is breached and the reader is given an insight into the production process of the news.[62] This would be in itself an important step towards more transparency. Nevertheless obstacles encountered by correspondents or journalists in general are almost never taken into account in the news narratives themselves.[63] On the contrary, they are rather treated as news themselves!

Perhaps one would expect the internet would offer some resolution, for the correspondent, as a mean to access an even greater variety of sources and to be able to check rumors and reports coming from not clearly identified sources. For news consumers, the internet would enable them to compare or check information, take a look behind the scenes and get a wider perspective on news events. Indeed internet sources are in principle accessible from all over the world, evidently for journalists as well, but authentic sources 'from the field' are only accessible by journalists who are based 'in the field'. This might seem an artificial distinction, as social media can provide journalists with authentic voices from the field as well. It should be emphasized though that despite all optimism about the growing accessibility of the internet, there are still too many 'enemies of the internet', some of them being international political and economic powers to reckon with. Moreover, a global digital divide still exists, particularly between western and non-western countries, between the wealthy parts of the world and poverty stricken areas and, in the context of our topic, last but not least, between free and non-free countries, that is democracies and dictatorships.[64]

Note: I would like to thank my colleague at the Erasmus University, Johannes von Engelhardt, for assisting me in processing the data.

---

[62] Broersma, M., 'The Unbearable Limitations of Journalism: On Press Critique and Journalism's Claim to Truth', *The International Communication Gazette* 72 (2010), no.1, pp. 21-33.

[63] Kester, B.C.M., 'The Art of Balancing. Foreign Correspondence in Non-Democratic Countries: The Russian Case', *The International Communication Gazette* 1 (2010), pp. 51-69.

[64] Abbott, J.P., *The Political Economy of the Internet in Asia and the Pacific Digital Divides, Economic Competitiveness, and Security Challenges* (New York, 2004).

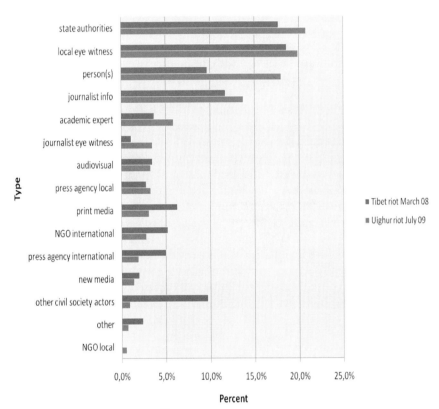

1. Sources Used in Coverage[65]

_____

[65] Every upper line represents the Tibetan case, the lower line the Uighur.

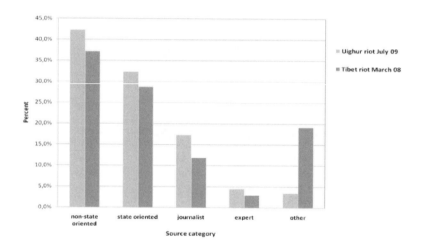

2. Categories of Sources[66]

---

[66] Every right column represents the Tibetan case, the left columns the Uighur

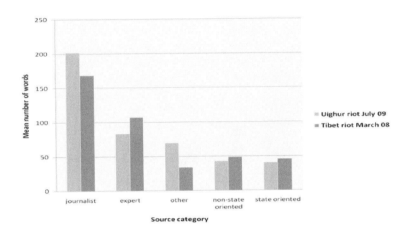

3. Categories of Sources[67]

---

[67] Every right column represents the Tibetan case, the left columns the Uighur

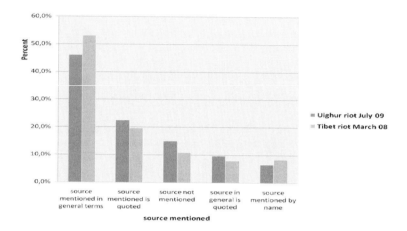

4. How Sources are Deployed in Reports[68]

---

[68] Every right column represents the Tibetan case, the left columns the Uighur.

BIBLIOGRAPHY

Adair, J. and Worthy, S., *Through Navajo Eyes: An Exploration in Film
    Communication and Anthropology* (Albuquerque, NM, 1972).
Adriaansen, M. L., Van Praag, P. and De Vreese, C. H., 'Substance Matters: How
    News Content can Reduce Political Cynicism', *International Journal of
    Public Opinion Research* 22 (2010), no. 4, pp. 433-457.
Aitchison, J., *The Word Weavers: Newshounds and Wordsmiths* (New York, 2007).
Altheide, D., *Creating Fear: News and the Construction of Crisis* (New York,
    2002).
'A Propos de la Nouvelle Formule', *Le Monde*, Internal Note, September 16, 2005.
Archetti, E.P., 'The Spectacle of a Heroic Life: The Case of Diego Maradona', in:
    Andrews, D.L. and Jackson S.J., eds, *Sport Stars: The Cultural Politics of
    Sporting Celebrity* (New York, 2001), pp. 151-163.
Arendt, H., 'Kultur und Politik', *Merkur: Deutsche Zeitschrift für Europäisches
    Denken* 130 (1958), no. 12, pp. 1122-1145.
———, *The Human Condition* (London, 1969).
———, *Das Urteilen: Texte zu Kants Politische Philosophie* (Zürich, 1998).
Aristotle., *Retorik* (Copenhagen, 2002).
Ashton, B., 'The Anchorman', *The Quill* 92 (2004), no. 7.
Aslama, M. and Pantti, M., 'Talking Alone: Reality TV, Emotions and
    Authenticity', in: *European Journal of Cultural Studies* 9 (2006), no. 2,
    pp. 167-184.
Assmann, J., *The Price of Monotheism* (Stanford, CA, 2010).
Atton, C. and Hamilton, J., *Alternative Journalism* (London, 2008).
Aucoin, J., 'Epistemic Responsibility and Narrative Theory: The Literary
    Journalism of Ryszard Kapuscinski', *Journalism* 2 (2001), no. 1, pp. 5-21.
Aufderheide, P., 'Public Intimacy: The Development of First-Person Documentary',
    Afterimage 25 (1997), no. 1.
Averbeck, S. and Kutsch, A., 'Thesen zur Geschichte der Zeitungs- und
    Publizistikwissenschaft 1900-1960', in: Duchkowitsch, W. et al., eds, *Die
    Spirale des Schweigens: Zum Umgang mit der Nationalsozialistischen
    Zeitungswissenschaft* (Berlin, 2004), pp. 55-66.
Author Unknown., 'Krant voor Nieuwe Nieuwsconsument', *NRC Handelsblad*,
    available from: http://vorige.nrc.nl/economie/article1869191.ece (15-08-
    2005).
Bahr, E., ed, *Was ist Aufklärung? Thesen und Definitionen* (Stuttgart, 2002).
Bail, A., 'Cosmétique Rédactionnelle: Le Marketing en Charge de la Modernisation
    de Nord Eclair', *Dissertation, Institute of Political Science* (Lille, 2009).
Baisnée, O. and Balland, L., 'France: Much Ado About (Almost) Nothing', in:
    Eberwein, T. et al., eds, *Mapping Media Accountability: In Europe and
    Beyond* (Koln, 2011), pp. 63-76.

Bakir,V. and Barlow, D. M., 'Exploring Relationships Between Trust Studies and Media Studies', in: Bakir, V. and Barlow, D.M., eds, *Communication in the Age of Suspicion: Trust and the Media* (New York, 2007), pp. 9-24.

Barbalet, J., *Emotion, Social Theory, and Social Structure: A Macrosociological Approach* (Cambridge, 1998).

Barboza, D., 'Pressed on Tibet, China Berates Foreign Media', The New York Times, March 25, 2008.

Bardoel, J., 'Het Einde van de Journalistiek? Nieuwe Verhoudingen Tussen Professie en Publiek', in: Bardoel, J. et al., *Journalistieke Cultuur in Nederland* (Amsterdam, 2005), pp. 357-372.

Bardoel J. and D'Haenens L., 'Media Meet the Citizen: Beyond Market Mechanisms and Government Regulations', *European Journal of Communication* 2 (2004), pp. 165-194.

———, 'Media Responsibility and Accountability: New Conceptualizations and Practices', *Communications* 1 (2004), pp. 5-25.

Barnes, B., 'CBS, Katie Couric Have Already Made Sweet Music Together,' *Wall Street Journal*, September 5, 2006, A1.

Barnouw, E., *Documentary: A History of Non-Fiction Film* (Oxford, 1993).

Barron, A., 'Toward New Goals in Documentary', in: Lewis, J., ed, *The Documentary Tradition* (New York, 1971), pp. 494-499.

Barsam, R., *Nonfiction Film: A Critical History* (Indiana, 1992).

Barthes, R., *Mythologies* (Paris, 1957).

———, 'The Rhetoric of the Image', in: Heath, S., ed, *Image, Music, Text* (New York, 1977), pp. 32-51.

Bauman, Z., *The Individualized Society* (Oxford, 2001).

Beattie, K., *Documentary Screens: Non-Fiction and Television* (London, 2004).

Beck, U., 'The Reinvention of Politics: Towards a Theory of Reflexive Modernization', in: Beck, U., Giddens, A. and Lash, S., eds, *Reflexive Modernization: Politics Tradition and Aestetics in the Modern Social Order* (Stanford, 1994), pp. 1-55.

Becker, K. E., 'Photojournalism and the Tabloid Press', in: Dahlgreen, P. and Sparks, C., eds, *Journalism and Popular Culture* (Thousand Oaks, 1992), pp.130-153.

Bennett, W.L., *The Governing Crisis* (New York, 1992).

Benoit, W. L., Stein, K. A. and Hansen, G. J., 'New York Times Coverage of Presidential Campaigns', *Journalism and Mass Communication Quarterly* 82 (2005), pp. 356-376.

Benson, R. and Neveu, E., *Bourdieu and the Journalistic Field* (Cambridge, 2005).

———, 'Introduction: Field Theory as a Work in Progress', in: *idem.*, eds, *Bourdieu and the Journalistic Field* (Cambridge, 2005).

Benson R. et al., 'Media Systems Online and Off: Comparing the Form of News in the United States, Denmark, and France', *Journal of Communication* 62 (2012), pp. 21–38.

Benson, R., 'Tearing Down the 'Wall' in American Journalism', *International Journal of the Humanities* 1 (2001), pp. 102-113.

———, 'La Fin du Monde. Tradition and Change in the French Press', *French Politics, Culture and Society* 22 (2004), pp. 108-126.

Berger, F., *Journaux Intimes: Les Aventures Tragi-Comiques de la Presse sous François Mitterrand* (Paris, 1992).

Berkowitz, D., 'The Ironic Hero of Virginia Tech: Healing Trauma through Mythical Narrative and Collective Memory', *Journalism* 11 (2010), pp. 643-659.

————, *Social Meanings of News: A Text-Reader* (Thousand Oaks, CA, 1997).

Berkowitz, M., 'Reporters and Their Sources', in: Wahl-Jorgensen, K. and Hanitzsch, T., eds, *The Handbook of Journalism Studies* (New York, 2009), pp. 102-115.

Berndsen, F.A.H., *Met Alle Respect: Over Literatuurkritiek* (Groningen, 2000).

Bertaux, D., *L'enquête et ses Méthodes: Le Récit de Vie* (Paris, 2005).

Bird, S.E. and Dardenne, R.W., 'Myth, Chronicle and Story: Exploring the Narrative Qualities of News', in: Berkowitz, D., ed, *Social Meanings of News: A Text-Reader* (Thousand Oaks, CA, 1997), pp. 333-350.

————, 'Rethinking News and Myth as Storytelling', in: Wahl-Jorgensen, K. and Hanitzsch, T., eds, *The Handbook of Journalism Studies* (New York, 2009), pp. 205-217.

Blin, F., 'Les Secrétaires de Rédaction et les éditeurs de Libération: Des Journalistes Spécialisés dans le Journal', *Réseaux* 111 (2002), pp. 163-190.

Blumler. J.G., 'Origins of the Crisis of Communication for Citizenship', *Political Communication* 14 (1997), pp. 395-404.

Bohrmann, H., 'Als der Krieg zu Ende war: Von der Zeitungswissenschaft zur Publizistik', in: Duchkowitsch, W. et al., eds, *Die Spirale des Schweigens: Zum Umgang mit der Nationalsozialistischen Zeitungswissenschaft* (Berlin, 2004), pp. 97-122.

Bond, M., 'Insular by Default? How the BBC Presents Europe to the British Public', *European Movement Policy Paper 3*, available from: www.euromove.org.uk (2005).

Bondebjerg, I., 'The Social and the Subjective Look: Socumentaries and Reflexive Modernity', *Paper presented at the Australian International Documentary Conference*, available from: http://www.modinet.dk/pdf/WorkingPapers/The_Social_and_the_Subjective_Look.pf (2003).

Boorstin, D.J., *The Image: A Guide to Pseudo-Events in America* (New York, 1992).

Bourdieu, P., *Distinction: A Social Critique of the Judgement of Taste* (Cambridge, 1984).

————, *On Television* (New York, 1998).

————, Opstellen over Smaak, Habitus en het Veldbegrip (Amsterdam, 1992).

————, State Nobility: Elite Schools in the Field of Power (Cambridge, 1996).

————, 'The Political Field, the Social Science Field, and the Journalistic Field', in:

Brady, A.-M., 'Guided Hand: The Role of the CCP Central Propaganda Department in the Current Era', *Westminster Papers in Communication and Culture* 1 (2006) pp. 58-77.

Brakhage, S., 'In Defence of Amateur', (1971), reprinted in: Brakhage, S., ed, *Essential Brakhage: Selected Writings on Filmmaking* (Kingston, 2001).

Brandewinder, M., 'Les Consultants et le Journalisme: Le Conseil Médias dans les Entreprises de Presse', *PhD, University Rennes I* (Rennes, 2009).

Branigan, T. and Ramesh, R., 'Tibet: Gunfire on the streets of Lhasa as Rallies Turn
        Violent', *The Guardian*, March 15, 2008, p. 24.
Brants, K. and Bardoel, J., 'Death Duties: Kelly, Fortuyn, and Their Challenge to
        Media Governance', *European Journal of Communication* 4 (2008), pp.
        471-489.
Brants, K. and De Haan, Y., 'Taking the Public Seriously: Three Models of
        Responsiveness in Media and Journalism', *Media, Culture & Society* 3
        (2010), pp. 411-428.
Brants, K. and Van Praag, P., *Politiek en Media in Verwarring: De
        Verkiezingscampagne in het Lange Jaar 2002* (Amsterdam, 2005).
————, 'Signs of Media Logic: Half a Century of Political Communication in the
        Netherlands', *Javnost—the Public* 13 (2006), pp. 25–40.
Brants, K. et al., 'The Real Spiral of Cynicism? Symbiosis and Mistrust between
        Politicians and Journalists', *The International Journal of Press/Politics* 15
        (2010), no. 1, pp. 25-40.
Brems, H., *Alweer Vogels die Nesten Beginnen: Geschiedenis van de Nederlandse
        Literatuur 1945-2005* (Amsterdam, 2006).
Brin, C., Charron, J. and De Bonville, J., eds, *Nature et Transformation du
        Journalisme: Théorie et Recherches Empiriques* (Laval, 2004).
Broersma, M. and Peters, C., 'Introduction: Rethinking Journalism: The Structural
        Transformation of a Public Good', in: Peters, C. and Broersma, M., eds,
        *Rethinking Journalism: Trust and Participation in a Transformed News
        Landscape* (London, 2012), pp. 1-12.
Broersma, M., *De Associatiemaatschappij: Journalistieke Stijl en de Onthechte
        Nieuwsconsument*, Unpublished Inaugural Lecture, available from:
        http://www.rug.nl/staff/m.j.broersma/Oratie_MarcelBroersma_170309.pdf
        (2009).
————, 'De Waarheid in Tijden van Crisis: Kwaliteitsjournalistiek in een
        Veranderend Medialandschap', in: Ummelen, B., ed, *Journalistiek in
        Diskrediet* (Diemen, 2009), pp. 23-40.
————, 'Form, Style and Journalistic Strategies: An Introduction', in: *Form and
        Style in Journalism: European Newspapers and the Representation of
        News, 1880-2005* (Leuven, 2007), pp. ix-xxix.
————, 'Journalism as Performative Discourse: The Importance of Form and Style
        in Journalism', in: *Journalism and Meaning-making: Reading the
        Newspaper* (New York, 2010), pp. 15-35.
————, 'The Unbearable Limitations of Journalism: On Press Critique and
        Journalism's Claim to Truth', *The International Communication Gazette*
        72 (2010), no.1, pp. 21-33.
————, 'Visual strategies. Dutch Newspaper Design between Text and Image 1900-
        2000', in: *idem.*, ed, *Form and Style in Journalism. European Newspapers
        and the Representation of News 1880-2005* (Leuven, 2007), pp. 177-198.
Brooker, P., *Non-Democratic Regimes* (Hampshire, 2009).
Brooten, L., 'Political Violence and Journalism in a Multiethnic State: A Case Study
        of Burma (Myanmar)', Journal of Communication Inquiry 4 (2006), pp.
        354-373.
Bruin, W. et al., *Tussen de Regels: Vijf Jaar Verslaggeving in De Volkskrant*
        (Amsterdam, 2006).

Brusini, H. and James, F., *Voir la Vérité: le Journalisme de Télévision* (Paris, 1982).

Buckingham, D. and Willett, R., eds, *Video Cultures: Media Technology and Everyday Creativity* (London, 2009).

Bucy, E. P. and Grabe, M. E., 'Taking Television Seriously: A Sound and Image Bite Analysis of Presidential Campaign Coverage, 1992-2004', *Journal of Communication* 57 (2007), pp. 652-675.

Bull, M., 'The World According to Sound', *New Media and Society* 3 (2001), no. 2, pp. 179-197.

Burke, P., *A Social History of Knowledge: From Gutenberg to Diderot* (Cambridge, 2000).

Cameron, D., 'Language. Truth or Dare?', *Critical Quarterly* 46 (2004), no. 2, 124-127.

Campbell, C.C., 'Journalism as a Democratic Art', in: Glasser, T.L., ed, *The Idea of Public Journalism* (New York, 1999), pp. xiii-xxix.

Campbell, J., *The Hero with a Thousand Faces* (London, 1993).

Cappella, J.N. and Jamieson, K.H., *Spiral of Cynicism: The Press and the Public Good* (New York, 1997).

Carter, C. et al., "Setting New(s) Agendas: An Introduction', in: Carter, C., Branston, C. and Allan, S., eds, *News, Gender and Power* (London, 1998), pp. 1-12.

Cater, D., *The Fourth Branch of Government* (New York, 1959).

Cathcart, R.S., 'From Hero to Celebrity: The Media Connection', in: Drucker, S.J. and Cathcart, R.S., eds, *American Heroes in a Media Age* (Cresskill, 1994), pp. 36-46.

CBS Early Show., 'Cronkite Remembers JFK: Newsman Walter Cronkite's Impressions on the Fallen President', *Early Show* (2003).

CBS Evening News., Newscast Aired on March 28th, 1979.

————, Newscast Aired on May 14th, 1979.

————, Newscast Aired on November 5th, 1979.

————, Newscast Aired on November 21st, 1979.

————, 'Katie Couric is Joining CBS News: Couric Will Become Anchor and Managing Editor of The CBS Evening News', *CBS News*, available from: http://www.cbscorporation.com/news/ (2006).

————, 'CBS Evening News With Katie Couric Will Become the First Network Evening News Broadcast to be Simulcast Live on the Internet', available from: http://www.cbsnews.com/sections/eveningnews/main3420.shtml (2006).

————, Newscast Aired on May 7th, 2007.

————, Newscast Aired on May 8th, 2007.

————, Newscast Aired on May 9th, 2007.

————, Newscast Aired on May 10th, 2007.

————, Newscast Aired on May 11th, 2007.

————, Newscast Aired on May 14th, 2007.

————, Newscast Aired on May 15th, 2007.

————, Newscast Aired on May 16th, 2007.

————, Newscast Aired on May 17th, 2007.

————, Newscast Aired on May 18th, 2007.

————, 'Couric & Co', *CBS News*, available from:
http://www.cbsnews.com/sections/couricandco/main500803.shtml (2008).

Champagne, P., 'Le Médiateur Entre Deux Monde, Actes de la Recherche en Sciences Sociales', *Actes de la Recherche en Sciences Sociales* 131-132 (2000), pp. 8-29.

Charon J.-M., 'Managers au quotidien', *Médiaspouvoirs* 16 (1989), pp. 112-123.

————, 'Le Lecteur à Satisfaire: Le Marketing en Presse Magazine', in: Dreyer E. and Le Floch P., eds, *Le lecteur. Approche Sociologique, Économique et Juridique* (Paris, 2004), pp. 19-45.

Charpentier, I., 'Une Pratique Rare et Sélective: La Lecture de la Presse d'information Générale et Politique', in: Legavre, J.-B., ed, *La Presse Écrite: Objets Délaissés* (Paris, 2004), pp. 315-335.

Children and Young People's Unit., *Young People and Politics: A Report on the Yvote?/ Ynot?Project* (London, 2002).

China: World Democracy Profile, *WorldAudit.org*, available from:
http://www.worldaudit.org/countries/china.htm (2001).

Chouliaraki, L., 'Aestheticization of Suffering on Television', *Visual Communication* 5 (2006), no. 3, pp. 261-285.

Chupin, I., Hubé, N. and Kaciaf, N., *Histoire Politique et Économique des Médias en France* (Paris, 2012).

Clayman, S.E. and Reisner, A., 'Gatekeeping in Action: Editorial Conferences and Assessments of Newsworthiness', *American Sociological Review* 63 (1998), pp. 178-199.

Cloostermans, M., 'Grunberg is God', *De Standaard*, available from:
http://www.standaard.be/artikel/detail.aspx?artikelid=3D29QKT4 (08-05-2009).

Coakley, J. and Dunning, E., *Handbook of Sports Studies* (London, 2000).

Colbert Report, The, 'Interview with Katie Couric', *Comedy Central*, Episode Aired on March 22nd, 2007.

Compton, J.R., 'Newspapers, Labor and the Flux of Economic Uncertainty', in: Allan, S., ed, *The Routledge Companion to News and Journalism* (New York, 2010), pp. 591-601. Conboy, M., *Tabloid Britain: Constructing a Community through Language* (New York, 2006).

————, *The Press and Popular Culture* (London, 2002).

Cook, T.E., *Making Laws and Making News* (Washington, 1989).

Cornu, D. and Borruat, R., *Les Médias en Suisse: Structures et Audiences* (Lausanne, 2007).

Cottle, S. and M. Rai., 'Between Display and Deliberation: Analyzing TV News as Communicative Architecture', *Media, Culture & Society* 28 (2006), no. 2, pp. 163-189.

Crick, B., *In Defence of Politics* (New York, 2005).

Clausen, L., 'Localizing the Global: "Domestication" Processes in International News Production', *Media, Culture and Society* 1 (2004), pp. 25-44.

Corner, J., 'Documentary in a Post-Documentary Culture: A Note on Forms and Their Functions", available from:
http://www.lboro.ac.uk/research/changing.media/index.html (2000).

————, 'Afterword. Framing the New', in: Holmes, S. and Jermyn, D., eds, *Understanding Reality Television* (London, 2004), pp. 290-299.

Cronkite, W., *A Reporter's Life* (New York, 1996).

Crouteau, D. and Hoynes, W., *The Business of Media: Corporate Media and the Public Interest* (Thousand Oaks, 2001).

Dahlgren, P., 'Media, Citizenship and Civic Culture', in: Curran, J. and Gurevitch, M., eds, *Mass Media and Society* (London, 2000).

———, 'TV News as a Social Relation', *Media, Culture and Society* 3 (1981), pp. 291-302. Dallmayr, F., 'Hermeneutics and Inter-Cultural Dialog: Linking Theory and Practice', *Ethics & Global Politics* 2 (2009), no. 1, pp. 23-39.

D'Angelo, P. and Lombard, M., 'The Power of the Press: The Effects of Press Frames in Political Campaign News on Media Perceptions', *Atlantic Journal of Communication* 16 (2008), no. 1, pp. 1-32.

Deacon, D. et al., *Reporting the 2005 UK General Election* (London 2005).

Deacon, D., Golding, P. and Billig, M., 'Press and Broadcasting: "Real Issues" and Real Coverage', in: Norris, P., ed, *Britain Votes 2001* (Oxford, 2001), pp. 103-114.

Dean, J., 'U.S. and European Heroism Compared', in: Drucker, S.J. and Gumpert, G., eds, *Heroes in a Global World* (Cresskill, 2008), pp. 19-45.

Deans, P., 'The Internet in the People's Republic of China: Censorship and Participation', in: Abbott, J.P., ed, *The Political Economy of the Internet in Asia and the Pacific: Digital Divides, Economic Competitiveness, and Security Challenges* (Connecticut, 2004), pp. 123-138.

De Montaigne, M., 'Wenn Man Einander des Lügens Bezichtigt', in: *Essais: Erste moderne Gesamtübersetzung von Hans Stilett. Vol II* (Frankfurt am Main, 2000).

Delli Carpini, M. and B. Williams., 'Let Us Infotain You: Politics in the New Media Environment', in: Bennett, W. L. and Entman. R. M., eds, *Mediated Politics: Communication in the Future of Democracy* (Cambridge, 2001), pp. 160-181.

De Jong, S., 'De krant Antwoordt', in: *NRC Handelsblad* (04-08-2007).

De Maulde, F., 'La Presse: Maggiori de me Voir si Belle: Un Entretien Avec le Zorro du Look', *Le Matin*, June 12, 1985.

De Nooij, W., *Richtingen en Lichtingen: Literaire Classificaties, Netwerken, Instituties* (Tilburg, 1993).

Desrosières, A., 'How to Make Things Which Hold Together: Social Science, Statistics and the State', in: Wittrock, B., Wagner, P. and Whitley, R., eds, *Discourses on Society: The Shaping of the Social Science Disciplines* (Dordrecht, 1991), pp. 195-218.

Deutsch Karlekar, K. and Cook, S.G., 'Access and Control: A Growing Diversity of Threats to Internet Freedom', in: *Freedom House Report Freedom on the Net: A Global Assessment of Internet and Digital Media* 1 (2009), pp. 34-45.

Deuze, M., 'Popular Journalism and Professional Ideology: Tabloid Reporters and Editors Speak Out', *Media, Culture & Society* 27 (2005), no. 6, pp. 861-82.

De Volkskrant (2002, Jan. 28). Statuut ombudsman. Internal document.

———, *Onderzoek Jansen van Galen en Kemper naar Martelprimeur in de Volkskrant* (Amsterdam, 2007).

De Vreese, C.H., *Framing Europe: Television News and European Integration* (Amsterdam, 2005).

De Vreese, C.H. and Elenbaas, M., 'Media in the Game of Politics: Effects of Strategic Metacoverage on Political Cynicism', *Harvard International Journal of Press/ Politics* 13 (2008), no. 3, pp.285-309.

De Vreese, C.H. and Semetko, H.A., 'Cynical and Engaged: Strategic Campaign Coverage, Public Opinion and Mobilisation in a Referendum', *Communication Research* 29 (2006), no. 6, pp. 615-641.

Dillon, M., 'Ethics in Black and White,' in: Good, H., ed, *Ethics in Black and White* (New York, 2007).

Directorate General Communication., 'Eurobarometer 66: Public Opinion in the European Union', *European Commission*, available from: http://ec.europa.eu/public_opinion/archives/eb/eb66/eb66_highlights_ en.pdf (2006).

———, 'Eurobarometer 72: Public Opinion in the European Union', *European Commission*, available from: http://ec.europa.eu/public_opinion/archives/eb/eb72/eb72_en.htm (2010).

Dorleijn, G. and Van Rees, C.J., *De Productie van de Literatuur: Het Literaire Veld in Nederland 1800-2000* (Nijmegen, 2006).

Drok, N., 'Civiele Journalistiek: Het Belang van de Professie voor het Publieke Domein', in: Bardoel, J., et.al, *Journalistieke Cultuur in Nederland* (Amsterdam, 2005), pp. 373-390.

Dovey, J., *Freakshow: First Person Media and Factual Television* (London, 2000).

Drucker, S.J., 'The Mediated Sports Hero', in: Drucker, S.J. and Gumpert, G., eds, *Heroes in a Global World* (Cresskill, 2008), pp. 415-432.

Drucker, S.J. and Cathcart, R.S., *American Heroes in a Media Age* (Cresskill, 1994).

Drucker, S.J. and Gumpert, G., *Heroes in a Global World* (Cresskill, 2008).

Dubied, A., 'L'information People, Entre Rhétorique du cas Particulier et Récit de l'intimité', *Communication* 27 (2009), no. 1, pp. 54-65.

———, 'Catalyse et Parenthèse Enchantée: Quand le Fait Divers Rencontre la Politique-People', *Le Temps des Médias* 10 (2008), pp.142-155.

Duffy, S., 'Heroes in a Global World', in: Drucker, S.J. and Gumpert, G., eds, *Heroes in a Global World* (Cresskill, 2008), pp. 205-225.

Dyer, R., *Stars* (London, 1979).

Eberwein, T. et al., *Mapping Media Accountability: In Europe and Beyond* (Cologne, 2011). Ellis, J., *Documentary: Witness and Self-Revelation* (New York, 2012).

Entman, R.M., *Projections of Power: Framing News, Public Opinion, and U.S. Foreign Policy* (London, 2004).

Enzensberger, H.M., *Einzelheiten I: Bewusstseins-Industrie* (Frankfurt am Main, 1964).

Ericson, et al., *Negotiating Control: A Study of News Sources* (London, 1989).

———, *Visualizing Deviance: A Study of News Organization* (Toronto, 1987).

Erignac, H., 'Quand Le Monde Fait sa Publicité', *Dissertation, Université Paris II-Assas* (Paris, 2000).

Esser, F., 'Editorial Structures and Work Principles in British and German Newsrooms', *European Journal of Communication* 13 (1998), no.3, pp. 375-405.

————, 'Metacoverage of Mediated Wars: How the Press Framed the Role of the News Media and of Military News Management in the Iraq Wars of 1991 and 2003', *American Behavioral Scientist* 52 (2009), no. 5, pp. 709-734

————, 'Tabloidization of News: a Comparative Analysis of Anglo-American and German Press Journalism', *European Journal of Communication* 14 (1999), pp. 291-324.

Esser, F. and D'Angelo, P., 'Framing the Press and Publicity Process: A Content Analysis of Meta-coverage in Campaign 2000 Network News', *American Behavioral Scientist* 46 (2003), no. 5, pp. 617-641.

————, 'Framing the Press and Publicity Process in German, British, and U.S. General Elections: A Comparative Study of Metacoverage', *Harvard International Journal of Press/Politics* 11 (2006), no. 3, pp. 44-66.

Esser, F., Reinemann, C. and Fan, D., 'Spin Doctors in the United States, Great Britain, and Germany: Metacommunication about Media Manipulation', *Harvard International Journal of Press/ Politics* 6 (2001), no. 1, pp. 16-45.

Esser, F. and Spanier, B., 'News Management as News: How Media Politics Leads to Metacoverage', *Journal of Political Marketing* 4 (2005), no.4, pp. 27-58.

'Ethiek: Code voor de Journalistiek', *Nederlandse Vereniging van Journalisten (NVJ)*, available from, http://www.nvj.nl/ethiek/code-voor-de-journalistiek (2008).

Fairclough, N., Media Discourse (London, 1985).

Falcous, M. and Maguire, J., 'Globetrotters and Local Heroes? Labor Migration, Basketball, and Local Identities', *Sociology of Sport Journal* 22 (2005), pp. 137-157.

Fallows, J., *Breaking the News: How the Media Undermine American Democracy* (New York, 1996).

Ferris, K., 'The Sociology of Celebrity', *Sociology Compass* 1 (2007), pp. 371-384.

Firat, A. and Dholakia, N., *Consuming People; From Political Economy to Theatres of Consumption* (London, 1998).

Fisher, W.R., 'The Narrative Paradigm - in the Beginning', *Journal of Communication* 35 (1985), pp. 74-89.

Fishman, M., *Manufacturing the News* (Austin, 1980).

Frank, R., 'These Crowded Circumstances: When Pack Journalists Bash Pack Journalism', *Journalism* 4 (2003), no. 4, pp. 441-458.

Franklin, B., ed, *The Future of Newspapers* (New York, 2009).

————, *Newzak and the News Media* (London, 1997).

————, *Packaging Politics: Political Communications in Britain's Media Democracy* (London, 2004).

Frus, P., *The Politics and Poetics of Journalistic Narrative: The Timely and the Timeless* (Cambridge, 1994).

Fulford, R., *The Triumph of Narrative: Storytelling in the Age of Mass Culture* (Toronto, 1999).

Fuller, J., 'The Collapse of the Old Order', in: *What is Happening to News: The Information Explosion and the Crisis in Journalism* (Chicago, 2010), pp. 1-11.

Furedi, F., *Therapy Culture: Cultivating Vulnerability in an Uncertain Age* (London, 2003).

Gaber, I., '"Dislocated and Distracted": Media, Parties and the Voters in the 2005 General Election Campaign', *British Politics* 1 (2006), no. 3, pp. 344–366.

———, 'Election 2010: a Policy-Free Environment', *Presented at the IPSA/ MPG Joint International Conference on Political Communication, Loughborough University* (November 2010).

Gadamer, H.-G., *Wahrheit und Methode* (Tübingen, 1975).

Gamson, J., 'Normal Sins: Sex Scandal Narratives as Institutional Morality Tales', *Social Problems* 48 (2001), pp. 185-205.

Gans, H., *Deciding What's News: A Study of CBS Evening News, NBC Nightly News, Newsweek and Time* (Evanston, 1979).

Gauntlet, D., *Making is Connecting* (London, 2011).

Gavin, N.T., *Press and Television in British Politics* (Basingstoke, 2007).

Gerhardt, V., *Partizipation: Das Prinzip der Politik* (Munich, 2007).

Gerring, J., *Case Study Research: Principles and Practices* (Cambridge, 2007).

Giddens, A., 'Living in the Post-Traditional Society', in: Beck, U., Giddens, A. and Lash, S., eds, *Reflexive Modernization. Politics Tradition and Aestetics in the Modern Social Order* (Stanford, 1994), pp. 56-109.

Glasser, T.L., 'Preface and Acknowledgments', in: *idem*, ed, *The Idea of Public Journalism* (New York, 1999), pp. xxxi-xxxiii.

———, 'The Idea of Public Journalism', in: *idem*, ed, *The Idea of Public Journalism* (New York, 1999), pp. 3-18.

Goud, J., '"De Toekomst is Niets dan Leegte: Wat Zal Ik Eens Gaan Doen?" Een Gesprek met Arnon Grunberg', in: Goud, J., ed, *Het Leven Volgens Arnon Grunberg: De Wereld als Poppenkast* (Kampen, 2010), pp. 126-147.

Goulet, V., 'Le Médiateur de la Rédaction de France 2: L'institutionnalisation d'un Public Idéal', *Question de Communication* 5 (2004), pp. 281-299.

Graber, D., 'The Infotainment Quotient in Routine Television News: A Director's Perspective', *Discourse & Society* 5 (1994), no. 4, pp. 483-508.

Grevisse, B., 'Le Journalisme Gagné par la Peoplisation: Identités Professionnelles, Déontologie et Culture de la Dérision', *Communication* 27 (2009), no.1, pp.179-197.

———, *Le Temps des Journalistes: Essai de Narratologie Médiatique* (Louvain-la-Neuve, 1997).

Guisnel, J., *Libération, la Biographie* (Paris, 1999).

Gumpert, G., 'The Wrinkle Theory: The Deconsecration of the Hero', in: Drucker, S.J. and Gumpert, G., eds, *Heroes in a Global World* (Cresskill, 2008), pp. 129-147.

Hachten, W.A. and Scotton, J.F., *World News Prisms: Global Information in a Satellite Age* (Oxford, 2007).

Hackett, R. and Zhao, Y., *Sustaining Democracy?: Journalism and the Politics of Objectivity* (Toronto, 1998).

Habermas, J., *Strukturwandel der Öffentlichkeit* (Frankfurt am Main, 1962).

Hagan, J., 'Alas, Poor Couric: But Pity Her Not', *New York Magazine*, available from: http://nymag.com/news/features/34452/ (2007).

Hahn, K., Iyengar, S. and Norpoth, H., 'Consumer Demand for Election News: The Horserace Sells', *Presented at the Annual Meeting of the American Political Science Association* (Boston, August 2002).

Hallin, D. 'The Passing of the "High Modernism" of American Journalism', *Journal of Communication* 42 (1992), no. 3, pp. 14-25.

Hallin, D. C. and Mancini, P., *Comparing Media Systems Beyond the Western World* (Cambridge 2012).

_____, *Comparing Media Systems: Three Models of Media and Politics* (Cambridge, 2004).

Hanitzsch, T., 'Deconstructing Journalism Culture: Toward a Universal Theory', *Communication Theory* 17 (2007), pp. 367-385.

Hannerz, U., *Foreign News: Exploring the World of Foreign Correspondents* (Chicago, 2004).

Harbers, F., 'Between Fact and Fiction: Grunberg on His Literary Journalism', in: *Literary Journalism Studies* 2 (2010), no. 1, pp. 74-83.

_____, 'Defying Journalistic Performativity. The Tension between Journalism and Literature in Arnon Grunberg's Reportage', in: Boucharenc, M., Martens, D. and Van Nuys, L., eds, *Interférences littéraires* (2011), no. 7, pp. 141-163.

Hardt, H., 'Am Vergessen Scheitern: Essay zur Jistorischen Identität der Publizistikwissenschaft, 1945-68', in: Duchkowitsch, W. et al., eds, *Die Spirale des Schweigens: Zum Umgang mit der Nationalsozialistischen Zeitungswissenschaft* (Münster, 2004), pp. 153-160.

Hargreaves, I. and Thomas, J., 'New News, Old News', *ITC/BSC Report*, available from: http://www.itc.org.uk/itc_publications/audience_research/index.asp (2002).

Harrop, M., 'Press', in: Butler, D. and Kavanagh, D., eds., *The British General Election of 1983* (London, 1984),

Hartley, J., *Understanding News* (London, 1983).

Hartsock, J. C., *A History of American Literary Journalism: The Emergence of a Modern Narrative Form* (Amherst, 2000).

Harvey, J. and Houle, F., 'Sport, World Economy, Global Culture, and New Social Movements', *Sociology of Sport Journal* 11 (1994), pp. 337-355.

Heikki, H. and Kylmala, T., 'Finland: Direction of Change Still Pending', in: Eberwein, T. et al., eds, *Mapping Media Accountability: In Europe and Beyond* (Koln, 2011), pp. 50-62.

Helmers, M. and Hill, C., 'Introduction', in: Hall, C. and Helmers, M., eds, *Defining Visual Rhetorics* (Mahwah NJ, 2004), pp. 1-24.

Henderson, J., 'Handing Over Control? Access, 'Ordinary People' and Video Nation', in: Buckingham, D. and Willet, R., eds, *Video Cultures: Media Technology and Everyday Creativity* (New York, 2009), pp. 152-171.

Herman, E. and Chomsky, N., *Manufacturing Consent: The Political Economy of the Mass Media* (New York, 1988).

Hermida, A., 'Let' s Talk: How Blogging is Shaping the BBC' s Relationship with the Public', in: Tunney, S. and Monaghan. G., eds, *Web Journalism: A New Form of Citizenship* (Eastourne, 2010), pp. 306-316.

Hibbing, J. and Theiss-Morse, E., *Stealth Democracy: Americans' Beliefs about how Government Should Work* (Cambridge, 2002).

Hirschman, E.C., 'The Interplay between Archetypes and Autobiography in Mass Media Preferences', *Advances in Consumer Research* 31 (2004), pp. 168-173.

Hill, C., *Rewind: Video Art and Alternative Media in the United States, 1968-1980* (Video Data Bank, 2008).

Hoebeke, T., Deprez, A. and Raeymaeckers, K., 'Heroes in the Sports Pages: The Troubled Road to Victory for Belgian Cyclist Tom Boonen', *Journalism Studies* 12 (2011), pp. 658-672.

Hockney, D., *Secret Knowledge: Rediscovering the Lost Techniques of the Old Masters* (London, 2006).

Holmes, S. and Redmond, S., *Framing Celebrity: New Directions in Celebrity Culture* (New York, 2006).

Holtz-Bacha, C., 'Videomalaise Revisited: Media Exposure and Political Alienation in West Germany', *European Journal of Communication* 5 (1990), pp. 78-85.

Houlihan, B., 'Homogenization, Americanization, and Creolization of Sport: Varieties of Globalization', *Sociology of Sport Journal* 11 (1994), pp. 356-375.

Høyer, S., 'Rumours of Modernity: How American Journalism Spread to Europe', in: Broersma, M., ed, *Form and Style in Journalism: European Newspapers and the Representation of News, 1880-2005* (Leuven, 2007), pp. 27-52.

Hubé, N, 'Face aux Pairs. Centralisation des Rédactions, Contraintes de Rôle et Publicité des Discussions', in: Dauvin, P. and Legavre J.-B., eds, *Les Publics des Journalistes* (Paris, 2007), pp. 85-106.

———, *Décrocher la 'Une'. Le Choix des Titres de Première Page de la Presse Quotidienne en France et en Allemagne (1945-2005)* (Strasbourg, 2008).

Hubé, N. and Kaciaf, N., 'Les Pages Société… ou les Pages Politiques en Creux', in: Chupin, I. and Nollet, J., eds, *Les Frontières Journalistiques* (Paris, 2005), pp. 189-211.

Hulshof, A. and Bronkhorst, D., *De Andere Kant van de Medaille: Een Journalistieke Gids voor China* (Amsterdam, 2007).

Ipsos-MORI., 'The Political Triangle 1987-2010', *Ipsos*, available from: http://www.ipsos-mori.com/researchpublications/researcharchive/poll.aspx?oItemId=85 (2010).

Iyengar, S., *Is Anyone Responsible? How Television Frames Political Issues* (Chicago, 1991).

Jackson, D., 'Framing Democratic Politics: An Investigation into the Presence and Effects of 'Strategy' News Frames in the UK', *PhD thesis, Bournemouth University* (2009).

———, 'Strategic Media, Cynical Public? Examining the Contingent Effects of Strategic News Frames on Political Cynicism in the UK', *The Harvard International Journal of Press/Politics* 16 (2011), no. 1, pp. 75-101.

———, 'Strategic News Frames and Public Policy Debates: Press and Television News Coverage of the Euro in the UK', *Communications* 36 (2011), no. 2, pp. 169-194.

Jacob, M.C., *The Radical Enlightenment: Pantheists, Freemasons and Republicans* (Lafayette, LA, 2006).

Jacobs, R. 'Producing the News, Producing the Crisis: Narrativity, Television and News Work', *Media, Culture and Society* 18 (1996), no. 3, pp. 373-397.

Jamieson, K.H., *Dirty Politics* (Oxford, 1992).

Jansen, T. and Drok, N., *Op Zoek Naar Vertrouwen in de Pers* (Amsterdam, 2005).

Jarvie, G. and Reid, I.A., 'Sport, Nationalism and Culture in Scotland', *The Sports Historian* 19 (1999), pp. 97-124.

Jenkins, H., *Convergence Culture: Where Old and New Media Collide* (New York, 2008). Jensma, F., 'De Lezer Schrijft over de Introductie van NRC.Next, de Nieuwe Ochtendkrant', in: *NRC Handelsblad* (18-03-2006).

Jobert, B., ed, *Le Tournant Néo-Libéral en Europe: Idées et Recettes dans les Pratiques Gouvernementales* (Paris, 1994).

Johnson, T. J. and Boudreau, T., 'Turning the Spotlight Inward: How Leading News Organizations Covered the Media in the 1992 Presidential Election', *Journalism and Mass Communication Quarterly* 73 (1996), no. 3, pp. 657-671.

Jones J., *Entertaining Politics* (New York, 2005).

Josephi, B., 'Journalism in the Global Age. Between Normative and Empirical', *The International Communication Gazette* 6 (2005), pp. 575-590.

Juhem, P., 'Alternances Politiques et Transformations du Champ de l'information en France après 1981', *Politix* 56 (2001), pp. 185-208.

July, S., 'Entretien', *Médiaspouvoirs* 19 (1990), pp. 81-87.

Just, M., 'Talk is Cheap: Thoughts on Improving Voter Information in Light of the 1992 Campaign', *Harvard International Journal of Press/Politics* 1 (1996), pp. 152-160.

Kaciaf, N., 'La Mort du Séancier. Les Transformations Contemporaines des Comptes-Rendus Parlementaires dans les Quotidiens Français', in: Ringoot, R. and Utard J.-M., eds, *Genres journalistiques. Savoirs et Savoir-Faire* (Paris, 2009), pp. 83-100.

Kerbel, M.R., Apee, S. and Ross, M.H., 'PBS ain't so Different: Public Broadcasting, Election Frames, and Democratic Empowerment', *The Harvard International Journal of Press/ Politics* 5 (2000), no. 8, pp. 8-32.

Kester, B.C.M.., 'Working at the End of the Assembly Line: A Conversation with Joris Luyendijk about the Impossibility of Doing Western-style Journalism in Arab Countries', *The International Journal of Press/Politics* 4 (2008), pp. 500-506.

——, 'The Art of Balancing. Foreign Correspondence in Non-Democratic Countries: The Russian Case', *The International Communication Gazette* 1 (2010), pp. 51-69.

Kirkup, J., 'Cameron Fails to end 'Punch and Judy' Politics', *The Daily Telegraph*, available from: http://www.telegraph.co.uk/news/politics/conservative/1908155/David-Cameron-fails-to-end-Punch-and-Judy-politics.html (2008).

Klaassen, J. and Klein, T., *Srebrenica in de Volkskrant: 1991-1995* (Amsterdam, 2002).

Klapp, O.E., 'Heroes, Villains and Fools, as Agents of Social Control', *American Sociological Review* 19 (1954), pp. 56-62.

————, 'The Creation of Popular Heroes', *The American Journal of Sociology* 54 (1948), pp. 135-141.

Koch, H., *Hvad er Demokrati?* (Copenhagen, 1995).

Kovach, B. and Rosenstiel, T., *Warp Speed: America in the Age of Mixed Media* (New York, 1999).

Kopper, G.G. and Bates, B.J., 'Political Economy of Foreign Correspondents', in: Gross, P. and Kopper, G.G., eds, *Understanding Foreign Correspondence: A Euro American Perspective of Concepts, Methodologies, and Theories* (New York, 2011), pp. 45-68.

Kostenzer, C., *Die Literarische Reportage: Über eine Hybride Form Zwischen Journalismus und Literatur* (Innsbruck, 2009).

Kracauer, S., *Die Angestellten* (Frankfurt am Main, 1929).

Kress, G. and Van Leeuwen, T., *Reading Images: The Grammar of Visual Design* (London, 1996).

Kristeller, P.O., *Renaissance Thought: The Classic, Scholastic and Humanist Strains* (New York, 1961).

Kuhn, R., 'The Media and Politics', in: Dunleavy, P. et al., eds, *Developments in British Politics* 7 (Hampshire: 2003).

Lallemand, A., *Journalisme Narratif en Pratique* (Brussels, 2011).

'L'Alsace, Projet Éditorial 2000', *Internal Document,* September 3, 1999, p. 13.

Lane, J., *The Autobiographical Documentary in America* (London, 2002).

Latour, B., 'A Dialogue on Actor-Network Theory with a (Somewhat) Socratic Professor', in: Avgerou, C. et al., eds, *The Social Study of Information and Communication Study* (Oxford, 2004), pp. 62-76.

Lawrence, R., 'Game Framing the Issues: Tracking the Strategy Frame in Public Policy News', *Political Communication* 17 (2000), pp. 93-114.

Le Bohec, J., *Les Mythes Professionnels des Journalistes* (Paris, 2000).

Le Figaro Économie, 'Le Figaro, a Newspaper that is Attentive to its Readers' Expectations', November 11, 1999, p. VIII.

Lehman, D., *Matters of Fact: Reading Nonfiction over the Edge* (Columbus, 1997).

'Le Parisien, En un Clin D'œil', *Publicity Brochure*, 2001, pp. 8-9.

'Le Parisien, En un Clin D'œil', *Publicity Brochure*, 1997, p. 7.

Lewis, J., 'News and the Empowerment of Citizens', *European Journal of Cultural Studies* (2006), no. 3, pp. 303-319.

Lewis, J., Williams, A. and Franklin, B., 'Four Rumours and an Explanation', *Journalism Practice* 2 (2008), no. 1, pp. 27 – 45.

'Libération, Principes D'Editing', *Internal Document*, October 1998, p. 9.

Lichter, R., 'Was TV Election News Better This Time: A Content Analysis of 1988 and 1992 Campaign Coverage', *Journal of Political Science* 21 (1993), pp. 3-25.

Lilleker, D. G., Negrine, R. and Stanyer, J., 'A Vicious Circle: Politicians and Journalists in Britain's Media Democracy', *Political Studies Review* (2002).

Lipsitz, K. et al., 'What Voters Want from Political Campaign Communication', *Political Communication* 20 (2005), pp. 337-354.

Lock, H., 'Transformations of the Trickster', *Southern Cross Review*, available from: http://www.southerncrossreview.org/18/trickster.htm (2002).

Louw, E. P., 'Journalists Reporting from Foreign Places', in: De Beer A. S. and Merrill, J. C., eds, *Global Journalism: Topical Issues and Media Systems* (Boston, 2004), pp. 151-162.

Lowrey, W. and Anderson, W., 'The Journalist Behind the Curtain: Participatory Functions on the Internet and Their Impact on Perceptions of the Work of Journalism', *Journal of Computer-Mediated Communication* 10 (2005), no. 3, available from: http://jcmc.indiana.edu/vol10/issue3/lowrey.html.

Lozano, E., 'The Force of Myth on Popular Narratives: The Case of Melodramatic Serials', *Communication Theory* 2 (1992), pp. 207-220.

Lule, J., *Daily News, Eternal Stories: The Mythological Role of Journalism* (London, 2001).

Luyendijk, J., 'Beyond Orientalism', *The International Communication Gazette* 1 (2010), pp. 9-20.

Ma, E. K.-W., 'Rethinking Media Studies: The Case of China', in: Curran, J. and Park, M.-J., eds, *De-Westernizing Media Studies* (London, New York, 2000), pp. 21-34.

MacDonald, M., 'Rethinking Personalization in Current Affairs Journalism', in: Sparks, C. and Tulloch, J., eds, *Tabloid Tales: Global Debates over Media Standards* (Oxford, 2000), pp. 251-266.

MacDonald, S., *A Critical Cinema 4: Interviews with Independent Filmmakers* (Berkeley, 2005).

MacIntyre, A., *After Virtue: A Study in Moral Theory* (Notre Dame, IN, 1984).

MacKinnon, R., 'Blogs and China Correspondence: Lessons about Global Information Flows', *Chinese Journal of Communication* 2 (2008), pp. 242-257.

Maguire, J., 'Sport and Globalization', in: Coakley, J. and Dunning, E., eds, *Handbook of Sports Studies* (London, 2000), pp. 356-369.

Manning, P., *News and News Sources: A Critical Introduction* (London, 2001).

Marchetti, D. and Ruellan, D., *Devenir Journaliste. Sociologie de l'entrée sur le Marché du Travail* (Paris, 2001).

Marchetti, D., 'The Revelations of Investigative Journalism in France', *Global Media and Communication* 5 (2009), pp. 353-388.

Marcuse, H., *One-Dimensional Man* (Boston, 1968).

Marshall, P. D., *Celebrity and Power* (London, 1997).
———, ed, *The Celebrity Culture Reader* (New York, 2006).

Matos, E., "I Have Cancer", *YouTube* (2007), available from: http://www.youtube.com/watch?v=0Q0Jo7JfbfE.

Maxwell Hamilton, J. and Jenner, E., 'Redefining Foreign Correspondence', in: *Journalism* 3 (2004), pp. 301-321.

Mazzoleni, G. and Schultz, W., '"Mediatization" of Politics: A Challenge for Democracy?', *Political Communication* 16 (1999), no. 3, pp. 247-261.

McCandless, H. E., *A Citizen's Guide to Public Accountability: Changing the Relationship Between Citizens and Authorities* (Victoria, 2001).

McChesney, R., 'September 11 and the Structural Limitations of U.S. Journalism', Zelizer, B. and Allan, S., eds, *Journalism After September 11: When Trauma Shapes the News* (London, 2002), pp. 91-100.

McManus, M., *Market Driven Journalism: Let the Citizen Beware?* (London, 1994).
McNair, B., *Cultural Chaos: Journalism, News and Power in a Globalised World* (London, 2006).
McNair, B., *Journalism and Democracy* (London, 2000).
————, *The Sociology of Journalism* (London, 2008).
McQuail, D., *McQuail's Mass Communication Theory* (London, 2005).
————, *Media Accountability and Freedom of Publication* (Oxford, 2003).
Mehl, D., 'La "Vie Publique Privée"', *Hermès* 13-14 (1994), pp.13-14.
Melnick, M.J. and Jackson, S.J., 'Globalization American-Style and Reference Idol Selection', *International Review for the Sociology of Sport* 37 (2002), pp. 429-448.
Mentink, H., *Veel Raad, Weinig Baat: Een Onderzoek naar Nut en Noodzaak van de Nederlandse Raad voor de Journalistiek* (Rotterdam, 2006).
Merton, R.K., *Social Theory and Social Structure* (New York, 1968).
Meyer, G. and Lund, A.B., 'Spiral of Cynicism: Are Media Researchers Mere Observers?' *Ethical Space: The International Journal of Communication Ethics* 5 (2008), no. 3, pp. 33-42.
————, 'International Language Monism and Homogenisation of Journalism', *Javnost — The Public* 15 (2008), no. 4, pp. 73-86.
Miles, M.B. and Huberman, A.M., *Qualitative Data Analysis: An Expanded Sourcebook* (Thousands Oaks, 1994).
Mitchell, J. and Blumler, J.G., 'In Conclusion: Beyond the State and the Market', in: *idem.*, eds, *Television and the Viewer Interest: Explorations in the Responsiveness of European Broadcasters* (London, 1994), pp. 227-240.
Moyo, L., 'The Global Citizen and the International Media: A Comparative Analysis of CNN and Xinhua's Coverage of the Tibetan Crisis', *International Communication Gazette* 72 (2010), no. 2, pp. 191-207.
Muhlmann, G., *A Political History of Journalism* (Cambridge, 2008).
Mutz, D.C., *Hearing the Other Side: Deliberative vs. Participatory Democracy* (New York, 2006).
Nederlands Instituut voor Oorlogsdocumentatie, (NIOD)., *Srebrenica, een 'Veilig' Gebied: Reconstructie, Achtergronden, Gevolgen en Analyses van de Val van een Safe Area* (Amsterdam, 2002).
Negrine, R. and Lilleker, D. G., 'The Professionalization of Political Communication', *European Journal of Communication* 17 (2003), no. 3, pp. 305-323.
Nerone, J. and Barnhurst, K.G., 'Visual Mapping and Cultural Authority: Design Changes in U.S. Newspapers, 1920-1940', *Journal of Communication* 45 (1995), pp. 9-43.
Neuberger, C. and Nuernbergk, C., 'Competition, Complementarity or integration?', *Journalism Practice* 3(2010), pp. 319-332.
Neveu, E., *Sociologie du Journalisme* (Paris, 2001).
Newton, K., 'Politics and the News Media: Mobilisation or Videomalaise?', in: Jowell, R., et al., eds, *British Social Attitudes: The 14th Report* (Aldershot, 1997), pp. 151-163.
New York Times Editorial., 'The Last Anchor', *New York Times*, available from: http://www.nytimes.com/2005/08/09/opinion/09tue4.html (August 9, 2005).

Nichols, B., *Blurred boundaries: Questions of meaning in contemporary culture* (Bloomington and Indianapolis 1994).
———, *Introduction to Documentary* (Bloomington, 2001).
———, *Representing Reality: Issues and Concepts in Documentary* (Bloomington, 1991).
Nord, D.P., *Communities of Journalism: A History of American Newspapers and their Readers* (Chicago, 2001).
Norris, P., *A Virtuous Circle: Political Communication in Post- Industrial Democracies* (Oxford, 2000).
Norris, P. et al., *On Message: Communicating the Campaign* (London, 1999).
North, A.C., Bland, V. and Ellis, N., 'Distinguishing Heroes from Celebrities', *British Journal of Psychology* 96 (2005), pp. 39-52.
O'Brien, M., 'Lost Cause? Network Executives Say Evening News Shows Remain Viable', *The Quill* 94 (2006), no. 1, pp. 24-31.
O'Donnell, M., 'Preposterous Trickster: Myth, News, the Law and John Marsden', *Media and Arts Law Review* 8 (2003), pp. 282-305.
Ofcom., *'Viewers and Voters: Attitudes to Television Coverage of the 2005 General Election'*, available from: http://www.ofcom.org.uk/research/tv/reports/election/ (2005).
O'Shaughnessy, N., 'The Symbolic State: a British Experience', *Journal of Public Affairs* 3 (2003), no. 4, pp. 297-312.
Padioleau, J.-G., 'Systèmes d'interaction et Rhétoriques Journalistiques', *Sociologie du Travail* 1 (1976), pp. 256-282.
———, Le Monde et le Washington Post: Précepteurs et Mousquetaires (Paris, 1985).
Pam, M., 'Reizen met Grunberg', in: *HP/De Tijd* (13-02-2009).
Pan, Z. and Kosicki, G., 'Framing Analysis: An Approach to News Discourse', *Political Communication* 10 (1993), pp. 55-75.
Parry, K.D., 'Search for the Hero: An Investigation into the Sports Heroes of British Sports Fans', *Sport in Society* 12 (2009), pp. 212-226.
Patterson, T.E., *Out of Order* (New York: 1993).
———, 'The News Media: An Effective Political Actor?', *Political Communication* 14 (1997), pp. 445-455.
Patton, M.Q., *Qualitative Evaluation and Research Methods* (Newbury Park CA, 1990).
Paulussen, S. et al., 'Doing it Together: Citizen Participation in the Professional News Making Process', *Observatorio Journal* 3(2007), pp. 131-154.
Pavlik, J., 'The Impact of Technology on Journalism', *Journalism Studies* 2 (2007), pp. 229-237.
Peters, C., 'Emotion Aside or Emotional Side?: Crafting an 'Experience of Involvement in the News', *Journalism: Theory, Practice and Criticism* 12 (2011), no. 3, pp. 297-316.
———, 'Even Better than being Informed: Media Literacy and The Daily Show', in: Peters, C. and Broersma, M., eds, *Rethinking Journalism: Trust and Participation in a Transformed News Landscape* (London, 2012), pp. 171-188.
———, 'No-Spin Zones: The Rise of the American Cable News Magazine and Bill O'Reilly', *Journalism Studies* 11 (2010), no. 6, pp. 832-51.

Porter, R., *Enlightenment: Britain and the Creation of the Modern World* (London, 2001).

Pinkleton, B.E. and Austin, E.W., 'Exploring Relationships among Media Use Frequency, Perceived Media Importance, and Media Satisfaction in Political Disaffection and Efficacy', *Mass Communication and Society* 5 (2002), pp. 113-140.

Pinto, L., *L'intelligence en Action: le Nouvel Observateur* (Paris, 1984).

Plaisance, P. L., 'The Concept of Media Accountability Reconsidered', *Journal of Mass Media Ethics* 4 (2000), pp. 257-268.

Price, V. and Tewksbury, D., 'News Values and Public Opinion: A Theoretical Account of Media Priming and Framing', in: Barnett, G. and Boster, F.J., eds, *Progress in Communication Science* (Greenwich, CT, 1997), pp.173-212.

Pritchard, D., *Holding the Media Accountable: Citizens, Ethics and the Law* (Bloomington, 2000).

Project for Excellence in Journalism (PEJ)., *State of the News Media 2004: An Annual Report on American Journalism*, available from: http://www.stateofthenewsmedia.org/2004/ (2004).

————, 'No-Spin Zones: The Rise of the American Cable News Magazine and Bill O'Reilly', *Journalism Studies* 11 (2010), no. 6, pp. 832-51. *State of the News Media 2006: An Annual Report on American Journalism*, available from: http://www.stateofthemedia.org/2006/ (2006).

————, 'No-Spin Zones: The Rise of the American Cable News Magazine and Bill O'Reilly', *Journalism Studies* 11 (2010), no. 6, pp. 832-51. *State of the News Media 2007: An Annual Report on American Journalism*, available from: http://www.stateofthemedia.org/2007/ (2007).

————, *State of the News Media 2008: An Annual Report on American Journalism*, available from: http://www.stateofthemedia.org/2008/ (2008).

————, *State of the News Media 2013: An Annual Report on American Journalism*, available from: http://www.stateofthemedia.org/2013/ (2013).

————, 'The Debate Effect: How the Press Covered the Pivotal Period of the 2004 Presidential Campaign', available from: http://www.journalism.org/node/163 (2004).

————, 'The Last Lap: How the Press Covered the Final Stages of the Campaign', available from: http://www.journalism.org/node/309 (2002).

Raad voor Maatschappelijke Ontwikkelingen, (RMO)., *Medialogica: Over het Krachtenveld Tussen Burgers, Media en Politiek* (Den Haag, 2003).

Raad voor het Openbaar Bestuur, ROB., *Politiek en Media: Pleidooi voor een LAT-relatie* (Den Haag, 2003).

Rais, C., 'Presse et Événement People: Une Subjectivité qui s'affiche', *Recherches en Communication* 26 (2007), pp.225-241.

Rennen, T., *Journalistiek als Kwestie van Bronnen. Ontwikkeling en Toepassing van Bron-Georiënteerde Benadering van Journalistiek* (Delft, 2000).

Renov, M., *The Subject of Documentary* (Minneapolis, 2004).

————, 'Video Confessions', in: Renov, M. and Suderburg, S., eds, *Resolutions: Contemporary Video Practices* (Minneapolis, 1996), pp. 78-102.

Reporters without Borders., available from: http://en.rsf.org/internet.html (2012).

Reuter, Y., 'Le Personnage', *Cahiers de Recherches en Didactique du Français* 1(1987), pp. 9-45.

Rich, F., 'The Weight of an Anchor', *New York Times*, available from: http://query.nytimes.com/gst/fullpage.html?res=9C06E5DC1439F93A A25756C0A9649C8B63# (May 19, 2002).

Richards, B., *Emotional Governance: Politics, Media and Terror* (Basingstoke, 2007).

Ricoeur, P., *Time and Narrative* (Chicago, 1984).

Rigney, A., 'Teksten en Cultuurhistorische Context', in: Brillenburg Wurt, K. and Rigney, A., eds, *Het leven van Teksten: Een Inleiding tot de Literatuurwetenschap* (Amsterdam, 2006), pp. 295-331.

Roggenkamp, K., *Narrating the News: New Journalism and Literary Genre in Late Nineteenth-Century American Newspapers and Fiction* (Kent, 2005).

Rowe, D., McKay, J. and Miller, T., 'Come Together: Sport, Nationalism, and the Media', in: Wenner L.A., ed, *MediaSport* (London, 1998), pp. 119-133.

Rowe, D., 'Sport and the Repudiation of the Global', *International Review for the Sociology of Sport* 38 (2003), pp. 281-294.

Ruby, J., 'Speaking For, Speaking About, Speaking With, or Speaking Alongside – an Anthropological and Documentary Dilemma', in: *Visual Anthropology Review* 7 (1991), pp. 50-67.

Ruellan, D., *Le Professionnalisme du Flou: Identité et Savoir-Faire des Journalistes Français* (Grenoble, 1993).

Rupar, V., 'Journalism, Political Change and Front-Page Design: A Case Study of the Belgrade Daily Politika', in: Broersma, M., ed, *Form and Style in Journalism: European Newspapers and the Representation of News 1880-2005* (Leuven, 2007), pp. 199-218.

Rusbridger, A., 'Politicians, the Press and Political Language', *The Hetherington Memorial Lecture: The University of Stirling*, available from http://www-fms.stir.ac.uk/ (2001).

Sabato, L.J., *Feeding Frenzy: How Attack Journalism has Transformed American Politics* (New York, 1993).

Safranski, R., *Goethe & Schiller: Geschichte einer Freundschaft* (Munich, 2009).

Salmon, C., *Storytelling: Bewitching the Modern Mind* (Brooklyn, 2010).

Sanchez, T.R., 'It's Time Again for Heroes - Or Were They Ever Gone?', *The Social Studies* 92 (2000), pp. 58-61.

Schlesinger, P., 'Is There a Crisis in British Journalism?', *Media, Culture & Society* 28 (2006), no. 2, pp. 343-351.

Schnädelbach, H., *Vernunft* (Stuttgart, 2007).

Schroeder , R. and Stovall, J., 'The Impact of the Internet on Foreign Correspondents: Work Routines', in: Gross, P. and Kopper, G.G., eds, *Understanding Foreign Correspondence: A Euro-American Perspective of Concepts, Methodologies, and Theories* (New York, 2011), pp. 187-193.

Schudson, M., 'The Objectivity Norm in American Journalism', *Journalism* 2 (2001), no. 2, pp. 149-170.

———, *The Power of News* (London, 2000).

———, 'Would Journalism Please Hold Still!', in: C. Peters and M. Broersma (eds.) *Rethinking Journalism* (London, 2012), pp. 191-199

Semetko, H. A. and Valkenburg, P. M., 'Framing European Politics: A Content Analysis of Press and Television News', *Journal of Communication* 50 (2000), no. 2, pp. 93-109.

Semetko, H.A. et al., *The Formation of Campaign Agendas* (Hillsdale, NJ: 1991).

Seymour-Ure, C., 'Fleet Street', in: Butler, D. and Pinto-Duschinsky, M., eds, *The British General Election of 1970* (London 1971).

——, 'The Press', in: Butler, D. and Kavanagh, D., eds, *The British General Election of February 1974* (London, 1974).

Shapin, S. and Schaffer, S., *Leviathan and the Air-Pump: Hobbes, Boyle, and the Experimental Life* (Princeton NJ, 1985).

Shirk, S.L., ed, *Changing Media, Changing China* (Oxford, New York, 2011).

Shoemaker, P.J. and Cohen, A.A., *News around the World: Content, Practitioners and the Public* (New York, 2006).

Shoemaker, P.J. and Reese, S., *Mediating the Message: Theories of Influence on Mass Media Content* (New York, 1996).

Shoemaker, P.J. et al, 'Proximity and Scope as News Values', in: Devereux, E., ed, *Media Studies. Key Issues and Debates* (London, 2007), 231-248.

Shuart, J., 'Heroes in Sport: Assessing Celebrity Endorser Effectiveness', *International Journal of Sports Marketing & Sponsorship* 8 (2007), pp. 126-141.

Sigal, L. V., 'Reporters and Officials: The Organization and Politics of Newsmaking', in: Tumber, H., ed, *News: A Reader* (Oxford, 1999), pp. 224-234.

Skorkjaer Binderkrantz, A. and Green-Pedersen, C., 'Policy or Processes in Focus?', *The Harvard International Journal of Press/ Politics* 14 (2009), pp. 166-185.

Smith, G., 'The Sport Hero: An Endangered Species', *Quest* 19 (1973), pp. 59-70.

Sociaal Cultureel Planbureau, SCP., *De Sociale Staat van Nederland 2009* (Den Haag, 2009).

Socolow, M., 'Anchors Away: Huntley, Brinkley, and Cronkite and the 1967 AFTRA Strike', *Journalism History* 29 (2003), no. 2, pp. 50-58.

Somers, M., 'The Narrative Construction of Identity: A Relational and Network Approach', *Theory and Society* 23 (1994), pp, 605-649.

Sparks, C. and Tulloch, J., *Tabloid Tales: Global Debates over Media Standards* (Oxford, 2000).

Sparks, C., 'Media Systems in Transition: Poland, Russia, China', *Chinese Journal of Communication* 1 (2008), pp. 7-24.

——, 'The Panic over Tabloid News', in: Tulloch, J. and Sparks, C., eds, *Tabloid Tales: Global Debates over Media Standards* (Oxford, 2000), pp. 1-40.

Splichal, S., 'Why be critical?', *Communication, Culture & Critique* 1 (2008), no.1, pp. 20-30.

'Statistics', *YouTube*, available from: http://www.youtube.com/t/press_statistics.

Stearns, P., *American Cool: Constructing a 20th Century Emotional Style* (New York, 1994).

Steensen, S., 'The Featurization of Journalism', in: *Nordicom Review* 32 (2010), no. 2, pp. 49-61.

Stephens, M., *Broadcast News* (New York, 1980).

Stockman, D., 'What Kind of Information Does the Public Demand? Getting the News during the 2005 Ant-Japanese Protests', in: Shirk S., ed, *Changing Media, Changing China*, pp. 175-201.

Strate, L., 'Heroes and/as Communication', in: Drucker, S.J. and Gumpert, G., eds, *Heroes in a Global World* (Cresskill, 2008), pp. 19-45.

Street, J., *Mass Media, Politics and Democracy* (London, 2001).

Strömbäck, J., 'Four Phases of Mediatization: An Analysis of the Mediatization of Politics', *The International Journal of Press/Politics* 13 (2008), no. 3, pp. 228-246.

Strömbäck, J. and Kaid, L.L., eds., *The Handbook of Election News Coverage around the World* (New York, 2008).

Strout, L.N., 'The Edward R. Murrow of Docudramas and Documentary', *Media History Monographs* 12 (2010), no. 1, pp. 1-21.

Swanson, D., 'Political Communication Research and the Mutations of Democracy', in: Gudykunst, W.B., ed, *Communications Yearbook 24* (Thousand Oaks, 2001).

Swift,T., 'Trust, Reputation and Corporate Accountability to Stakeholders', *Business Ethics: A European Review* 1 (2001), pp.16-26.

Taslé D'Heliand, G., 'Le Parisien: L'Innovation au Quotidien', *Ibidem*, p. 110.

Temple, M., 'Dumbing Down is Good for you', *British Politics* 1 (2006), pp. 257-273.

Tolson, A., *Mediations: Text and Discourse in Media Studies* (London, 1996).

Toulmin, S., *Cosmopolis: The Hidden Agenda of Modernity* (New York, 1990).

Tuchman, G., *Making News: A Study in the Construction of Reality* (New York, 1978).

Toussaint-Desmoulins, N., 'Comment le Management Vint aux Médias?', *Médiaspouvoirs* 16 (1989), pp. 100-105.

Trujillo, N. and Vande Berg, L., 'From Wild Western Prodigy to Ageless Wonder: The Mediated Evolution of Nolan Ryan', in: Drucker, S.J. and Cathcart, R.S., eds, *American Heroes in a Media Age* (Cresskill, 1994), pp. 221-240.

Tsfati,Y., 'Media Skepticism and Climate of Opinion Perception', *International Journal of Public Opinion Research* 1 (2003), pp. 64-82.

Tuchman, G., *Making the News: A Study in the Construction of Reality* (New York, 1978).

Tunstall, J., *Journalists at Work* (London, 1971).

Turner, G., 'The Mass Production of Celebrity: "Celetoïds", Reality TV and the "Demotic turn"', *International Journal of Cultural Studies* 9 (2006), no. 2, pp. 153-165.

Underwood, D., *From Yahveh to Yahoo: The Religious Roots of the Secular Press* (Chicago, 2008).

————, *When MBAs Rule the Newsroom* (New-York, 1995).

Valentino, N.A., Beckmann, M.N. and Buhr, T.A., 'A Spiral of Cynicism for Some: The Contingent Effects of Campaign News Frames on Participation and Confidence in Government', *Political Communication* 18 (2001), pp. 347-367.

Vaessens, T., 'Realiteitshonger: Arnon Grunberg en de (Non-)Fictie', in: *Tijdschrift voor Nederlandse Taal- en Letterkunde* 126 (2010), no. 3, pp. 306-326.

————, 'Making Overtures: Literature and Journalism, 1968 and 2008', in: *Literary Journalism Studies* 3 (2011), no. 2, pp. 55-72.

Vande Berg, L., 'The Sports Hero Meets Mediated Celebrityhood', in: Wenner, L.A., ed, *MediaSport* (London, 1998), pp. 134-153.

Van Cuilenburg, J. and McQuail, D., 'Media Policy Paradigm Shifts: Towards and New Communications Policy Paradigm', *European Journal of Communication* 18 (2003), no. 2, pp. 181-207.

Van Cuilenburg, J., 'On Competition, Access and Diversity in Media, Old and New', *New Media & Society* 2 (1998), pp. 183–207.

Van Dam, L. and De Jong, B., 'Winstgevendheid is een Waarborg voor Onafhankelijkheid', in: Van Dijck, J., *The Culture of Connectivity: A Critical History of Social Media* (New York, 2013).

Van Dijck, J., *The Culture of Connectivity: A Critical History of Social Media* (New York, 2013).

Von Krogh, T., 'Introduction: Media Accountability: A 60-year-old Compromise that Still Holds Promise for the Future', in: Von Krogh,T., ed, *Media Accountability Today... and Tomorrow: Updating the Concept in Theory and Practice* (Göteborg, 2008), pp. 1-12.

Van Zoonen, L., 'Desire and Resistance: Big Brother and the Recognition of Everyday Life', in: *Media, Society, Culture* 23 (2001), pp. 669-677.

————, 'I-Pistemology: Changing Truth Claims in Popular and Political Culture', in: *European Journal of Communication* 27 (2012), no.1, pp. 56-67.

————, 'One of the Girls?: The Changing Gender of Journalism', in Carter, C., Branston, G. and Allan, S., eds, *News, Gender and Power* (London, 1998), pp. 33-46.

Vasterman, P., *Mediahypes* (Amsterdam: 2004).

Vullings, J., 'Onder Sergeanten: Literaire Reportages van Arnon Grunberg', in: *Vrij Nederland* (14-02-2009), pp. 102.

Wahl-Jorgensen, K. and Hanitzsch, T., *The Handbook of Journalism Studies* (New York, 2009).

Wahl Jorgenson, K., 'The Strategic Ritual of Emotionality: A Case Study of Pullitzer Prize-winning Articles', in: *Journalism* (2012), pp. 1-17.

Ward, S., *The Invention of Journalism Ethics: The Path to Objectivity and Beyond* (Montreal, 2005).

Weber, M., *Politik als Beruf* (Stuttgart, 1992).

————, *The Methodology of the Social Sciences* (New York, 1949).

Welcome to Life, Dear Little One (1963), broadcast: January 15, 1964, 16 mm. black-white with sound, partially post-synchronised, running time: 36' 00" (EYE Institute).

Wells, K., 'Narratives of Liberation and Narratives of Innocent Suffering: The Rhetorical Uses of Images of Iraqi Children in the British Press', *Visual Communication* 6 (2007), no. 1, pp. 55-71

Wesch, M., 'Digital ethnography: YouTube statistics', *YouTube*, available from: http://mediatedcultures.net/smatterings/youtube-statistics/.

Whannel, G., Media Sport Stars: Masculinities and Moralities (London, 2002).

White, C., Bruce, S. and Ritchie, J., Young People's Politics: Political Interest and Engagement Amongst 14 to 24-year –olds (London 2000).

White, M., 'Television, Therapy and the Social Subject; Or, The TV Therapy Machine', in: Friedman, J., ed, *Reality Squared: Televisual Discourse on the Real* (New Brunswick, 2002), pp. 313-321.

Wieten, J., *Srebrenica en de Journalistiek: Achtergronden en Invloed van de Berichtgeving over het Conflict in Voormalig Joegoslavië in de Periode 1991-1995: Een Onderzoek naar Opvattingen en Werkwijze van Nederlandse Journalisten* (Amsterdam, 2002).

Wijfjes, H. and De Jong, B., eds, *De Hoofdredacteur: Over Ondernemend Leiderschap in de Journalistiek* (Diemen, 2011), pp. 45-54.

Wijfjes, H., *Journalistiek in Nederland: Beroep, Cultuur en Organisatie 1850-2000* (Amsterdam, 2004).

————, 'Kranten voor de Zondvloed? Het Krantenlandschap in de Lage Landen anno 2010', in: *Ons Erfdeel* 53 (2010), no 1, pp. 46- 55.

Wijman, E., 'De Column als Literair Genre', in: *Bzzltetin* 17 (1989), no. 164, pp. 27-31.

Wildenmann, R. and Kaltefleiter, W., *Funktionen der Massenmedien* (Frankfurt am Main, 1965).

Willett, R., 'In the Frame: Mapping Camcorder Cults', in: Buckingham, D., and Willet, R., eds, *Video Cultures: Media Technology and Everyday Creativity* (London, 2009).

Williams, B., *Ethics and the Limits of Philosophy* (London, 1993).

Williams, K., 'Anglo-American Journalism: The Historical Development of Practice, Style and Form', in: Broersma, M., ed, *Form and Style in Journalism: European Newspapers and the Representation of News, 1880-2005* (Leuven, 2007), pp. 1-26.

Williams, P., *The Sports Immortals: Deifying the American Athlete* (Bowling Green, 1994).

Wines, M., 'In latest Upheaval, China Applies New Strategies to Control Flow of Information', *The New York Times*, July 8, 2009.

Wines, M. and LaFranière, S., 'In Baring Facts of Train Crash, Blogs Erode China Censorship', in: *New York Times* (July 29, 2011).

Worcester, R. and Mortimore. R., *Explaining Labour's Second Landslide* (London, 2002).

Woo, S., 'China Clings to Control. Press Freedom in 2009', *International Federation of Journalists, Brussels* (2010).

Worth, S., 'Toward An Anthropological Politics of Symbolic Form', in: Gross, L., ed, *Studying Visual Communication* (Philadelphia, 1981), pp. 85-86.

Wright, B., 'The Hero in Popular Stories', *Journal of Popular Film & Television* 32 (2005), pp. 146-148.

Wring, D. and Deacon, D., 'Patterns of Press Partisanship in the 2010 General Election', *British Politics* 5 (2010), no. 4, pp. 436–454.

Wring, D., 'The Media and the Election', in: Geddes, A. and Tonge, J., eds, *Labour's Landslide: The British General Election 1997* (Manchester, 1997), pp. 70-83.

Ybema, S., *De Koers van de Krant: Vertogen over Identiteit bij Trouw en de Volkskrant* (Amsterdam, 2003).

Yin, J. and G. Payne., 'Asia and the Pacific', in: De Beer, A. S. and Merrill, J. C.,
    eds, *Global Journalism: Topical Issues and Media Systems* (Boston,
    2004), pp. 347-397.
Yin, R.K., *Case Study Research: Design and Methods* (London, 1989).
Zaller, J., 'A New Standard of News Quality: Burglar Alarms for the Monitorial
    Citizen', *Political Communication* 20 (2003), no. 1, pp. 109-130.
————, *A Theory of Media Politics: How the Interests of Politicians, Journalists,
    and Citizens Shape the News*, unpublished manuscript (1999).
Zehnder, S.P. and Calvert, S.L., 'Between the Hero and the Shadow: Developmental
    Differences in Adolescents' Perceptions and Understanding of Mythic
    Themes in Film', *Journal of Communication Inquiry* 28 (2004), pp. 122-
    137.
Zelizer, B. and Allan, S., *Keywords in News and Journalism Studies* (New York,
    2010).
Zelizer, B., 'Foreword', in: Sparks, C. and Tulloch, J., eds, *Tabloid Tales: Global
    Debates over Media Standards* (Oxford, 2000), pp. ix – xi.
————, 'Journalists as Interpretive Communities', *Critical Studies in Mass
    Communication* 10 (1993), pp. 219-237.
————, *Taking Journalism Seriously: News and the Academy* (Thousand Oaks CA,
    2004).
Zhao, Y., *Communication in China: Political Economy, Power and Conflict* (New
    York, 2008).
Zoglin, R., '10 Questions for Walter Cronkite', *Time* 162 (2003), no. 8.

INDEX